Funding Local Governance

Urban Management Series

Series Editor: Nick Hall

Funding Local Governance
Small Grants for Democracy and Development

Jo Beall

ITDG
PUBLISHING

Published by ITDG Publishing
The Schumacher Centre for Technology and Development,
Bourton Hall, Bourton-on-Dunsmore, Rugby, CV23 9QZ, UK
www.itdgpublishing.org.uk

First published in 2005

ISBN 1 85339 597 8

ITDG Publishing is the publishing arm of the Intermediate
Technology Development Group.
Our mission is to build the skills and capacity of people in developing
countries through the dissemination of information in all forms,
enabling them to improve the quality of their lives and
that of future generations.

Cover photograph by Neil Cooper

Typeset by J&L Composition, Filey, North Yorkshire
Printed in Great Britain

Contents

The Urban Management Series

The Urban Management Series focuses on the impacts of demographic and economic change in developing countries. The series offers a platform for practical, in-depth analysis of the complex institutional, economic and social issues that have to be addressed in an increasingly urban and globalized world. One of the UN's Millenium Development Targets calls for significant improvement in the lives of at least 100 million slum dwellers by 2020. This is a depressingly modest target as over 600 million people currently live in life and health threatening homes and neighbourhoods.

By 2025 it is estimated that two-thirds of the poor in Latin America and a third to almost half the poor in Africa and Asia will live in cities or towns. The urban poor face different issues and livelihood choices in comparison to the rural poor. The reduction of urban poverty requires carefully designed policies and determined commitment on the part of governments, in particular. The livelihoods and rights of the poor must be at the centre of any strategy to reduce poverty and develop an inclusive society. This is equally true in urban areas.

Cities and towns, and the industrial and commercial activities located in them, are a positive force for national economic growth. This is why cities are popular: where you find the mass of bees is where to look for honey. Urban areas provide consumer markets and services for agricultural producers. They are also gateways to larger national, regional, and international markets. But the opportunities from urban development have not been maximized by poor people. Their rights are curtailed and they are often excluded from accessing secure land, shelter, services, employment and social welfare due to the discriminatory practices of government, the private sector and civil society.

This series of books addresses the many challenges facing urban management professionals. First and foremost, they aim to improve understanding of the impact of urbanization on the livelihoods and living conditions of poor people. With better understanding the institutional and political conditions for poor people to participate and benefit from the urban development process may be improved. The lessons from research and dialogue should show how best to involve the private sector and civil society in mobilizing the necessary resources for inclusive and sustainable development; how to mitigate the impact that poor environments and natural hazards have on the poor; how to enhance the social and economic synergy between rural and urban populations; and how to strengthen efforts by the international community to coordinate support for a positive urbanization process.

Funding Local Governance is a provocative analysis about new ways to manage aid. Local funds have become popular thanks to the failure of conventional strategies by national states and aid agencies to successfully address problems of mass poverty in the South. Locally managed development funds are thought to help resources flow more directly for the benefit of households and communities. Local funds have also emerged as an important vehicle for strengthening representative organizations of the urban poor and of supporting creative relationships between urban poor groups and development agencies operating at the local level. By analysing original research and secondary sources from around the world this book explores the rationale, the practicalities, and the results of many attempts to ensure that development funds are spent effectively.

Donor agencies command a range of aid instruments for development support and government-to-government financial aid in the form of Budgetary Support may be seen as the optimum instrument for ideal circumstances. But, even when a central government does demonstrate commitment and capacity for pro-poor development, macro-level budget support can never be sufficient nor appropriate in all circumstances. In the poorest developing countries where government policies and capacities are weak, Local Funds targeted at the local and micro-level can be the most effective way to hit development targets. In any country, they should never be ignored. In a globalizing world where local, national, and international development conditions are ever changing, micro level instruments such as local funds designed to support the voice of civil society will always be needed. This book convincingly explains why they are important.

Nick Hall
Series Editor

Preface

The origins of this book rest with a long-standing intellectual commitment to finding ways in which international development and donor aid do no harm and ideally do some good. Recognizing the importance of political economy and global and national economic and political institutions, the study is nevertheless animated by the belief that what happens locally counts, and it is at this level that most people encounter the state. Local level interventions are limited in their effect if macro-level economic and social policy conditions are hopeless and power and political relationships are skewed. However, without them macro-level policy can be without tangible impact. When this happens state society relations (governance) are at risk. This book takes a hard look at local funds as one way of keeping governance alive and at best promoting local democracy and development. At a time when all are focused on globalization and international economic institutions and regimes, and when donor aid is taking the form of general budget support given directly to national ministries of finance, it is worth remembering Schumacher's (1974: 52) point in *Small is Beautiful* that 'Large units tend to break up into smaller units'. Like him I would say that 'whether we approve of it or not, it 'should at least not pass unnoticed'. This book is also the product of a professional engagement with local funds in both Africa and Asia over the last five years or more. In Africa I led a three-year evaluation of the City-Community Challenge Fund (C3) pilot programme, funded by the Department for International Development (DFID) and overseen in Uganda by Local Government International Bureau (LGIB) and in Zambia by Care International UK. In Asia I have been a long-term external adviser to a human rights and governance fund in Bangladesh, Manusher Jonno, funded by DFID and managed by Care International. These encounters I have processed through the analytical and policy frameworks I employ in the context of my academic work on urban policy, governance, and management.

The debts that I have accumulated along the way and in all these directions are many. First and foremost I wish to thank the people engaged at the pit face of local funds delivery and management who have shared with me openly and frankly not only their successes but also their dilemmas and disappointments. In Uganda I was enormously assisted by Raphael Magyezi of the Uganda Local Authorities Association and Dr John Kiyaga-Nsubuga, Deputy Director of the Uganda Institute of Management. In Zambia I received remarkable cooperation and willingness to share and reflect from Liseli Bull-Kamanga, Elizabeth Ndhlovu, Florence Zulu, and David Kalaba of Urban Insaka and Care Zambia, and proficient research assistance from Dr Webby Kalikiti from the Centre of Development and Management at University of Zambia. The international team working on C3 were equally generous with their ideas and time and were a pleasure to know. Heartfelt thanks are due to Nick Hall and David Sanderson on the Care International team and Mark Sheldrake, Joanna Wright, and Jim Beadle from LGIB. Support was also forthcoming from Michael Mutter and Ilias Dirie, then of DFID, Theo Schilderman and Lucky Lowe at Intermediate Technology, Tony Lloyd-Jones from University of Westminster, and Ian Roberts for his patient facilitation during the international steering group and management committee meetings. It was great fun working with Sanjiv Lingayah, then with the New Economics Foundation, during the early months of the evaluation. I learnt a lot from his approach both to evaluation and to life. In Bangladesh I have had the pleasure of working with the Manusher Jonno team in Dhaka with particular thanks to the Director Shaheen Anam. I am also grateful to the Care International team, particularly Navaraj Gyawali in Bangladesh and Katie Wiseman in London. Most particularly I would like to thank David Lewis, my colleague at the London School of Economics (LSE) and co-adviser to Manusher Jonno. His wisdom, friendship, and knowledge of Bangladesh are deeply valued.

It takes a lot to turn theoretical ideas and practical experience into a manuscript and many thanks are due in this regard. Additional funds from DFID for the production of this book allowed me to assemble a wide range of comparative material beyond my own direct experience. I am grateful to Michael Parkes for this. I owe a special debt to Francisco Cos-Montiel for his help with the chapter on Mexcio, to Jez Hall and the Community Pride Initiative in Salford for their assistance on the participatory budgeting chapter, to Katie Wiseman for giving me interview time and access to material on the Civil Society Fund in Tanzania, to Neil Johnson and the Paddington Development Trust for their time and documentation towards the chapter on challenge funds, and to David Archer and Chike Anyanwu of ActionAid for the same for the chapter on innovative approaches. The book also benefited from documents, contacts, and insights from Carine Clert, Nick Devas, Daniel Esser, Chris Rogerson, Kim Segel, and Carla Sutherland.

Completion of the manuscript would not have been possible without research and editorial support from Tom Goodfellow and Charlie Beall, and the professionalism and eagle eye of Andie Ball. Thanks too are due to Toby Milner and Sarah Silvester at ITDG Publications, as well as Nick Hall in his role as Series Editor, for their steady steerage of this endeavour. At the Development Studies Institute (DESTIN) at the LSE special thanks are due to Stephanie Davies, Drucilla Daley, and Sue Redgrave for their unfailing good nature and much appreciated assistance. I have also been encouraged in completing this project by DESTIN and LSE colleagues Teddy Brett, Cathy Campbell, Tim Dyson, Jean Paul Faguet, Tim Forsyth, John Harriss,

James Putzel, Dennis Rogers and Robert Wade, who while not all sharing my passion for things local have supported me in all sorts of ways. Finally, my eclectic family have once again had to deal with my physical and mental absences and have done so willingly and with understanding. To them all I offer love and gratitude. This book is dedicated to Malcolm Alexander.

Jo Beall
January 2005

Boxes

Figures

Tables

Acronyms and abbreviations

ABO	Area-based organization
ACP	African, Caribbean and Pacific
AGETIPS	*Agence d'Execution de Travaux d'Interet Public*
AGETUR	*L'Agence d'Execution des Travaux Urbains (a haute intensite de main d'oeuvre)*
ANC	African National Congress
ANCEFA	Africa Network Campaign on Education
BLCF	Business Linkages Challenge Fund
C3	City Community Challenge Fund
CADEC	Cancel Debt for the Child Campaign
CAP	Community action plan
CAS	World Bank Country Assistance Strategy
CAREZ	Care Zambia
CAVI	*Centro de Apoyo a la Violencia Intrafamiliar*
CBA	Capacity building for advocacy
CBI	Confederation of British Industry
CBO	Community-based organization
CCCF	Climate Change Challenge Fund
CCF	City Challenge Fund
CF	Challenge Fund
CEF	Commonwealth Education Fund
CEPEPE	*Centre de Promotion et d'Encadrement des Petites et Moyennes Enterprises*
CHOGM	Commonwealth Head Governments Meeting
CIDA	The Canadian International Development Agency
COP	Council of Participatory Budgeting
CPI	Community Pride Initiative
CPRC	Chronic Poverty Report
CRC	Community Relations Office
CRS	Westminster City Council Civic Renewal Strategy
CSACEFA	Civil Society Campaign for Education
CSCF	Civil Society Challenge Fund
CSO	Civil society organization
CSP	Civil society programme
CSR	Corporate social responsibility
DBS	Direct Budget Support
DAC	Development Assistance Committee

DCI	Development Cooperation Ireland
DFI	Direct Funding Initiative
DFID	Department for International Development
DRD	*Democratiser Radicalement la Democratie*
EFA	Education For All
ERF	European Refugee Fund
FCO	Foreign and Commonwealth Office
FCS	Foundation for Civil Society
FDCF	Financial Deepening Challenge Fund
FDD	District Development Fund
FODESAF	*Fondo de Desarallo Social y Asignaciones Familiares*
GAD	Gender and Development
GAPLAN	Planning Office
GBS	General Budget Support
GCE	Global Campaign for Education
GDP	Gross Domestic Product
GNECC	Ghana National Education Campaign Coalition
GP	Governance and policy dialogue
GTS	Global technical support
IAD	Integrated area-based development
IADB	Inter-American Development Bank
IBRD	International Bank of Reconstruction and Development
IDA	International Development Association
IFI	International Financial Institution
ILO	International Labour Organization
IMC	International Management Committee
IMF	International Monetary Fund
IPMU	International Management Project Unit
IUDD	Infrastructure and Urban Development Division
JFS	Joint Funding Scheme
LC	Local council
LCC	Lusaka City Council
LDA	London Development Agency
LDFs	Local Development Funds
LDP	Local Development Programme
LGIB	Local Government International Bureau
LIFE	United Nations Development Programme's Local Initiative Facility for Urban Environment
LIU	Local Implementation Unit
LLCF	Lifelong Learning Challenge Fund
LMU	Local management unit
MDFs	Municipal Development Funds
MDGs	Millennium Development Goals
MJ	Manusher Jonno
MPF	Ministry of Planning and Finance
MWAWODE	Mwanayamala Women's Development Group

NAFTA	North America Free Trade Agreement
NAG	National Advisory Group
NCC	National Coordination Committee
NCC	Ndola City Council
NGO	Non-governmental organization
NGOAB	NGO Affairs Bureau
NIMBY	Not in my back yard
NLP	New Life for Paddington Programme
NORAD	Norwegian Agency for Development
NPE	National Policy on Education
NPM	New Public Management
NRM	National Resistance Movement
NSC	National Steering Committee
ODA	Overseas Development Assistance
OECD	Organization for Economic Cooperation and Development
OT	Organizational transformation
PAMSCAD	Programme of Action to Mitigate the Social Cost of Adjustment
PAN	*Partido Accion Nacional*
PB	Participatory budgeting
PBs	Participatory budgets
PNB	*Prefeitura nos Barrios*
PDD	District Development Plan
PDT	Paddington Development Trust
PPA	Participatory Poverty Assessment
PPP	Public–private partnership
PRA	Participatory Rapid Appraisal
PRGU	Project of Urban Rehabilitation and Management
PRI	*Partido Revolucionario Institucional*
ProGenero	Gender Equity Project
Progressa	*Programa Nacional de Educacion, Salud y Alimentacion*
Pronasol	*Programa Nacional de Solidaridad*
PRSPs	Poverty Reduction Strategy Papers
PSB	*Partido Socialist Brazil*
PT	*Partido Trabalhista*
RDC	Resident Development Committees
SAFE	Social activities for environment
SAP	Structural Adjustment Policy
SCF	Save the Children Fund
SDC	Swiss Agency for Development and Cooperation
SEDESOL	Social Development Ministry
SEFs	Social Emergency Funds
SERHAUSEM	*Society d'Etudes Regionales d'Habit et d'Amenagement Urbain*
SHD	Sustainable Human Development

SIDA	Swedish International Development Agency
SIFs	Social Investment Funds
SLF	Sustainable Livelihoods Framework
SMMEs	Small, Medium and Micro-Enterprises
SPU	Social Protection Unit
SRBCF	Single Regeneration Budget Challenge Fund
SRM	Social Risk Management
SWAp	Sector Wide Approach
TAC	Technical Appraisal Committee
TAYOA	The Tanzania Youth Aware Trust
UAMPA	Federation of Neighbourhood Associations of Porto Alegre
UI	Urban INSAKA
UK	United Kingdom
ULAA	Uganda Local Authorities Association
UMP	Urban Management Programme
UNCDF	United Nations Capital Development Fund
UNDP	United Nations Development Programme
USAID	United States Assistance for International Development
WID	Women in Development
WTO	World Trade Organisation
ZAMSIF	Zambian Social Investment Fund
ZC	Zero Capacity

PART I

LOCAL FUNDS AND THE POLICY ENVIRONMENT

CHAPTER ONE

Local funds and development

INTRODUCTION

Governments, donors, and development agencies like to believe that their interventions help poor people and enhance their capacity to help themselves. Unfortunately, however, this is all too rarely the case. Instead, large amounts of money directed at alleviating poverty and empowering low-income and marginalized people end up in the wrong hands, or give rise to ambiguous outcomes. The intentions are often good but either the conditions are not propitious or the mechanisms through which funds are disbursed are not appropriate. International agencies have experimented with a wide array of instruments for providing development assistance, ranging from full interest-bearing loans, to concession-based finance, tied aid, unconditional grants, and various forms of conditionality. Decisions as to what kind of assistance to provide, where to direct it, and how to deliver it, are based on factors such as the priorities and capabilities of recipient countries; what donors want out of the process; what is being done by the private sector, other donors or non-governmental organizations (NGOs), and changing trends and fashions in development thinking and practice. Aid modalities are responsive to debates on aid effectiveness and are often associated with ensuring that the impact of assistance is felt not only at the national but also at the sub-national, local, and micro-levels.

The failure of successive policies and international development strategies to address problems of persistent poverty has led to notes of cynicism being struck in commentaries on development. Sometimes criticism is directed at the institutional level, for example donor ineptitude, weak states, or the lack of accountability on the part of NGOs. Alternatively, the means by which development assistance is delivered becomes the focus of negative inspection. Local funds are a mechanism for aid delivery that has gained increasing currency in recent years as a response to perceived problems of aid ineffectiveness but which are themselves a form of development assistance that is not without its critics. At their core, local funds are an administrative vehicle for selecting, funding, and implementing community or locally identified and managed small-scale public projects targeted at disadvantaged groups or areas. They are invariably externally funded, usually through grants, and are used to channel small amounts of money to a large number of local and micro-level projects (Jack, 2001).

Local funds are typically characterized as being quick-disbursing, relatively autonomous from government structures and procedures, and driven by a demand-led approach in which the public voice informs project design, implementation, and monitoring. Sometimes presented as a depoliticized way of allocating resources on the basis of need or willingness of beneficiaries to participate, local funds can also be used as a vehicle for enhancing governance. This can mean politicizing development and promoting democracy but often, in seminal World Bank (1992: 1) parlance, 'good governance' is understood as 'sound development management'. This post-Washington consensus approach to governance can see local funds being used to promote particular modes of reform or to engage communities and other local-level organizations in taking over some of the functions of the state. This book takes a hard look at the assumptions behind local funds being used as an aid instrument, particularly those that promote democracy and governance (understood as state society relations) alongside issues of development (understood as improvements in people's well-being).

The early development decades of the post-war era were not particularly concerned with democracy except that alongside social development it was thought to be a likely by-product of economic growth. In terms of aid delivery, this period was characterized by indirect efforts to influence macro-economic policy and project-based lending. Both areas came in for criticism in the 1970s, giving way to more direct intervention at the level of macro-economic policy, notably through the Structural Adjustment Programmes (SAPs) of the World Bank and the International Monetary Fund (IMF) in the 1980s. While projects remained tenacious, from the 1980s onwards they increasingly gave way to programme aid, usually directed at particular sectors such as health and education or public sector reform, which operated alongside macro-economic reform efforts. The latter came in for mounting criticism in the face of incontrovertible negative social consequences resulting from SAPs, and programme aid was focused at longer-term economic and human development. It was in this context that a funds approach was born when, in the late 1980s, the World Bank set up social funds as compensatory measures to ameliorate the adverse social effect of macro-economic reforms. Since then local funds have evolved considerably.

Currently there is a growing trend towards the delivery of aid through Direct Budget Support (DBS), where financial support is channeled directly to a recipient government, usually through a ministry of finance, in a context where conditionality is arguably less oppressive and negotiated in advance in the context of policy dialogue and development partnerships. As an aid instrument DBS is considered to be less patronizing and more efficient than earlier modes of delivery as it does not require the creation or replication of institutions but rather allows governments to use their own systems, instead of conforming to the project management cycles and reporting systems of donors. Nevertheless DBS has its weaknesses and is not sufficient or appropriate in all circumstances. In most contexts there will be groups, regions, or sectors that are relatively neglected. Moreover, national governments often face similar problems to donors in ensuring the wide reach of resources and services. As a result meso- and micro-level instruments will always be necessary. This is an important factor in understanding why local funds have become a favoured strategy for targeting assistance to the local and micro-levels. They are seen as an effective way of reaching the parts that other aid instruments cannot reach.

A further factor explaining the popularity of local funds as a contemporary aid instrument relates to politics. In the past, development assistance was associated primarily with economic policy interventions and social and human development. The political arena was the terrain of foreign affairs and interventions beyond the military realm were largely confined to support for or monitoring of elections. In the post-1989 world, following the economic and political transitions that took place in Eastern Europe and the former Soviet Union, this changed. Public sector reform, institutional support, and promotion of democracy all became areas of fair game for development cooperation. Indeed, the policy dialogue and negotiated conditionality associated with DBS was critically bound up with issues of 'good governance' and democratization. In this context local funds have become an important mechanism employed by donors to ensure that in addition to top-down aid measures for governments, some resources are also directed towards what is invariably called 'bottom-up development' or 'civil society strengthening'. This approach allows donors both to foster engaged citizenship and to help hold governments to account without getting overtly involved with party politics, which is anathema to conventional development practice. While the rationale for donors adopting local funds is fairly clear, it is also important to point out that there are disadvantages as well as advantages to their use as an aid instrument and that international development agencies are not necessarily the best organizational vehicle for their delivery. These issues are taken up and illustrated throughout this volume.

THE CHARACTERISTICS OF AND ARGUMENTS FOR LOCAL FUNDS

Local funds operate across a wide front, are diverse in scope and focus and change and adapt in response to particular local political, social, institutional, and fiscal contexts. They include the World Bank's social funds, which involve quite large sums of money, alongside smaller charitable donations, which are as old as political philanthropy itself. Many funds today have additional empowerment objectives or are concerned with democracy promotion. As such, local funds are quite difficult to define. Nevertheless, drawing on Jørgensen and Van Domelen's (2001) definition of

World Bank social funds, the definition adopted for the City-Community Challenge Fund (C3), Beall (2002a), and the description of local funds by Satterthwaite (2002), the following definition is offered:

> *Local funds are both financing instruments and funding agencies created to disburse resources for local development. They are a response to local needs and demands and encourage addressing these through local partnerships. The objective of these funds is usually to reduce risk and to enhance the livelihood opportunities of disadvantaged people through development initiatives that remove barriers to voice, the realization of rights and delivery and accountability on the part of a broad range of local governance institutions.*

Almost by definition local funds are the product of external agents, whether the result of the charity of individual benefactors and welfare organizations, the corporate social citizenship of private sector companies, or the development aid of donor agencies. There are more strings attached to some funds than others but in all cases, the givers are in a stronger position than the recipients, simply by virtue of holding the purse strings and through information and power asymmetries. Herein lies one of the ambiguities of such funds, especially if they are intended to empower people. When funds are designed with the additional aim of promoting local democracy, the contradictions multiply. This is because most donors across the scale find themselves more comfortable with poverty reduction than with encouraging political activity.

At their least controversial local funds aim to alleviate poverty through the financing of activities that include social service programmes and infrastructure such as schools, clinics, water supply, and sanitation facilities; economic programmes such as support to micro-credit, SMMEs (Small, Medium and Micro-enterprises), and other forms of local economic development; and environmental protection and physical infrastructure such as roads, civil works, irrigation, land reclamation, and natural resource management (Jørgensen and Van Domelen, 2001; Narayan and Ebbe, 1997). It is believed that supporting such activities improves the well-being of poor people and communities. Further, it is often claimed that they are in turn better equipped to exercise greater control over their own lives and to exercise leverage over local governments and other local institutions. This is more controversial. Local funds can be directed towards involving residents and local governments in the co-production of infrastructure and services, supporting decentralization processes in local government, assisting civil society organizations advocate for increased effectiveness and accountability on the part of government departments, or towards citizens monitoring the performance of politicians and government officials. When local funds are used to get local governments to listen and respond they are seen as a tool for the empowerment of poor people and marginalized groups and of increased democratization.

What are some of the more generic features of local funds? First, they are a means by which *small resources* are targeted directly towards disadvantaged groups or local communities, according to predetermined criteria. Individual grants can be very small, covering the cost, for example, of a couple of sewing machines for a neighbourhood women's income-generating group or the materials for digging drainage in an informal settlement. Nevertheless, considerable amounts of money are spent on local funds overall. As of May 2001 the World Bank alone had spent 3.5 billion dollars on social and local funds projects (World Bank, 2002: 1).

Second, because local funds are dispersed closer to where they are needed, it is believed that they will be better *targeted*, with local people being more able to decide what they need and to influence what they get. In social policy, the rationale behind targeting is to increase the efficient use of scarce resources by ensuring that they get to those most in need, low-income households for example. However, targeting can be notoriously expensive as it is not always easy to identify and reach the target group. It is for this reason that welfare states have so often opted for universal benefits, such as child maintenance grants for all children up to a certain age, or pensions for all those over a certain age. In the case of local funds, targeting is done through the criteria imposed and through the rules of disbursement, and the group to be targeted is mainly dictated by the priorities of a particular funding agency. These invariably relate to poverty reduction. A common way of targeting is through identity-based eligibility criteria, for example widows and orphans, the homeless, women-headed households, children in difficult circumstances, and so on. While an effective method of channeling funds to identifiable groups, it can lead to perverse incentives and is open to problems of leakage to non-poor groups. To counter this some funds employ self-selection to discourage the non-poor from using them. The most obvious examples here are food-for-work and low-wage public works programmes (Marc et al., 1995: 57). Such approaches have been heavily criticized and are akin to social policies for the 'deserving poor', where benefits are set deliberately low in order to exclude all but the most desperate.

An alternative approach to targeting is prioritizing projects that are likely to have a particularly strong impact on poor people, such as primary health care, primary education and vocational training, or school meals programmes. Another approach is geographical targeting through area-based strategies, for example, by focusing on informal settlements. The criticism here is that spatial communities are not homogenous and contain within them significant levels of inequality and exclusion. Hence this strategy is inappropriate for income support but might be useful in the case of infrastructure provision and services, where some areas are clearly in greater need than others – although when there are multiple infrastructure-poor areas there can be problems over how one is chosen over another. The funds discussed in Chapter Four, on Mexico and in Chapter Nine on Bangladesh provide examples of targeting on the basis of issues and identity, while the local funds in francophone Africa discussed in Chapter Five and the discussion of the C3 Pilot Programme in Uganda and Zambia in

Chapters Six and Nine respectively demonstrate the issues involved when local funds are associated with area-based strategies.

A third dimension of local funds is that they are supposed to be *demand-driven*, operating in response to expressions of need and initiatives proposed by local actors themselves. The original social funds were unequivocally supply-driven by the Bretton Woods organizations, providing a human face to structural adjustment (Cornia et al., 1987). Contemporary local funds, by contrast, are part of an evolving process where design encourages a more demand-driven approach in which community-based groups (CBOs), civil society organizations (CSOs), or their representatives are able to influence what projects get taken up and in what way. In reality, requests come mainly from NGOs although some do come from membership organizations, local governments, and even private firms. Proposals are presented to the organization managing the funds and, subject to acceptance, the agency disburses the resources to the (usually intermediary) organization requesting them. The demand-led feature of local funds is often offered as a mechanism for effective targeting as only those in need will apply. However, in reality, local funds often go to those who know how to apply and report on their activities according to donor monitoring and evaluation requirements, rather than those in need. Biggio (1998: 37) points out that in the case of social funds, for example, the poorest are those least likely to be capable of presenting project proposals and implementing them. This is why it is so important that procedures and practices are kept short and simple to ensure that funds are less likely to exclude.

A fourth feature of local funds is that they are supposed to *stimulate partnerships* for development, which are thought to have positive side effects for all involved. One of the ideas at work here is that the process of eliciting and utilizing local funds will lead to *increased participation* and possibly greater confidence on the part of local actors. Another is that partnerships will mobilize or *leverage resources* locally and that this will lead to cooperation among multiple local stakeholders. As will be shown by some of the case studies presented in this book, local funds do have positive effects on local people and the engagement of local organizations in governance. Tendler and Serrano (1999: 20) argue, in reference to social funds, that their success depends to a large degree on how autonomous they are from governments and indeed donors. This is confirmed by research on some but not all of the local funds reviewed for this book. While some local funds are best when autonomous of government control, if empowerment and democratization are among the aims, then it is likely that the most successful development initiatives will be those that engage government officials and agencies, albeit at arm's length.

A fifth characteristic of local funds is that they offer grant funding as opposed to loans – but they require *co-financing*. In other words, there is no obligation to pay back moneys received but applicants have to provide match funding. This is believed to have a number of advantages; It is thought to restrict the benefits on offer to those who actually need the service and to avoid 'free-riding', as well as creating a sense of ownership among the applicants. While this requirement undoubtedly has some merit there is also a danger that it serves to limit those who can take advantage of local funds. At a stakeholder workshop attended in Lusaka, in my role of external evaluator of a local fund in Zambia (described in more detail in Chapter Nine), the problems posed by match funding for poor communities were described by one of the participants as follows:

> *A chicken and a pig were travelling together. After a hard night's travelling they woke up bright and early. The chicken [read donor] said that they ought to have some breakfast. The chicken said it would contribute an egg. The pig [read community] asked what it was expected to contribute. 'Bacon, of course' replied the chicken. 'Bacon is not like an egg' said the pig. 'To give you bacon for your breakfast I must die.'*

If their grant aid is premised on principles and mechanisms that exclude the poorest, this poses a problem for donors, particularly as most purport a pro-poor agenda and most local funds have grown out of the 'small-grants' element of aid budgets, which historically have been directed towards NGOs working with very poor communities. It has been argued, regarding social funds, that the requirement of match funding has only transpired in practice among a small percentage (Tendler, 2000: 117). Increasingly common is for 'match funding' to be guaranteed through non-financial contributions such as labour, participation in processes and procedures, or particular behaviours. While it is sometimes the case that contributions disproportionately fall on some members of a community rather than others, there are examples of creative ways in which match funding has been solicited and delivered, as described in the case of C3 in Zambia in Chapter Nine.

A sixth feature of local funds is that they are deemed to be *swift and flexible*. Well-performing local funds are celebrated for being able to respond in ways that reduce the time that local groups need to spend accessing resources. Moreover, they are intended to be sufficiently malleable to respond to a multiplicity of poverty-alleviating and risk-reducing efforts. This derives from their origin with social funds, which as policy instruments were designed to transfer resources quickly and efficiently under emergency conditions, 'in order to mitigate temporary states of deprivation caused by economic crisis and adjustment' (Fumo et al., 2000: 4). However, there is as much of an imperative not to engage disadvantaged people and resource-strapped organizations in long and complicated processes that involve them in difficult opportunity costs. There are good practice examples of funds where a lot of time and effort has been spent on simplifying and refining procedures for reviewing and supporting applications and projects, and for monitoring their progress and advance.

Nevertheless, there are a number of constraints that impede speed and compliance. On the side of recipients, even with simple procedures some of the more disadvantaged applicants need a lot of support in making applications, and communities and groups often need considerable time to consult, identify, and negotiate priorities and to muster match funding. On the side of donors and local fund agencies it is often difficult to break the habits of a lifetime and reduce the levels of managerial scrutiny to which they are accustomed. Resistance primarily relates to issues of accountability but it is argued that if application procedures and decision-making processes are open and transparent, then accountability is fostered through the wide availability of information and the fact that local funds lie with local organizations (Satterthwaite, 2002: 182). There are obvious elements of risk for donors but no more than with some of the mega-projects of the past. Moreover, an arm's-length approach is increasingly characteristic of macro-level aid instruments such as DBS. A more hands-off approach requiring not micro-management but oversight and stewardship is as much a crucial element of good practice in terms of local funds and applies all the way up the chain, from the organization assessing applications and dispersing funds up to the donor agency itself. As shown in a number of the case study chapters across the book, this can be done but often with great difficulty.

A seventh feature of local funds is that *management is devolved* from donor agencies to other organizations that are responsible for oversight and day-to-day management. It is for this reason more than any that they are popular with donors. Because other organizations vet the projects, disburse the money, and monitor progress, the transaction costs of overseeing a large number of small projects are transferred. This is especially important when multiple small grants are involved. As Satterthwaite (2002: 179) has argued:

> *Ask any staff member from an official bilateral agency or the World Bank to manage fifty times the number of projects with an average cost of one-fiftieth of their current project portfolio, and they would resign. Any international agency would face an impossible administrative burden and far higher staff costs if its central offices had to support a multiplicity of (often) low-cost, diverse, distant initiatives, especially if each proposal had to be reviewed on the ground and monitored and evaluated to ensure compliance with its initial objectives.*

Additionally, local funds are devoid of the complications and delays attached to large-scale aid packages or the political sensitivities of bilateral government-to-government aid. As such, local funds fit in well with a development climate where international donors are often criticized for agenda-setting and unwarranted interference in domestic policy agendas. Increasingly, local funds are being designed so that the delivery agencies or trusts become autonomous organizations and independent of donors at some stage. In this way, international development agencies, if they are prepared to let go, can adopt an arm's-length approach while directing resources to poor people and civil society organizations. For those donor agencies pursuing a policy of Direct Budget Support, where no strings attached transfers are made to partner governments and/or sectors, local funds offer a compatible mechanism to channel much smaller amounts to less ambitious and more circumscribed initiatives at the local level. Local funds are therefore coming to replace the 'small projects' budgets of many bilateral and multilateral donor agencies that previously went exclusively to NGOs.

However, local funds as an aid instrument come at a price. International development agencies love to put their stamp on things and local funds do not always lend themselves to logos. Indeed, for some donors having their name over a programme or project is their *raison d'être*, whether it is the European Union supporting area-based urban renewal projects in British inner cities or WaterAid installing communal taps in a Dhaka slum. This tendency on the part of donors is one of the reasons that large-scale infrastructure projects have been so popular for so long. They are highly visible and it is easy to claim the credit for them. Most international agencies are now convinced of the efficacy and value of more behind-the-scenes assistance such as capacity building and institutional support. Nevertheless, it is still possible to proudly say 'we supported that' or 'we assisted there' when a sector improves its performance or a country's public administration is reformed. There is seemingly less obvious impact or kudos to be gained from claiming support for a kilometre of drainage in a low-income city settlement, for which the community offered their labour in kind. Moreover, this is even more the case where the funding mechanism is several times removed from the donor and what credit there is to be had goes elsewhere. Yet funds for these sorts of interventions really can make a difference to people's lives and enable them to draw out of government institutions the support they deserve as citizens. They are replete with problems but when well executed they can be of great value.

Funds for local development and particularly the World Bank's social funds, are controversial. They have been widely criticized in development studies literature and often for good reason. At worst, funds get enmeshed in bureaucracy or are siphoned off – either way failing to reach the people for whom they are meant. At their most innovative, they can swiftly and flexibly bring valuable resources to where they are needed most. The intention here is neither to advocate for local funds, nor to write them off as futile or misdirected. Rather it is to situate local funds within broader development paradigms and more particularly the strategies characteristic of recent decades. For better or worse, local funds are a firm part of contemporary development cooperation. Of policy interest is to understand their current salience. Of operational interest is to identify not so much whether they work or not but rather under which conditions or circumstances they best flourish and towards what goals they are most effectively employed. With this in mind the questions pursued in this book are as follows: Under what circumstances can the provision of limited resources directed at the local level both alleviate poverty and enhance state society relations? Can a focus on social or economic development on the part of local funds contribute indirectly to enhanced governance or democratization and vice versa? Are local funds strengthened or weakened by having multiple aims, including poverty reduction strategies alongside democracy promotion, for example? Can donors and governments, with their demanding electorates and lofty goals, be satisfied with the sometimes meagre or invisible results achieved by local funds? How can those implementing local funds let go, balance stewardship with risk, and allow both to inform the way they manage them and measure their success?

THE CRITIQUE OF LOCAL FUNDS

There are a number of objections that are commonly leveled at local funds. The most important of these relates to their potential to depoliticize development. This fear is reinforced when their origins are contemplated. As ameliorative measures to soften the impact of macro-economic reforms, social funds were informed by clear political objectives in that the intention was to reduce domestic opposition to the SAPs being imposed from the outside by the International Financial Institutions (IFIs). It can be argued that social funds represented economic compensation to influential or potentially oppositional groups in society, which might otherwise have disrupted the implementation of adjustment policies in one way or another. Ever since – despite their evolution from emergency funds, to social investment funds, to local funds promoting democracy alongside development – local funds have remained open to political manipulation and interference. In different contexts they have become a political tool to reward constituents, recruit new voters, and win back the disaffected, alongside compensating for losses suffered under austerity programmes. It is for this reason that Tendler and Serrano (1999) are emphatic that the funds that work best are those most distanced from government. However, if local funds are designed to enhance people's voice, then they should not be so distant from government that citizens cannot be heard.

Donors have not been shy in using local funds towards political ends, whether to strengthen weak states or bypass recalcitrant governments, to provide civil society assistance under conditions of tenuous state society engagement, or to promote the fortunes of the private sector in determining development futures. Depending on one's normative position, the use of local funds to address political and institutional change alongside poverty reduction and social development can be regarded as a good thing. For example, few, from the vantage point of the early twenty-first century, would retrospectively object to the local funds model adopted by, among others, the European Union and the Scandinavian bilateral donor agencies, towards supporting the liberation and anti-apartheid movements, which also addressed both social and political disadvantage in South Africa. In assessing the potential impact of local funds on democracy and development, it is these experiences that need to be kept in mind, alongside anxieties about social engineering. Moreover, local funds do not have to bring down illegitimate governments to be regarded as effective. In his assessment of civil society assistance in Asia, Golub (2000: 136) distinguishes between assistance for 'Big D' and 'small d' democracy. While the former refers to making more effective and accountable elections, judiciaries, legislatures, political parties, and so on, the latter is more closely associated with development work, employing a range of strategies such as community mobilization, civic education, and advocacy, all 'important threads in the fabrics of many sturdy democracies'.

Beyond political objections, other shortcomings of local funds have been well documented, particularly in relation to assessments and evaluations of social funds (Cornia, 2001; Fumo et al., 2000; Jørgensen and Van Domelen, 2001; Narayan and Ebbe, 1997; Parker and Serrano, 2000; Tendler, 2000; Tendler and Serrano, 1999; World Bank, 2002). They include among other things that social funds are not good at targeting poverty, are heavily dependent on external funding and are therefore not sustainable, and that even when located in government they are not well integrated into the rest of the public sector. However, it is worth reiterating at this point that many local funds are much smaller, less dependent, and more agile than most social funds, which on the contrary are becoming increasingly bureaucratized. Nevertheless, local funds are not immune to criticism. The following are a number of key areas where there are unresolved issues in relation to local funds, some of which are inherited from or shared by social and challenge funds and some of which have emerged in the course of implementing the new generation of local funds themselves. Excluded from this discussion are the more detailed problems of implementation, relating to project design and management matters, as these are covered in some detail in Chapter Nine.

Poverty reduction and social protection

Kanji (2002: 246–7) argues that the evolution of social funds from social transfers with a temporary and ameliorative function into those with longer-term developmental ambitions, has implications for the way in which funds address poverty reduction and social protection. Moreover, she suggests that this has been inadequately thought through in terms of how they articulate with wider national policies. Growing out of their origins as emergency funds, strategies such as public works employment have persisted, enabling 'survival but not security nor accumulation'. Furthermore, she argues that projects with a more developmental focus – such as infrastructure for social services – while worthy, may not be best tackled through social funds. Similarly Tendler (2000) has argued that social funds have not contributed significantly to the reduction in unemployment and to poverty alleviation in the countries where they operate, when compared to other more supply-driven and centralized programmes with the same goal. She also argues that the jobs created tend to be of a poor quality, badly remunerated, and often temporary in nature. These critiques are borne out in part by the discussion of the *Agence d'Execution de Travaux d'Intéret Public* (Public Works and Employment Agency) (AGETIP) in Chapter Five. However, in situations of critical need and in the absence of proper safety nets and other means for social protection, local funds might represent the only option available and under such conditions the grant element commends itself over loans and micro-credit. However, local funds should never be the last word on poverty reduction and social protection, which as Kanji (2002: 247) points out, requires a more far-reaching panoply of policy approaches.

Other doubts about local funds already hinted at in the discussion above include the fact that despite 'strong rhetorical commitment to poverty targeting' (Fumo et al., 2000: 21) they do not necessarily reach the poorest, and that as a mechanism for targeting they have not been particularly successful. In other words, a large proportion of those benefiting from local funds are not poor and there is considerable danger of local elites capturing the projects. The targeting mechanisms discussed above under social funds, along with the innovative disbursement mechanisms discussed in Chapter Six, are used by local funds to increase the degree of participation by the groups and communities they hope to reach. Sometimes the funds go directly to community representatives who manage them on behalf of community members. Another model is for funds to be overseen by elected committees chosen by communities. At other times the funds go from the disbursing agency straight to contractors, but equally there are examples of community procurement and contracting. Whichever model is used, Jørgensen and Van Domelen (2001: 21) have pointed out that if the goals of 'community empowerment' and ownership are to be advanced, a bias can creep in towards those communities or groups that are more effective communicators and better connected. Moreover, demand-driven approaches – which are also frequently characteristic of local fund design – often see representatives of local communities overruling the poverty targeting goals of donors or local fund agencies. Fumo et al. (2000: 22) cite the case of *Red de Solidaridad* (Solidarity Network) in Colombia. This project was initially designed with poverty alleviation objectives and technical instructions for targeting based on regional and municipal level poverty mapping. However, local partners demanded greater flexibility and responsiveness towards their needs and demands in a context where violence, corruption and poor governance required the restoration and strengthening of civil society as a priority.

Demand orientation

It has been intimated already that the demand orientation of local funds is not without its problems. One difficulty is that local funds invariably have to conform to criteria set by the funding agency. This can limit their demand-driven character because local actors have to choose their activities from within a predetermined set of options (Narayan and Ebbe, 1997: 2). Even when local fund agencies are open as to what they fund and genuinely try to be responsive to innovations from the ground, it is the case that people only know what they know. In other words, where the impetus for an initiative and requests for funding emanate from users, demand orientation is constrained by the fact that local communities often cannot envisage what things could be like or what they themselves might achieve with a little assistance. As a result they only request funding for things they have seen other people do, and hence innovation is more limited than is anticipated by those engaged with local funds at the design stage. There are a number of examples of this in the case studies reviewed in this volume. For example, the City–Community Challenge Fund was taken up by communities in Kampala, Uganda to support micro-enterprises rather than pursuing more innovative strategies to engage local government towards much needed improvements in service delivery. Similarly, Manusher Jonno and its partners in Bangladesh have found it difficult to move beyond welfare-oriented projects in order to take advantage of the much more ambitious human rights and governance agenda set for the organization. Thus there is sometimes a real tension between demand-driven and supply-driven approaches, with the former often being more conservative.

In real life, demand orientation often involves having to choose from a menu of project options presented by local funds managers, leading to requests for funding for the same activities that people have seen initiated by a neighbouring community or group. These may parallel real needs and concerns on the part of both old and new applicants. However, there is the possibility that preconceived notions of development operating at the macro-level might re-orient what happens on the ground in ways that diverge from client understandings of development needs. Alternatively, a proliferation of local funds doing the same thing and copycat sub-projects may lead to certain ways of doing things becoming entrenched, without them necessarily being best or even good practice.

Another classic problem with demand-driven approaches is that while they may be beneficial to some sections of the client population, they can tend to keep the poorest or most marginalized groups out of the frame. It is often people who are disadvantaged or relatively deprived but not totally destitute who are best able to participate in partnerships and rise to the challenge of deliberative democracy. The poorest often have a more limited capacity to articulate their demands, to come up with match funding, and to sustain projects that meet all the criteria and requirements laid down by donors and local fund agencies. As a result of this and the inevitable power differentials within a locality, it has been argued that local funds often advance the interests of those who are already better off (Fumo et al., 2000; Tendler and Serrano, 1999). This points to one of the dilemmas that arise when local funds are designed both to alleviate poverty and to enhance governance or state society relations. When pro-poor local funds are accompanied by objectives such as participation and poverty reduction these objectives are not necessarily compatible.

Beyond elite capture of local funds, another problem is that intermediaries often benefit more than the intended beneficiaries. This can include the local funds agency itself – which absorbs both capital and running costs – intermediary and advocacy NGOs that require the same, as well as a whole slew of new supply-side characters who come in on the back of local funds programmes and their sub-projects, such as technical cooperation personnel and local contractors. They in turn absorb significant resources and often determine the direction of initiatives. While their advice may be important and their skills indispensable, especially in the early phases, they can limit the demand orientation of local funds and sabotage, wittingly or otherwise, the effective participation of local partners. Ultimately, the demand orientation of local funds will always be limited so long as local funds are not informed by genuine partnerships in which realistic menus of development options are negotiated in relation to a broad and inclusive definition of priorities and need.

Participation

While earlier social funds, such as the Social Emergency Funds (SEFs), were singularly unconcerned about participatory approaches, the latter have become an act of faith in contemporary local funds. The conventional wisdom here is that by broadening client participation in the development projects supported by local funds, connection to and ownership of the project is built and fostered. Participatory approaches are also thought to ensure that the aims and objectives of projects match those of the people involved with and impacted by them, and to increase government accountability through the involvement of active and engaged citizens. For much of the 1980s and 1990s participation was a central tenet of alternative approaches to development (Chambers, 1983, 1993, 1995, 1996) and later came to inform mainstream development practice (Narayan et al, 2000a; Narayan et al., 2000b). Today there is a new cynicism about the value and purpose of participation (Cooke and Kothari, 2001; Mosse, 2001) and the effectiveness of institutions to deliver on this agenda (Cleaver, 2001). In the case of local funds there are a range of issues around how participation operates, who participates and on whose terms, as well as who benefits. Sometimes those who are given voice through participatory approaches use the opportunity to advance their own rather than collective interests, and conflicts develop between individuals and groups in the community that undermine the good intentions informing local funds and the sub-projects they support.

Participation in local funds is also sought through the principle of co-financing or match funding which is believed to ferment buy-in on the part of those who have raised or provided the match funding. Here, the dangers associated with who participates and who benefits are very real. It is not unknown for the least powerful in a community, often women or the youngest members, to be the ones who provide the time and labour while more powerful members are most likely to benefit. For example, a road may be built with community participation outside a local notable's house or business. When things like this happen, the empowerment claims of local funds have to be regarded with circumspection. It is admittedly difficult for funders, and sometimes no less difficult for local funds agencies, to identify – let alone control – social relationships at the local level. Nevertheless, as others have pointed out (Cleaver, 2001; Uphoff, 1992), there is a tendency in development more generally to recognize the ways in which informal institutions operate but nevertheless to concentrate on perfecting the operation of formal institutions. This certainly holds true in the case of local funds and one of the critical challenges of implementation is to understand and work creatively with both formal and informal institutions operating in and on the local level.

Sustainability and balance

One of the biggest anxieties about local funds is their sustainability outside of external funding arrangements. For those who are broadly supportive of local funds, concerns coalesce around whether, in the absence of donor support, local funds can be sustained over the long term (Satterthwaite, 2002: 185). This is a particular concern in countries where affordability on the part of poor people makes cost recovery more difficult, and where leveraging resources from local partners, especially those in the private sector, can also be a challenge. For those who do not necessarily hold a brief for local funds or are critical of them, the question is whether local funds are an appropriate instrument for addressing poverty or supporting community participation in the first place (Fumo et al., 2000: 32). Kanji (2002: 247) has cogently argued regarding social funds that they 'are no substitute for wider economic and social policies which address the distribution of material and social assets in highly unequal societies'. Furthermore, to the extent that local funds are initiated to promote participation and local governance agendas, this too can be fraught with danger; and caution needs to be exercised as to the political use made of 'the local'. As Mohan and Stokke (2000: 263) have argued, '[L]ocal participation can be used for different purposes by very different ideological stakeholders'.

Clearly local funds cannot and should not be the first or last word on social development and democracy assistance. They have to be part of broader social and economic policy repertoires and governance strategies. However, as has been argued by Mitlin and Satterthwaite (2004) and as is demonstrated through the examples highlighted in this volume, they can make a useful contribution to both development and democracy if they are well executed. Moreover, whether we like them or not, local funds are likely to be part of development cooperation for some time. This book is a contribution to ensuring that they do more good than harm, recognizing that this means, above all, that a correct balance must be achieved between support to local funds and wider support for social protection, and representative democracy.

ORGANIZATION OF THE BOOK

The book is divided into three sections. This first section on local funds and the policy environment seeks to situate the local funds phenomenon within a broader discussion of development policy and practice as it has evolved over recent decades. The following chapter looks at the origins of local funds, both in the World Bank's adoption of social funds and in the partnership models that grew up in the industrialized countries of North America and Western Europe, which were subsequently exported to late developing countries in the context of development assistance. The chapter concludes with a review of the various critiques of local funds as a platform by which to measure the achievements and shortcomings of some of the case studies reviewed in Part II. Chapter Three situates local funds within changing approaches to social development policy, governance, and democracy promotion. Chapter Four traces the trends identified in the first three introductory chapters through the experience of national level policy in a single country, Mexico. At the same time the chapter reflects on the gender impact and implications for women of evolving policy approaches.

Part II looks at experience of local funds in practice through a series of case studies. Chapter Five locates local funds within the context of current trends in development assistance and provides examples – drawn from multilateral aid to funds in Africa – of how local funds have been devised and delivered as an aid instrument, notably the AGETIP developed in francophone West Africa under the aegis of the World Bank and the International Labour Organization (ILO), and the introduction of the United Nations Capital Development Fund in local development in Mozambique. Chapter Six continues the discussion of local funds as an aid instrument in the context of DBS, making the argument that aid directed at the macro-level is not sufficient or appropriate in all circumstances and that meso- and micro-level instruments will always be needed. The chapter looks at the advantages of organizational plurality and flexibility in delivery of local funds through a review of two local funds programmes initiated by the United Kingdom's Department for International Development; the Foundation for Civil Society in Tanzania, and the Commonwealth Education Fund. Chapter Seven highlights lessons transmitted from the South to the North through a focus on participatory budgeting as it developed in Brazil and was taken up and adapted by cities in Southern Europe and the North of England. By contrast, Chapter Eight reviews the transmission of models from the North to the South through a focus on challenge funds, in particular the New Life for Paddington programme in West London, England and the City-Community-Challenge Fund pilot programme in Kampala and Jinja in Uganda.

The third and final part of the book focuses on issues of implementation and the day-to-day challenges of designing, managing, and assessing the impact of local funds. Chapter Nine considers in some detail the experience of two local funds which the international NGO, Care International manages. They are the City-Community Challenge Fund in Zambia and the human rights and governance fund in Bangladesh, called 'Manusher Jonno'. Chapter Ten concludes the book by looking at the future of local funds and drawing out some critical lessons from the design and management of local funds, considering the implications of these for a policy environment that seeks to promote both social well-being and democracy.

CHAPTER TWO

Local funds, governance, and democracy

INTRODUCTION

Local funds as they are currently deployed in development cooperation, have roots both in the social fund and challenge fund models. However, they have also evolved. Some are designed to reduce poverty and vulnerability, others to enhance local governance and promote democracy. Some try to do both, often with considerable difficulty. Local funds are delivered through a wide range of organizational forms, for example through existing NGOs, local government structures, or special purpose agencies. They can also involve a variety of funding instruments from block grants to soft loans. They have been influenced by social development policies developed in both industrialized and developing countries and, in some ways they constitute a meeting place for the implementation of both. What holds them together is a policy approach that recognizes poverty as multidimensional, and as linked to a lack of empowerment or political voice (Narayan et al., 2000a; Narayan et al., 2000b). In international development a sustainable livelihoods perspective has often framed the implementation of local funds, while in Europe the principal organizing concept is more commonly that of social exclusion. These concepts are discussed more fully in Chapter Three. Here, the endeavour is to trace the evolution of contemporary local funds from their origins with social funds – originally designed and implemented by the World Bank – as well as their roots in the challenge fund approach. These had their origins in industrialized countries but have increasingly become an important element of funding development cooperation.

THE ORIGINS AND EVOLUTION OF SOCIAL FUNDS

Social funds are mechanisms for social protection and social development that have now been part of the repertoire of international development agencies for nearly 20 years. They have evolved over time and currently come in a variety of shapes and forms. There is no universally agreed definition of a social fund although Jørgensen and Van Domelen have come close (2001: 91):

We propose to define social funds as follows: agencies that finance projects in several sectors targeted to benefit a country's poor and vulnerable groups based on a participatory manner of demand generated by local groups and screened against a set of eligibility criteria. There are agencies that would meet these criteria but are not called social funds and there are agencies that are called social funds that do not meet these criteria.

The first social funds schemes were implemented during the 1980s in Latin America and Africa with the assistance of the Bretton Woods institutions, notably the World Bank and the Inter-American Development Bank (IADB), as emergency relief funds. In fact, some social funds appeared prior to the 1980s, such as Costa Rica's *Fondo de Desarollo Social Y Asignaciones Familiares* (FODESAF), which was introduced as a welfare measure in 1975, although wider experience during the 1970s was limited. However, during the 1980s social emergency funds developed across Latin America in the wake of macro-economic reform. Between 1986 and 2000 the World Bank, which was the key driver of social funds, approved over 100 social fund loans, mostly in Latin America, where most countries now have social funds averaging US$240 million (Batkin, 2001).

Social funds were developed extensively from the early 1980s as a strategy to counteract the social costs of the macro-economic SAPs promoted and supported by the World Bank and the IMF. SAPs included a range of measures designed to stabilize macro-economic indicators and restore economic growth. They also signaled a shift in international social development policy from one that addressed basic needs through direct interventions targeted at poverty reduction and human development during the 1970s, to an emphasis on economic growth as an indirect but more effective route to poverty reduction in the 1980s. SAPs were first introduced in Latin America and Africa but the macro-economic reforms associated with them were a broader phenomenon that extended to many other parts of the world in both the North and the South. In addition to debt repayment, which was a particular feature of economic policy for indebted developing countries, they included supply side mechanisms such as trade liberalization and the introduction into public sector reform of the market principles that were a feature of industrialized countries, particularly those espousing welfare states. This shift was part of a globalized neoliberal policy agenda that at the time Toye (1987) called a 'counter-revolution' and one in which 'the World Bank explicitly argued that poverty reduction belonged to the future' (Kanji, 2002: 233).

However, not only was the task of poverty reduction put on hold but the demand for poverty alleviation increased as the social impact of macro-economic policies began to bite. Public sector reforms saw massive job losses and rising unemployment, while the loss of subsidies on public services and food staples, along with the introduction of cost recovery and user charges, saw living costs escalating with a particularly negative impact on the urban poor. In this context, social funds were initially conceived of as compensatory measures or social safety nets. They later became integral to and an essential component of the three-pronged strategy that made up the 'Washington Consensus' – broad-based economic growth as the main route to poverty reduction; human development as a long-term approach to social development; and social safety nets as a means of supporting the poorest and reducing risk for most vulnerable.

Initially an attempt was made to distinguish between the 'adjustment poor' and the 'chronic poor'. The first category was that section of the population made poor by the impact of SAPs and seen to be in temporary poverty as a result. For example, this group might include redundant workers from downsized public sector organizations or those who were formally employed in firms that had moved towards employing casualized workers. The chronic poor were deemed to be those who were already poor, well before the introduction of macro-economic reforms, and who were likely to remain so; for example the long-term unemployed. However, this distinction was very difficult to effect in practice and was later dropped. During the early stages, social funds programmes were supposed to compensate the 'adjustment poor' through anti-cyclical income maintenance and social expenditure programmes. In the later phases, the poor in general – both adjustment poor and chronic poor – were addressed through promotional measures that involved them in productive activities, such as employment creation or public works programmes, as well as through the community-based provision of social services (Cornia, 1999: 2). Two schemes typify these two phases in the development of social funds: the first were the SEFs and the second, the Social Investment Funds (SIFs).

The SEFs, which were introduced in tandem with SAPs, had as their goal the transfer of resources to the poor through multi-sectoral programmes such as employment generation and support for social services. The first SEF was the *Fondo Social de Emergencia* in Bolivia, established in 1987. It functioned largely as a Keynesian-type counter-cyclical 'employment fund' (Tendler, 2000: 114). It had as its objective to address the plight of mine workers who were unemployed as a result of the collapse of tin prices and the closure of state-run mines. The Programme of Action to Mitigate the Social Cost of Adjustment (PAMSCAD) was set up in Ghana in the same year, with similar aims. SEFs were mainly managed outside of state institutions and were entirely reliant on external funding. The emergency funds were presented as an innovative alternative to the conventional welfare systems that were not adequate to the task and which could respond more swiftly and effectively than such systems, not least because of their relative autonomy from governments.

With time it became clear that SAPs were not going to be a quick fix. The notion of 'no pain, no gain' continued to prevail but it was clear that the pain was going to be around for some time. As such, short-term emergency funds were an inappropriate response to the worsened conditions of the majority of the population in adjusting economies. With this in mind, SEFs were replaced by SIFs, which were designed to operate over a longer time horizon. They were also funded to a greater extent by governments, as well as donors, and were not necessarily set up as independent organizations. Some, such as the AGETIP in Senegal, are still in place and are autonomous agencies with non-profit legal status. Others such as the Zambian Social Investment Fund (ZamSIF) are located within government ministries and have become important vehicles for decentralization. The aim of SIFs is also different. They characterize a shift from support for basic welfare to support for basic services. Cornia (2001: 8) has argued that SIFs are 'aimed at the alleviation of poverty by means of activities intended to expand the supply and utilization of services in the field of health, education, training and water and sanitation'. Thus it was during this formative period that social funds acquired a more permanent footing as a sustained social development strategy. It was also during this time that notions of partnership and co-funding emerged as an important component of local funds.

In addition to the World Bank, the United Nations Capital Development Fund (UNCDF), the United Nations Development Programme (UNDP), and UN-HABITAT, as well as a number of bilateral donors – including the United Kingdom's Department for International Development (DFID) and the Swedish International Development Agency (SIDA) – have taken up a range of local funds, either directly or indirectly, modelled on or offered as an improvement to social funds. Through the involvement of a broader range of organizations and the influence of NGOs with their greater experience of working at the local level, social funds have evolved further, and in a third phase of development are now seen as an important response to the challenge of 'social risk management' which constitutes the current operational framework of the World Bank's social funds (Jørgensen and Van Domelen, 2001). This echoes the emphasis on livelihoods and social exclusion, both important concepts informing social development practice in the North and the South and considered in more depth in the following chapter.

A fourth evolution in the development of social funds was to emerge out of this focus on social funds as mechanisms for social risk management. This was a stress not only on alleviating poverty but also on creating an enabling environment in which this could happen. This coincided with a turn in development thinking during the late 1990s towards questions of how the state functions (World Bank, 1997). It would probably not be unfair to say that during the heyday of neoliberal orthodoxy in the 1980s, when social funds were initially conceived, they were seen as vehicles for bypassing the state and showing up ineffective and recalcitrant governments. Certainly to the extent that they involved strategies to strengthen civil society, the intention was initially as much to circumvent inefficient government institutions as to enhance the capacity of people to make demands of them. However, by the end of the 1990s the emphasis had moved towards the latter objective and towards eliciting 'good governance', a now familiar if contested notion in the development lexicon and

public–private partnerships, as a critical component of sound development management. It is in this context that local funds were increasingly
informed by the design and aims of challenge funds, discussed below and
in more detail in Chapter Eight.

CHALLENGE FUNDS AND PARTNERSHIP

The challenge fund model has increasingly come to influence international
development cooperation and the nature of local funds. Contemporary
local funds contain two critical components that parallel social funds as
well as having a new element in the mix, deriving from the influence of
challenge funds. In terms of parallels, like early social funds there is a
poverty reduction focus and like later social funds, this often relates to the
development of infrastructure and services. In terms of innovation, the
influence of the challenge fund model on contemporary local funds has
been in the promotion of partnerships and particularly in the involvement
of the private sector. This has been a critical dimension that for better or
worse has come to inform the design and implementation of local funds in
countries of the South.

Challenge funds are a child of the industrialized countries and most particularly the United States, where they are manifold in number and where
they constitute an important part of the funding repertoire of many local
authorities, state governments, private companies, charitable trusts,
libraries, museums, research organizations, and universities. The idea
behind challenge funds is to get people, groups, or communities to compete
for resources on the basis of putting forward innovative and efficient projects. There is also an element of agenda setting in the operation of most
challenge funds, as awards are granted to those who tailor their proposals to
the aims and objectives of the award-making bodies. This can be restrictive,
for example, when research funding or education grants are geared towards
immediate or vocational aims and preclude 'blue sky thinking'. However,
challenge funds can be employed to good effect as, for example, with the
City Community Challenge Fund (C3) in Uganda, highlighted in Chapter
Six, aimed at reducing poverty while at the same time contributing towards
a more open political and social environment. Challenge funds are often
associated with area-based development strategies. For example, local
authorities or civil society organizations are encouraged to take on the role
of civic leadership in forming partnerships that harness resources, talent,
and energy from a wide range of actors and sectors. In industrialized countries this approach was put in motion to address the problems of urban
decay, while in the developing countries it became a vehicle for addressing
urban poverty as well as promoting local development partnerships.

In industrialized countries Public–Private Partnerships (PPPs) came to
dominate policy discourse from the 1980s onwards. The approach origi-
nated in the United States but it was the United Kingdom that pioneered

new models of partnership and private sector involvement in service delivery, grounded in the principles of New Public Management (NPM). These received high praise from the IFIs, as is evident in the *World Development Report* on infrastructure (World Bank, 1994), for example. Beginning with the 1992 Conservative administration in the United Kingdom, market mechanisms were introduced into areas of public service provision that for political reasons could not be privatized. From the late 1990s the approach was subsequently adopted and extended by Britain's New Labour government, to include not only utilities such as electricity and telecommunications but also key aspects of social policy such as health care and education (Le Grand and Bartlett, 1993). The challenge fund approach afforded the inclusion of community or social sectors in partnership arrangements at the local level and this became a strong feature of local funds.

Community involvement and participatory development has a long pedigree in international development cooperation. However, as was the case more generally, this often meant little more than the perfunctory consultation of communities or the instrumental use of community energies in the implementation of pre-determined development goals. Designers of local funds sought to eschew these shortcomings and to involve users and representatives of the social sector in decision-making. The clarion call of development organizations from NGOs through to the World Bank was one of promoting the 'voices of the poor' at all stages of the development policy process (Narayan et al., 2000a, 2000b). This was not particularly new in development practice, even if it was innovative for the large multilateral and bilateral donor agencies, as Penrose (2000: 243) has pointed out:

> For most development agencies, particularly northern-based non-governmental organizations (NGOs), 'partnership' is not seen as an option but as an obligation. It has been Oxfam's policy, for example, to work through local partners wherever possible since the 1960s. It is assumed that local organizations representative of the local population are essential to the long-term development process.

Nevertheless, the understanding and practice of partnership has broadened and deepened. Initially associated only with public-private relationships, partnerships are increasingly understood in broader terms to include NGOs, CSOs, and CBOs. Moreover, it is increasingly recognized that they need to be inclusive and participatory, with social partners involved in policy dialogue and decision-making as well as implementation. Furthermore, ways of collaborating need not be simply contractual but can include consortia, networks, alliances, and coalitions working in tightly or loosely bound association, with greater or lesser hierarchy among the partners, towards shared or negotiated development goals.

The benefits of a partnership approach can broadly be summarized as follows: they can lead to complementarity of effort (Evans, 1996a, 1996b) and co-production, with different partners bringing different strengths to the partnership (Ostrom, 1996); they can increase provider responsiveness to users (Brett, 1996); and they can lead to efficiency gains from public participation (Moser, 1993). Social and political gains are thought to relate to increased equity and reduced social exclusion (Osborne, 2000), the generation of social capital and democracy (Coleman 1990; Putnam, 1993), and increased synergies between state and society (Evans, 1996a, 1996b). The conditions for successful partnership are outlined in Table 2.1.

This is an idealized perspective. Just as local funds cannot promote democracy or sound governance on their own, so there are considerable constraints to their fostering equitable partnerships. Relationships between partners can be difficult and confound the most well resourced and astutely designed local funds. These include hierarchies that inhibit participation by social partners, as well as the inability of many government agencies to make a successful shift from the dominant to one of a number of partners, albeit in a coordinator role. Nevertheless, Peters (1998) sees the value of partnerships in the fact that they reduce transaction costs through continuous rather than transient relationships founded on consensus or conflict management models of collective action. Experience suggests that local funds that are able to sustain partnerships that are at least based on a common language are better able to negotiate priorities and even develop shared agendas. The biggest challenge for local funds seeking to reduce poverty and promote democracy is to hold hierarchies and power relations between partners in check. Under such conditions, proponents of partnerships are convinced that they can lead to better access to improved services, can foster demand-driven approaches, and allow people more influence over the type of services they receive. As illustrated by some of the case study examples in the chapters that follow, such as the experiments with participatory budgeting discussed in Chapter Seven, partnerships can be creative and enhance user involvement in ways that go beyond technocratic approaches to 'good governance'. However, genuine partnerships – which enable community organizations and citizens' representatives to negotiate priorities and monitor the implementation of policies and programmes – are difficult to achieve, let alone partnerships that promote democratic governance.

Table 2.1   Conditions for successful partnership

1. Two or more actors are involved, at least one of which is a public partner.
2. Each participant can bargain without reference back to other sources of authority.
3. Each partner is willing to make a stable commitment.
4. The partnership is an enduring relationship and not just a contract.
5. The parameters of the partnership are negotiated.
6. Each partner brings resources, whether material or symbolic.
7. There is shared responsibility for outcomes.
8. All partners are treated with respect.
9. The strengths and limitations of different partners are recognized.
10. Conflict is accommodated and not disallowed by consensus goals.

Source: Adapted from Peters (1998)

FUNDING 'GOOD GOVERNANCE'

The term 'governance' has been around for a long time and has a number of meanings. It is often seen as a technical term for describing the administrative effectiveness and efficiency of state institutions. This is not the way it is used here. At its simplest, governance refers to the manner in which power is exercised in the management of a country's social and economic resources. It focuses particularly on the relationship between 'government' and 'citizen' (Painter, 2000). There are two ways in which the concept of governance is used to refer to this relationship:

- The first and narrower definition relates to sound development supervision and is concerned with administration and management.
- The second and broader definition is also concerned with democratic politics and policy.

It is argued here that both characteristics are fundamental to advancing democracy. Stoker (1998: 38) defines governance as:

[. . .] the action, manner or system of governing in which the boundary between organizations and public and private sectors has become permeable [. . .] The essence of governance is the interactive relationship between and within government and non-governmental forces.

According to Stoker this implies joint action, a common purpose and value framework, as well as continuous interaction towards a shared agenda. In this perspective, good governance requires a democratic and engaged civil society that is able to ensure that neither the political nor economic system is 'captured' by elite interest groups and distorted to serve their needs. This can only be achieved when citizens are able to hold their institutions to account – as voters (in the case of political systems), as consumers (in the case of economic systems), and as users (in the case of service delivery) (Archer, 1994).

However, the term 'good governance' has also become associated with attempts to restrain government and reduce the influence of the state. The good governance agenda rose to prominence in international development agencies at the beginning of the 1990s. Here it is a normative concept about how development should be practiced and was used to identify a cluster of policy ideas, which its proponents (especially the World Bank) saw as a model for effective and beneficial economic and political management. It quickly developed the status of an international orthodoxy, and for the past decade has served as a general guiding principle for major donor agencies in the distribution of development and relief assistance (Goetz and O'Brien, 1995; Nunnenkamp, 1995; Robinson, 1995).

In particular, the notion of good governance has informed the approach adopted by international development agencies in assisting the countries of Eastern Europe to move from state-managed economic systems to market-based systems (Archer, 1994). Two factors coincided to ensure the popularity of 'good governance' in relation to the global development agenda. The first was the collapse of communism, graphically signified by the fall of the Berlin Wall in 1989. In looking for reform policies for the former Soviet Union and the countries of eastern Europe, Western governments and the IFIs turned to what they saw as the tried and tested policies associated with macro-economic structural adjustment, but sought to avoid some of their earlier failings in the countries of Latin America and Africa by trying to create an 'enabling environment' for the economy. This they did by focusing on institutional reform and more particularly, by strengthening partnerships for public service delivery, such as infrastructure, services, health, and education. They were less successful in strengthening the capacity of key elements of the state, but the principles of 'good governance' were nevertheless set in place by this experience, which is how the concept of governance became associated both with the notion of rolling back the state and the promotion of PPPs. The second factor was the remarkable economic success of the East Asian 'tiger economies', which began to reinforce the importance of strong and interventionist states as a means of protecting and enabling private markets, which in turn reinforced the importance accorded to the good governance agenda.

For the World Bank (1992: 1), good governance is understood as follows:

Good governance, for the World Bank, is synonymous with sound development management [. . .] Good governance is central to creating and sustaining an environment which fosters strong and equitable development, and it is an essential complement to sound economic policies. Governments play a key role in the provision of public goods. They establish the rules that make markets work efficiently and, more problematically, they correct for market failure. In order to play this role, they need revenues, and agents to collect revenues and produce the public goods. This in turn requires systems of accountability, adequate and reliable information, and efficiency in resource management and the delivery of public services.

In this understanding, good governance is barely different from good government except that the former works more efficiently and effectively with markets. This technical approach to governance owes more to public administration and management than it does to political theory. A political approach to governance, such as is adopted here, sees it not so much as a set of functions but as an expression of power.

In the context of international development the good governance framework is also controversial because it has emanated from donor discourse and in parallel with arguments about the universality of human rights, it is asked: how universal are the standards of good governance given the very many different ways in which state society relations can be structured? This question is raised with particular reference to good governance as a feature of aid conditionality (Doornbos, 2003). Second, there is the question of whether an approach that sets itself the task of 'manufacturing' from the outside principles, values, processes, and even institutions, which are not organic to the societies in which they are being promoted, is desirable and can be sustainable. For example, it is argued that civil society is not a concept universal to all societies and rather emerged at a distinctive point in European history, rendering it potentially meaningless in different social and political contexts (Lewis, 2002). Third, critics argue that at heart the good governance agenda remains a market-driven competitive model that is antithetical to development (Archer, 1994). Moreover, the consensus orientation of good governance seeks, in principle, the greatest good for the greatest number, but it operates in contexts where the playing field is not level; contexts that favour the strong over the weak, the powerful over the powerless, and that serve to undermine conflictual processes through which voiceless people are sometimes better able to express their dissatisfaction. Thus it is possible that in countries with widespread disadvantage and weak institutions of governance, poverty and poor governance can come together in a vicious rather than a virtuous circle.

While there is little consensus as to what constitutes good governance, there is general agreement that bad governance, whether understood in managerial or political terms, is not good for most and is especially bad for the poor. Combating it is critical to achieving effective development (Goetz and Gaventa, 2001). To create a virtuous circle of governance means going beyond technical approaches and addressing state society relationships as suggested by Painter (2000). This in turn does not mean imposing Western models of democracy but rather referring to the manner in which power is exercised in decision-making and understanding how this impacts on the management of a country's social and economic resources. Against this background, a growing number of proponents and supporters of local funds have sought to use such funds to create an atmosphere in which poor people can have greater control over their lives and greater voice. This has prompted an expansion of local funds aimed at fostering local development and democracy. For example, the World Bank expanded its social funds portfolio to include Municipal Development Funds (MDFs), which are designed to strengthen institutional capacity at local level. The UNCDF created the Local Development Funds (LDFs) with similar goals and philanthropic organizations have joined in, for example the Ford Foundation's Asset Building and Community Development Programme.

Factors militating against democratic governance are multiple and no one seriously expects local funds on their own to transform difficult governance relationships and institutional environments. Moreover, as pointed out in the introductory chapter, there are tensions associated with democracy promotion in the context of development. Western notions of democracy, whether in the Tocquevillian or Westminster traditions, do not necessarily travel and transplant well and are not always well received. Further, donor governments and aid agencies are habitually uncomfortable with the idea of democracy enhancing governance, 'fearing that grassroots political activity would veer into leftist political movements' (Carothers and Ottaway, 2000: 7). It is for this reason that local funds though starting out with the objective of promoting democracy, often fall into a concern with the more technical dimensions of governance. This tension is paralleled in the different approaches to decentralization, of which local funds have often been an integral part.

LOCAL FUNDS AND DECENTRALIZATION

From the mid-1980s countries throughout the world began experimenting with forms of decentralization, early examples in sub-Saharan Africa being Ghana, Nigeria, Tanzania, and Zambia (Conyers, 1983). By the mid-1990s, 80 per cent of countries, all with very different political dispensations, were engaged in some form of decentralization (Crook and Manor, 2000). Whether understood in an administrative sense as a policy framework 'in which public goods and services are provided primarily through the revealed preferences of individuals by market mechanisms' (Rondinelli et al., 1989: 59) or in relation to an explicit democratizing function (Manor 1999, 5), decentralization has become one of the core components of political conditionality in international development cooperation (World Bank, 1997). While the decentralization agenda is heavily donor-driven, disenchantment with bloated central bureaucracies is not confined to international development agencies. Across the political spectrum decentralization has been favoured as a mechanism for improving accountability and transparency and for improving state society relations. In other words, strengthening local government has been justified not only as a means of making government more efficient but as a way of increasing democratic participation (Heller 2001).

Decentralization nevertheless has its sceptics. Heller (2001) points out that there are no a priori reasons why more localized forms of governance are necessarily democratic and suggests that under some contexts decentralized authority can be quite pernicious. The most obvious example of this is indirect rule under colonialism, when local despots in the service of an imperial power exercised decentralized authority. Localized forms of governance offer no automatic improvement on central government. Local government has as much, if not more, potential for elite capture and might not have the human or financial resources to cope with the demands made upon it by decentralization strategies (Samoff, 1990; Schuurman, 1997; Slater, 1989). Indeed, it has been pointed out that there is little empirical evidence to support or refute the efficacy of decentralization (Faguet, 2004; Manor, 1999). What is clear is that local government occupies an ambiguous and perhaps even contradictory role. On the one hand it is undoubtedly part of the state but on the other, it can appear as a relatively autonomous sphere of government given that it is close to if not actually part of civil society. As such, achieving effective local governance – a sound relationship between the local state and society at the local level – is crucial to the project of democratic decentralization. It is to this end that a number of local funds programmes have been employed. However, the question is, how is the notion of 'sound' governance understood and does it relate to increased local democratization or efficient and effective management or, ideally, both?

Decentralization can apply both to local funds themselves and to the governments with which they interact. In government this occurs where central governments devolve responsibilities to district councils and municipalities. In terms of local funds, decentralization refers to the devolving and outsourcing of responsibility and activities to other providers such as NGOs or CSOs on the grounds that they will provide a better and more demand-oriented service. Local funds are themselves seen as an important feature of decentralization and they often have as part of their objectives the building of administrative or consultative capacity within lower tiers of government. Moreover, social funds that used to be more centralized are increasingly giving way to more decentralized local fund models. A recent study of social funds and decentralization showed that those social funds that were decentralized found it easier to engage with and involve local governments in development initiatives (Parker and Serrano, 2000).

Recent studies suggest that the decentralizing of social funds is taking place in a growing number of countries because it is seen as an opportunity to increase the involvement of local governments as partners (Fumo et al., 2000: 14–15; Parker and Serrano, 2000), although Tendler (2000: 115) argues that the majority of social funds do not fully devolve power, resources, and responsibility to the district and local governments with which they work. She posits that at best social funds represent deconcentration where power does not devolve from central government but is merely redeployed away from the centre to regional or local sites. The World Bank supported social fund in Zambia, Zamsif, is an example where this has happened and where the fund is employed in support of decentralization to the district level over and above a focus on enhanced governance, understood in terms of state–society relations. In seeking to analyse local funds in relation to decentralization, therefore, it is important to identify whether a genuinely decentralized or a deconcentrated model is at work, as different dynamics will unfold in either case. These in turn will affect the extent and nature of both government and public participation in local funds as well as the use made of resources.

The early generation of local funds, emerging in the wake of the critique of social funds, was less likely to be located within government. Taking the form of civil society assistance through NGOs or CSOs, problems sometimes arose through local funds setting up parallel institutions, thereby failing to have an influencing effect on existing government organizations. Thus, local funds ran the risk of setting in motion a substitution effect, whereby they or the organizations they support took on duties that should have been performed by government. Linked to this was the problem of fungibility, with government agencies reducing their allocations to areas covered by local funds. This has been particularly documented in relation to social funds. In Egypt, for example, which has one of the largest social funds, central government allocations to local government were explicitly cut back because of anticipated resources coming from the social fund. Similarly, in Honduras allocations to the Ministries of Health and Education declined when the local government received resources from the social fund (World Bank, 1997, cited in Fumo et al., 2000: 12 and Tendler and Serrano, 1999: 19). This in turn led to further problems of facilitating the mismanagement of local government resources. Thus it could under-mine attempts at enhancing the transparency and accountability of government (Parker and Serrano, 2000: 44–5).

A further anxiety regarding the relationship between local funds and decentralization is that strengthening local institutional capacity could be at odds with state-driven efforts towards decentralization. By financing projects outside the remit of line ministries, local funds are thought to potentially erode the commitment and interest of government towards the promotion of local development. At one level this objection is fairly simply overcome by promoting sub-projects and criteria that engage government institutions, rather than exclude or bypass them. At another level, how-ever, a different mindset is required. After all, decentralization is not just a technical exercise. Heller (2001: 133) puts the case well:

> Strengthening and empowering local government has been justified not only on the grounds of making government more efficient but also on the grounds of increasing accountability and participation [...] in its contemporary incarnation, decentralization in the developing world, especially when driven by international development agencies, has more often than not been associated with the rolling back of the state, the extension of bureaucratic control and the marketization of social services.

Where then do local funds fit in? Are they part of a technicist or managerial agenda or can they serve to democratize decentralization?

CONCLUSION

Social funds were not initially directed at the local level. Indeed, as pointed out above, they were initially introduced as national level interventions meant as an antidote to the adverse effects of SAPs. However, they increas-ingly came to be used as a means of decentralizing the management and financing of small infrastructure and service delivery projects. In articula-tion with other forms of local level development assistance, social funds joined a wider range of local level approaches that advocated community-driven development. As such they moved to the heart of the World Bank's decentralization agenda and its accompanying valorization of 'the local' in pursuit of managerial efficiency. Indeed some might argue that develop-ment interventions that emphasize local demand-based or community driven approaches are an essential component of the World Bank's notion of good governance, understood in purely technical terms. Here local actors, organizations, or their representatives are enticed into taking over some of the roles of poorly functioning states, or into engaging the local state in non-contestational forms of state–society relations that contribute to development as an 'anti-politics machine' (Ferguson, 1990).

Mohan and Stokke (2000: 255) argue that the emphasis in development on 'local participation and empowerment' and 'localism', which represents community relations in the 'non-threatening language of trust, networks, reciprocity and associations' rather than the potential for collective action is depoliticizing. This has been the approach of the World Bank which, as Fine (2001) and Harriss (2002) have pointed out, renders participation, social capital, and decentralization as part of Ferguson's 'anti-politics machine'. While this is no doubt true, the response should not simply be to eschew local level initiatives. Directing development assistance exclusively at central government is not the answer. Nor are all local funds derivative of social funds or dominated by World Bank thinking and agendas. It is argued here that local funds can also assist towards a process of democratic deepening. Democratization involves the exercise of citizenship rights and associational autonomy (Fox, 1994) as a generalized approach to political action. This in turn means confronting the deficiencies of bureaucratic and party political practice. In this respect, local funds can play a useful role by providing arenas in which people can participate in decision-making processes around local initiatives. They can also trigger institutional transition by requiring more transparency and accountability on the part of local government organizations. This is not to suggest that local funds always do this. However, the way in which they are designed and implemented can keep an eye trained on opportunities for political engagement and voice, alongside policy, planning, and service delivery. It is to these issues, and to the relationship between local funds and social policy, that the following chapter turns.

CHAPTER THREE

Local funds, social policy, and development

INTRODUCTION

Donors are increasingly including local funds as a critical component of development practice, particularly in relation to social development goals. For this reason the present chapter seeks to situate local funds within evolving social policy frameworks, particularly as they relate to international development. By way of introduction, three observations are made. First, local funds are not typically associated with traditional welfare states. Here central governments are the main providers of benefits, which in turn are linked to contributions made in the context of formal employment. However, cradle-to-grave employment and state welfare support are a fast fading experience for citizens of many industrialized countries. They have never been the experience of citizens of most developing countries. In this context, efforts to reduce poverty and combat social exclusion are more diverse and often piecemeal. Although local funds can be an integral part of state welfare policy, they do not equate with conventional social security because they are small in size and of finite duration. Nevertheless, they are an increasingly significant component of post-welfare state social policy approaches.

Second, because of their size and scale, local funds can easily promote or fall into a residual model of welfare that sees responsibility for social support lying at the micro-level, for example with family support and individual charity. Under this approach the provision of state welfare benefits is minimal and private philanthropy is common. Alternatively, local funds fall into what might be called an 'enterprise approach' whereby people are assisted to help themselves, for example through micro-enterprise support, micro-credit schemes, or as in more industrialized countries, 'welfare to work' programmes. Either way, local funds constitute short-term and finite interventions and as such are no magic bullet for enhancing social security. When they rely primarily on the agency and social networks of people with already scarce resources, their impact can be extremely limited and they are no substitute for more thorough-going social protection. As such, they are simply one quite circumscribed mechanism towards improving people's life chances. However, when well executed they can provide safety nets and can effectively kick-start a process that is more sustaining and sustainable.

A third observation is that local funds are founded on very different organizational arrangements from those funds associated either with traditional welfare or developmental states. Whereas the former are predicated on state involvement in delivery, contemporary frameworks of social policy assume multi-sectoral approaches with strong involvement on the part of both the private and social sectors. Inter-organizational relationships can be either slackly coordinated – for example where service providers are in loose association with one another – or they can be more tightly drawn into more formal partnerships. Local funds fit firmly within this institutional landscape and are thought to often flourish best when not too tightly bound in their relations with government.

In order to understand the strengths and limitations of local funds as a vehicle for social development, it is important to understand how social policy approaches and institutional relationships have evolved. This chapter first defines social policy and traces its evolution within the context of broader shifts in development policy. Second, the chapter traces shifts in institutional responsibility for social and development policy. This is in order to demonstrate how local funds are situated within broader policy frameworks, and relate to the current emphasis in international development on institutional reform and improved governance. While different paradigms and approaches are treated discretely for the purposes of descriptive and analytical manageability, it should be noted at the outset that the evolution of policy goals and implementation strategies is an iterative rather than a linear process. As with most categorizations, few policies are pure in form and most are hybrids. Similarly, few local funds fit straightforwardly into one single paradigm and, as ensuing chapters demonstrate, the design of local funds is often informed by more than one policy goal – for example aiming both to reduce poverty and to improve governance, or to enhance livelihoods and advance human rights. Indeed, local funds themselves evolve over time, adapting their aims and mutating in practice as a response to changing development paradigms and to demand on the ground.

THE FOUNDATIONS OF SOCIAL POLICY

Social policy is difficult to define as the term is used to refer both to the academic discipline 'Social Policy' and to what it studies, social policies themselves. The accusation is sometimes made that social policy is 'much more concerned with practicalities than it is with ideas' (Mullard and Spicker, 1998: 3), having as its critical focus how well-being can be supported through social action. However, there is a tension within the discipline of Social Policy between those who are primarily concerned with how to administer welfare and assess its effectiveness and those who are concerned about what sorts of welfare should be administered in the first place (Alcock et al., 1998: 9). The first position is often characterized as pragmatic, while bald ideologies are often said to inform the second. Both approaches have led to social policy being characterized as atheoretical. However, theoretical ideas underpin the value frameworks on which social policies and political ideologies are based, and there is a very close relationship between them. Theory has always influenced social policy, either implicitly or explicitly, whether it was the Marxist ideas that informed the social security system of the former Soviet Union, the social democratic underpinnings of many European welfare states, or the liberal individualism that characterizes the minimalist welfare provision of 'bootstrap capitalism' (Stoesz, 2000) in the United States. The theoretical foundations of social policy are therefore generally considered to be normative; put another way, they are not value free but rather guided by social objectives.

There have been many typologies of social policy and the normative theory that informs it (Esping-Anderson, 1990; Hewitt, 1992; Moser, 1989; Pinker, 1973; Taylor-Gooby and Dale, 1981; Titmuss, 1974). Most approaches generally fail to include in their analysis countries from developing countries (MacPherson and Midgley, 1987), although increasingly there is a focus on the global economy and its impact on social policy (Deacon, 2000; Deacon et al., 1997; Mullard and Spicker, 1998; Yeates, 2001). Exceptions include the work of Midgley (1993, 1995) on social development, which relates very specifically to the international context. Midgley (1995: 1) has defined social development as an attempt to harmonize social and economic objectives within wider development processes. For Midgley, it is this harmonization that 'differentiates social development from the other approaches for promoting social welfare'. He identifies three dominant ideological traditions in social development – 'individualism', 'collectivism', and 'populism' – which broadly mirror liberal, Marxist, and communitarian approaches to social theory respectively. While a detailed discussion of social theory is beyond the scope of this book, it is worth paying some regard; because as Mullard and Spicker (1998: 3) have argued:

> Social theory [. . .] helps, first, to describe what is happening in society by putting the material into some kind of classification or order. Second, theory makes analysis possible, by identifying the relationships between the different factors and explaining what is happening. Third, theory makes it possible to work out principles for action.

With this in mind it is useful to identify the theoretical basis for the development of local funds in order to understand the philosophy behind them, where they fit within a broader repertoire of social action, and what they can and cannot do.

Social policy is conventionally associated with state provision of social services. Indeed, social policy has been defined as 'a deliberate intervention by the state to redistribute resources amongst its citizens so as to achieve a welfare objective' (Baldock et al., 1999: xxi). In nineteenth century Britain this was confined to policies such as the Poor Law, which sought to address only the immediate needs of the most destitute. Government only intervened when family support and local charity was insufficient or unavailable. This approach is known as residualism. A residualist approach characterizes contemporary social policy in the United States, which is focused only on the 'deserving poor'. However, in Europe in the post-war era, government involvement in social policy was dramatically enhanced as welfare states were formed with the aim of ensuring certain fundamental living standards for all citizens. The welfare state in Britain, for example, saw economic planning along Keynesian lines that sought to guarantee full employment and to provide unemployment and social security benefits in its absence. The social wage was also enhanced through public investment in key social sectors such as education and housing, as well as a national health service. Similarly, in developing countries social policy in the colonial era was equated with state provision of services and, apart from the obvious differentials in the resources involved, largely mirrored policy trajectories in industrialized countries at the time.

SOCIAL POLICY AND DEVELOPMENT IN THE TWENTIETH CENTURY

During the early development decades of the 1950s and 1960s it was believed that modernization and industrialization would lead to levels of economic growth that would allow benefits to 'trickle down' so that the employment prospects and welfare of everyone would improve. A residual model of welfare also informed the policy frameworks of post-colonial governments. Here interventions in support of social need were minimal, being confined to addressing social pathologies such as crime and the destitute such as widows and orphans (Hardiman and Midgley, 1982). However, the residual model was unable to cope with the mass poverty that grew up in many developing countries from the 1960s onwards and the accompanying demand for basic social services. Hence residualism gave way to what has been dubbed an incremental welfare model, whereby state social sector spending on health, education, and housing increased according to available resources and in response to public pressure. It was driven very much by a desire to achieve political legitimacy and was focused on the demands of urban middle-class elites (Hardiman and Midgley, 1982). Hall and Midgley (2004: 5) argue that 'this incremental approach is still characteristic of social sector planning in most of the developing and much of the industrialized world', except in places where it gave way to the new right policies of the 1980s. These were forged by Ronald Reagan in the United States and Margaret Thatcher in the United Kingdom, and came to permeate international development policy as well.

Nevertheless, there was an intervening period associated with the 'redistribution with growth' paradigm. It included a focus on basic needs and the provision of basic goods and services to the poor (Stewart, 1985; Streeten et al., 1981). Initiated during the 1970s, it was particularly linked to World

Bank policy under the presidency of Robert McNamara. In social policy terms Moser (1993) has usefully identified this as an 'anti-poverty approach'; the state was still regarded as the primary institutional actor, but international development agencies were also seen to have an increasingly important role in social development. However, rather than providing social protection or social security, the focus was on supporting the self-help and cooperative activities of poor people themselves. It is in this context that the concept of social development arose, defined by the United Nations as 'a shift in emphasis from protection to development, from remedial activities to more positive forms of action' (Economic and Social Council of the UN, 1969). A more recent manifestation of this enterprise approach to poverty reduction is the current sustainable livelihoods framework (SLF), which is discussed below and which focuses on 'the wealth of the poor' through efforts to enhance their capabilities or assets. It is possible to see these early trends in social policy – residualism, basic needs, and an enterprise approach to poverty reduction – reflected in the design of local funds in that they are both premised on the view that social needs should be met through individual effort in the market place, supplemented by family and community support. This was reinforced by the neoliberal turn in development policy from the 1980s onwards.

The neoliberal turn was most clearly manifest in the SAPs, imposed by the World Bank and the IMF, as a form of conditionality on countries seeking soft loans. It has been driven since by the so-called 'Washington consensus', which advocates market deregulation and competition, export-led economic growth with increased incentives for foreign investment, an end to nationalized industries and state monopolies, and a reduction in public expenditure, including on social services. Social sectors such as health and primary education bore the brunt of spending cutbacks in many countries implementing SAPs, and social indicators worsened (Kanji and Manji, 1991; Moser, 1996), while poverty and vulnerability increased (Cornia et al., 1987; Ghai, 1991; Stewart, 1995). As a response to the negative social impact of structural adjustment, social policy became focused on compensatory measures or 'social safety nets' and enterprise support for the new poor rendered unemployed by cutbacks and downsizing. As indicated in the introductory chapter, these compensatory measures largely took the form of social funds, which were deemed to be finite and dispensable once the adjustment period was over. As they evolved, an anti-poverty approach became more evident in the design of local funds, with some adopting a clear enterprise approach.

CONTEMPORARY PERSPECTIVES IN SOCIAL AND DEVELOPMENT POLICY

Neoliberalism continues to impact upon contemporary development policy and is keenly felt in European social policy too, with increasing stress being placed on the role of the market in social welfare. This can be clearly seen in the promotion of private pensions and insurance as the bedrock of social protection, as well as in more institutional manifestations of an enterprise culture, such as the development of internal or quasi-markets in the provision of public services (Bartlett, et al., 1998; Le Grand and Bartlett, 1993; Leys, 2001). This represents a growing fusion between the paradigms informing policy approaches in industrialized and developing countries, as both respond to the inexorable forces of global economic integration. It has been claimed that economic globalization has rendered social democratic policies unviable, as national governments are unable to continue delivering the modern welfare state (Gray, 1996). It has also been suggested that the effect of the 'neoliberal thrust of globalization [. . .] is to strengthen market forces and the economic realm at the cost of the institutions of social protection' (Mishra, 1998: 32). Hence the contemporary social policy arena is one of atrophying welfare states and shrinking formal employment where these existed, and resignation that these are unattainable where they do not. This is the current policy framework into which local funds are being inserted.

Poverty reduction

Direct poverty alleviation was a key goal of development aid during the 1970s but was displaced during the high tide of neoliberalism in the 1980s, when the focus shifted towards efficiency and economic growth, with poverty being tackled indirectly through the 'trickle down' of the benefits of growth. However, direct poverty reduction became a more explicit focus of development once again in response to the negative social impact of macro-economic reforms. This can be seen, for example, in World Bank (1990, 2000) policy from the 1990s onwards and Britain's DFID's (1997, 2000; Lipton and Maxwell, 1992) emphasis on poverty from about the same time, culminating towards the end of the decade in the first and second white papers on international development cooperation. Over the last decade or so, increasing attention has been paid to understanding the 'multidimensional' nature of poverty. Until this time, most standard definitions of poverty used in the context of development cooperation focused solely on the issue of economic deprivation; poverty was defined in terms of having enough income to survive or food to eat. The success of poverty intervention strategies was determined by the movement of population above or below a particular income level threshold. There was an attempt to broaden the conceptualization of poverty under the basic needs approach, which emphasized that even the most minimal fulfilment of human needs demanded a wider range of material requirements than simply food or a cash income. In particular, access to basic health, education, and other essential services was stressed from the 1970s onwards, alongside the need for individuals to have access to employment opportunities and the right to participate in community life.

The work of Amartya Sen became particularly influential on the debates on reconceptualizing poverty and human development during the 1990s. His notions of 'functionings', 'capabilities', 'opportunities', and 'entitlements' contributed to an important paradigm shift in how poverty was understood and how human development was addressed (Sen and Drèze, 1999; Sen, 2001). *Functioning* concerns those actions or circumstances that a person may value doing or being, such as living a long life, being healthy or well educated. The concept encompasses relatively elemental states such as being adequately nourished, through to complex personal states such as the capacity to participate in community life. *Capability* refers to the ability of a person to realize different combinations of functionings. A central component of capability is the notion of choice (or lack of it) in the way in which a person lives a life that he or she values. Using this approach, poverty can be understood in terms of the absence or *deprivation* of certain basic capabilities. Hence, from this perspective, poverty refers not only to the impoverished state in which a person actually lives, but also to the lack of real *opportunity* to lead a valuable and valued life as a result of his or her impoverishment.

This multifaceted perspective challenged the focus on absolute poverty measured in purely quantitative terms. Poverty came to be seen as a multifaceted phenomenon that had material and non-material dimensions and that could not be reduced to a poverty datum line, whether expressed in terms of money, a basket of goods, or incomes below a US dollar a day (Brock and McGee, 2002; Chambers, 1995; Narayan et al., 2000a, 2000b; Tjonneland et al., 1998; Wilson et al., 2001). Qualitative methods and participatory approaches were used alongside quantitative methods to investigate both the extent and nature of absolute and relative poverty (Booth et al., 1998; Townsend and Gordon, 2002) in absolute and relative terms, and poverty was more systematically disaggregated, for example on the basis of gender and household status (Beall, 1998, 2002c; Chant, 1997; Jackson, 1996; Kabeer, 1994, 1997).

These influences have had an impact on the assessment of poverty and poverty reduction. Approaches to poverty reduction differ among the various donor agencies; none advance overtly redistributive policies such as land reform and many bear the neoliberal watermark of the 1980s, with poverty reduction strategies being strongly influenced by the World Bank's three-pronged approach to poverty – economic growth, human capital development, and social protection. However, the United Nations Human Development Index, although limited, has been important in going beyond money-metric measurement, and the World Bank has taken up the perspectives of poor people drawn from participatory poverty assessments

(Narayan et al., 2000a, 200b). Other examples of the impact of these changing approaches to poverty, which were important in feeding these shifts, include the series of country poverty assessments undertaken by the World Bank during the 1990s. The Department for International Development contributed to the process by supporting background papers drawn from participatory poverty assessments that brought to light some of the texture and experience of poverty (Norton, et al., 2001; Norton and Stephens, 1995). More recently, a process for producing national Poverty Reduction Strategy Papers (PRSPs) has been developed, and PRSPs have replaced old SAPs as a new form of conditionality for countries seeking development assistance from both multilateral and bilateral donors. They are particularly considered to be a prerequisite for DBS, an aid instrument advanced by some bilateral donors such as DFID. Such donors hope to move beyond project and programme support and even sector-wide approaches in order to provide long-term and arm's length assistance direct to governments that are implementing pro-poor development policies. As is argued in Chapters Five and Six, which discuss local funds as an aid instrument, they constitute an important vehicle for reaching poor groups and areas that might otherwise be overlooked or neglected in the context of DBS.

Another example of broadening the conceptualization of social disadvantage while maintaining a 'league table' approach to encouraging poverty reduction is the Millennium Development Goals (MDGs). This is an international compact that was introduced at the turn of the century and is aimed at reducing poverty to half current levels by the year 2015 (UNDP, 2003). The eight goals – which are outlined in Table 3.1 – although not without their critics, represent a more widely accepted common denominator for poverty reduction strategies that has the support of organizations beyond the Washington Consensus, including a range of national governments across the world and many NGOs and civil society organizations (CSOs) operating at different levels. Nevertheless, only Goal Two sets a universal target: primary education for all children. Moreover, as the *Chronic Poverty Report* (CPRC, 2004: 58) points out, the MDGs are unlikely to be met and 'cannot be viewed in isolation from other international policies and negotiations, some of which result in conditions in which chronic poverty is sustained and may even increase'.

Social exclusion

The concept of social exclusion, which is not synonymous with but is closely related to poverty, entered the development lexicon around the turn of the millennium. The concept derives from French social thought and was originally concerned with the relationship between citizens and the nation state. René Lenoir (1974) is commonly credited with popularizing the term in France, seeking to explain how *les exclus* were systematically overlooked by the French Republican social contract, and arguing that people's marginalization from formal labour markets and from benefits

Table 3.1 The Millennium Development Goals

The Goals	Implementation
1. Eradicate extreme poverty and hunger	■ Reduce by half the proportion of people living on less than a US dollar a day ■ Reduce by half the proportion of people who suffer from hunger
2. Achieve universal primary education	■ Ensure that all boys and girls complete a full course of primary schooling
3. Promote gender equality and empower women	■ Eliminate gender disparity in primary and secondary education preferably by 2005, and at all levels by 2015
4. Reduce child mortality	■ Reduce by two-thirds the mortality rate among children under five
5. Improve maternal health	■ Reduce by three-quarters the maternal mortality ratio
6. Combat HIV/AIDS, malaria, and other diseases	■ Halt and begin to reverse the spread of HIV/AIDS ■ Halt and begin to reverse the incidence of malaria and other major diseases
7. Ensure environmental sustainability	■ Integrate the principles of sustainable development into country policies and programmes; reverse loss of environmental resources ■ Reduce by half the proportion of people without sustainable access to safe drinking water ■ Achieve significant improvement in lives of at least 100 million slum dwellers by 2020
8. Develop a global partnership for development	■ Develop further an open trading and financial system that is rule-based, predictable, and non-discriminatory. Includes a commitment to good governance, development, and poverty reduction – nationally and internationally ■ Address the least developed countries' special needs. This includes tariff- and quota-free access for their exports; enhanced debt relief for heavily indebted poor countries; cancellation of official bilateral debt; and more generous official development assistance for countries committed to poverty reduction

The Goals	Implementation
	■ Address the special needs of landlocked and small island developing states
	■ Deal comprehensively with developing countries' debt problems through national and international measures to make debt sustainable in the long term
	■ In cooperation with the developing countries, develop decent and productive work for youth
	■ In cooperation with pharmaceutical companies, provide access to affordable essential drugs in developing countries
	■ In cooperation with the private sector, make available the benefits of new technologies – especially information and communications technologies

Source: UNDP (2003)

under the French welfare state constituted a rupture of the social bond that underpinned the rights and responsibilities of citizenship.

Either as an analytical or an operational framework, the notion of social exclusion was never going to translate easily to developing countries, where the vast majority of people were already excluded from formal labour markets and were never in their lives likely to benefit from state welfare or formal social security. Here social exclusion is more appropriately used to refer to people who have been denied ever attaining rights of access in the first place (Clert, 1999). However, the concept gained deeper resonance in developing countries, or in particular parts of these countries, as conditions of poverty and deprivation were exacerbated by globalization. Developing countries have been persistently excluded by global economic processes or have been incorporated under adverse conditions detrimental to the livelihoods and well-being of their poorest citizens (Beall, 2002b). As Castells (1998: 162) has put it, 'Globalization proceeds selectively, including and excluding segments of economies and societies in and out of the networks of information, wealth and power that characterize the new dominant system.' Within the context of these debates, social exclusion was seen as a problematic concept if the primary goal of policy was to encourage inclusion in mainstream development agendas without allowing for critique of alternatives to these agendas.

The relationship between global economic processes and increasing social differentiation was a critical issue debated at the United Nations World Summit on Social Development held in Copenhagen in March 1995 (UN, 1995), with contributors seeking to explain the polarization between countries incorporated into and excluded by the global economy and the patterns of inclusion and exclusion that resulted (Gore and Figueiredo, 1997; Rodgers et al., 1995). From a neoliberal perspective, social exclusion was presented as an unfortunate but inevitable side effect of globalization, the necessary result of global economic realignments. No longer protected by artificial trade barriers, it was considered unavoidable that formerly protected workers in industrialized countries had to lose their social security and formal employment conditions. Those on the left saw social exclusion as an obfuscating concept that deflected attention from the real issues of poverty and inequality. Those espousing a social democratic perspective saw social exclusion as an important opportunity within the context of development for countering the worst excesses of neoliberal social policy, and it is this approach that most informs its advocates within the context of international development.

Despite the growing salience of social exclusion as an organizing concept, it has not displaced poverty as the most critical focus in international development cooperation. Nevertheless, the concept of social exclusion continues to hold purchase not only within Europe but also within the arena of international development (DFID, 1997; IILS/UNDP, 1996; UNRISD, 1994, Wolfenson, 1997; World Bank, 1998b), particularly among those concerned to include an understanding of social relations and institutional frameworks alongside analyses of poverty (Beall, 2002b; Clert, 2000; de Haan, 1998; de Haan and Maxwell, 1998; Kabeer, 2000). Moreover, in addition to its obvious link to social protection policies, the social exclusion perspective is compatible with a rights-based approach to development (which is discussed further below), as it is concerned with the social contract and emphasizes both the rights and responsibilities of citizenship. Social exclusion is significant with regard to local funds in three important ways. First, in very general terms a social exclusion perspective invites a focus on social relations and institutional dynamics, both of which are important for the understanding and analysis of local funds. Second, and more specifically, the ILO has been important in advancing a focus on social exclusion and social protection. This in turn has influenced its approach to local funds such as the AGETIPs in West Africa, which are discussed in Chapter Five and which the ILO supports through capacity building. Third, social exclusion has become an important analytical and operational framework for area-based development programmes in the United Kingdom, which are also the focus of challenge funds and local initiatives such as New Life for Paddington, discussed in Chapter Eight.

Sustainable livelihoods

The Sustainable Livelihoods Framework (SLF) has become very influential both as an analytical and an operational concept, being taken up within the context of a broadening social policy agenda, and a more holistic approach to development. The SLF seems to have achieved more resonance in the context of international development cooperation than the concept of social exclusion, which – apart from its vigorous promotion by the ILO and its take-up by some bilateral aid agencies – remains primarily associated with the social policy frameworks of industrialized countries. By contrast, the livelihoods perspective has been welcomed by those in the international development community keen to move beyond a money-metric approach to poverty analysis but wanting to maintain an enterprise approach to poverty reduction. Influenced by Sen's analysis of poverty and deprivation (Chambers and Conway, 1992), and associated with shifts in policy thinking towards more integrated approaches to development – including environmental protection and sustainability (Scoones, 1998) – the SLF has emerged as a widely accepted way of understanding and dealing with poverty and deprivation. It has been taken up in different forms – for example by UNDP, DFID, and one of the largest international development NGOs, Care International – and operationalized in ways that incorporate the broader perspectives of each of these development institutions. This can be seen from Figure 2.1, which shows DFID's sustainable livelihoods framework, and Figure 2.2, which is a representation of the livelihoods framework used by Care International. The DFID framework foregrounds the vulnerability of poor people but also emphasizes their assets or 'capitals', while Care International's livelihoods framework places the livelihoods of low-income households at the centre and is less focused on assets. Both pay attention to the institutional context, but Care gives greater prominence to this aspect and to development partnerships, reflexively including the organization itself among the stakeholders involved.

At one level it is the portmanteau qualities of the framework that help explain its acceptability and popularity across a large number of international donor agencies and NGOs. It contains something for everyone. For example, it appeals to progressive thinkers because it captures historical processes and social relations (Bebbington, 1999: 2021). It also appeals to conventional thinkers because the SLF is focused on supporting people's assets and capabilities. The philosophical roots of the livelihoods approach, as espoused by many of its proponents, lie in liberal concerns with individual property rights. This said, there is more than one livelihoods approach and they have been informed by a variety of development perspectives (Beall, 2002c; Bebbington, 1999; Carney et al., 1999; Ellis, 2000; Rakodi, 2002). Some of the funds discussed in this book were designed according to a livelihoods framework, which is elaborated in more detail in the relevant chapters.

Social protection

There is a growing awareness of the significant role to be played by social protection policies and programmes, particularly in developing countries characterized by high levels of poverty and income insecurity. However, contemporary approaches to social protection do not give pre-eminence to

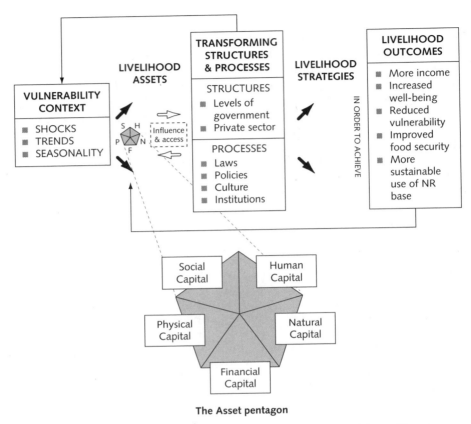

The Asset pentagon

Figure 3.1   Department for International Development's Sustainable Livelihoods Framework

the role of the public sector in providing social assistance and social safety nets (Holzmann and Jørgensen, 2000). The World Bank Social Protection Unit, for example, has been developing theories of social protection that go beyond traditional conceptions of social security. While in some ways these approaches approximate earlier residual approaches to social policy, Hall and Midgley (2004: 10) argue that the contemporary approach to social protection 'departs from the mere provision of charity since it is intended to support people's own livelihood strategies in the longer-term during times of vulnerability or high risk'. The conceptual framework for this is Social Risk Management (SRM) (Holzmann and Jørgensen, 2000; World Bank, 2001). An asset-based approach to social risk management in the World Bank is not new (Moser, 1998; Siegel and Alwang, 1999), although it has more recently become entrenched in Bank policy. The concept of SRM emerged in the context of developing the most recent Sector Strategy Paper of the World Bank's Social Protection Unit (SPU), which assessed the past

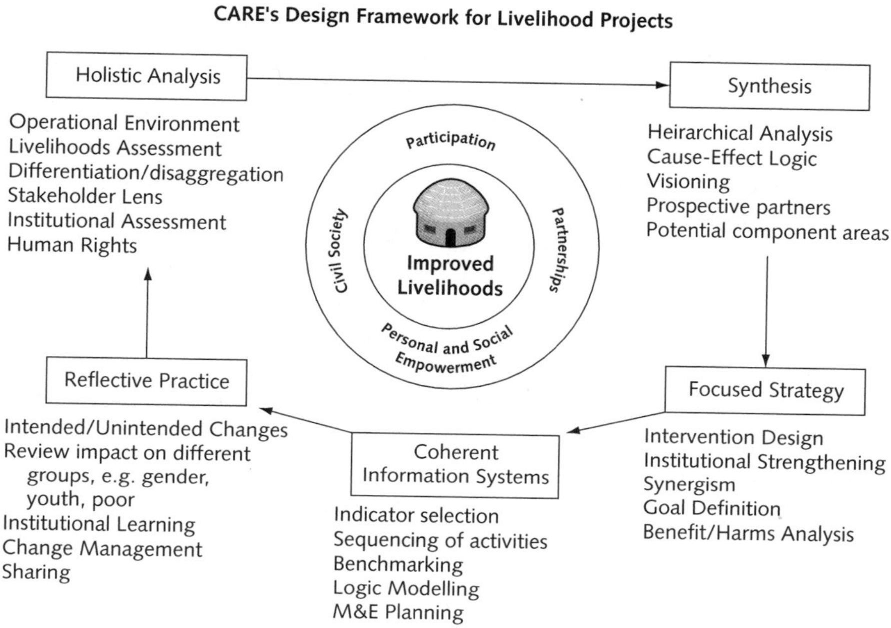

CARE's Design Framework for Livelihood Projects

Holistic Analysis

Operational Environment
Livelihoods Assessment
Differentiation/disaggregation
Stakeholder Lens
Institutional Assessment
Human Rights

Synthesis

Heirarchical Analysis
Cause-Effect Logic
Visioning
Prospective partners
Potential component areas

Participation
Civil Society
Partnerships
Improved Livelihoods
Personal and Social Empowerment

Reflective Practice

Intended/Unintended Changes
Review impact on different
groups, e.g. gender,
youth, poor
Institutional Learning
Change Management
Sharing

Coherent Information Systems

Indicator selection
Sequencing of activities
Benchmarking
Logic Modelling
M&E Planning

Focused Strategy

Intervention Design
Institutional Strengthening
Synergism
Goal Definition
Benefit/Harms Analysis

Figure 3.2 Care International's Livelihoods Framework

performance of social protection strategies. These were deemed to have been weak and failing, both in terms of their impact on poverty and in relation to institutional acceptance and delivery (Holzmann and Jørgenson, 2000: 3).

Four key conceptual underpinnings can be identified in the SRM framework. First, social protection is seen as both a safety net and a springboard to better opportunities, protecting poor people against adversity while encouraging them towards greater economic risk-taking. Second, social protection programmes are viewed not as a cost but as an investment in human capital formation. Third, it is argued that social protection should aim to focus more on the causes of poverty rather than on its symptoms. Fourth, the framework is premised on the fact that as less than a quarter of the world's population has access to formal social protection programmes, a realistic approach has to be adopted in the face of a massive need well beyond the fiscal capacity of most developing countries (Holzmann and Jørgensen, 2000). Within the broad panoply of poverty reduction strategies, social protection or SRM comprises three elements: risk prevention strategies, which seek to reduce the probability of vulnerability and risk; risk mitigation strategies, which are *ex-ante* strategies to help reduce the impact of potential stresses and shocks; and coping strategies, which are *ex-poste* efforts designed to soften the impact of adversity once it occurs (World Bank, 2002: 29).

Three things are clear from this emphasis on risk management. First, as one of the World Bank's three-pronged approaches to poverty, social protection is now much more conceptually intermeshed with the other two prongs of economic growth and human capital development. Second, with its focus on the assets and capabilities of individuals and households, SRM places far less emphasis on public transfers as a means of reducing poverty than does, say, the social exclusion approach. However, as with both social exclusion and a livelihoods perspective, SRM also pays consideration to the institutional environment in which social protection needs to take place. Third, the focus on assets and capabilities brings social protection and the SLF together within a single paradigmatic approach to social development. This is evident from the following extract from the United Kingdom's Department for International Development's guidelines on the sustainable livelihoods framework:

> *A livelihood comprises the capabilities, assets and activities required for a means of living. A livelihood is sustainable when it can cope with and recover from stresses and shocks and maintain or enhance its capabilities and assets both now and in the future, while not undermining the natural resource base.*

> *(DFID, no date)*

A review of social funds, from the time they were initiated in the late 1980s through to the local funds of the present, provides a microcosmic view of the way social development policies have shifted from a situation where they were focused solely on short-term safety nets to a springboard approach with a longer-term vision. Whereas early social funds were informed by a welfare-oriented approach to social protection, later funds and local funds with a social protection focus are more likely to be informed by the principles of sustainable livelihoods and social risk management.

The rights-based approach to development

A rights-based approach attempts to integrate the norms, standards, and principles of the international human rights system into the policies and processes of development (Moser and Norton, 2001). The Universal Declaration of Human Rights was adopted by the United Nations in 1948 and subsequently reaffirmed in 1993. Along with the International Covenant on Economic, Social and Cultural Rights and the International Covenant on Civil and Political Rights, it constitutes the International Bill of Rights. Over 160 countries have ratified one or both of these covenants, so they are binding in most places. Other treaties crucial to development practitioners include the Convention on the Rights of the Child, the Convention Eliminating All Forms of Discrimination against Women, and the Convention against Racial Discrimination – all of which have been ratified by a majority of governments. There is a difference between human rights and a rights-based approach to development. Human rights are commonly understood as being those rights that are inherent in a human being and that are legally guaranteed by human rights law. They are enshrined in treaties, declarations, guidelines, and principles that have been agreed under the auspices of the United Nations since 1945 (DFID, 2000). Closely related but not synonymous, a rights-based approach to development is a conceptual and operational framework for advancing the process of human development, which is normatively based on international human rights standards and directed towards promoting and protecting human rights (United Nations, 2003). Such an approach is thought to add value because it provides a normative framework of obligations with legal power to render governments accountable, which in turn can be calibrated with efforts to enhance governance.

Rights-based approaches have been taken up by a range of international development NGOs such as Oxfam and ActionAid, and have considerable purchase among development workers and activists in developing countries. The following definition of a rights-based approach, drawn from the Asia Forum for Human Rights and Development (cited in O'Neill, 2003: 1), illustrates how a distinction between rights and needs is drawn:

> *What does a rights approach mean? First, it means clearly understanding the difference between a right and a need. A right is something to which I am entitled solely by virtue of being a person. It is that which enables me to live with dignity. Moreover, a right can be enforced before the government and entails an obligation on the part of the government. A need, on the other hand, is an aspiration that can be quite legitimate, but it is not necessarily associated with an obligation on the part of the government to cater to it; satisfaction of a need cannot be enforced. Rights are associated with 'being', whereas needs are associated with 'having'.*

It is commonly believed that rights derive from the relationship between governments and their citizens, with citizens as right-holders and governments as duty-bearers, as implied in this second definition from the Asia Forum for Human Rights and Development (cited in O'Neill, 2003: 1):

> *A rights-based approach is founded on the conviction that each and every human being, by virtue of being human, is a holder of rights. A right entails an obligation on the part of the government to respect, promote, protect, and fulfil it. The legal and normative character of rights and the associated governmental obligations are based on international human rights treaties and other standards, as well as on national constitutional human rights provisions. Thus a rights-based approach involves not charity or simple economic development, but a process of enabling and empowering those not enjoying their economic, social and cultural rights to claim their rights.*

This understanding of a rights-based approach comes close to Sen's thesis of development as the expansion of human freedoms. Sen sees freedoms as embodied in social, economic, and cultural rights, such as access to health care, education, shelter, work, and nourishment. He also sees them as embodied in civil and political rights, such as participation in public and associational life (Moser and Norton, 2001).

A rights-based approach fits with the normative foundations of social policy as a discipline and a framework for action. Moreover, given that an aim of rights-based programming is that development workers use the principles of a *progressive* realization of rights to get governments to improve their performance, it has echoes of the incremental approach to social policy discussed above. In this, governments are encouraged to incrementally increase social sector spending as and when resources became available. However, with the contemporary rights-based approach, development actors and organizations other than governments are also thought to be accountable for rights violations. International development agencies are urged to support the full realization of human rights, and a wide range of organizations are seen as responsible for engaging with policies and practices that lead to the fulfilment or prevent the denial of human rights (O'Neill, 2003).

As with other social and development policy approaches and in the nature of normative theory, the rights-based approach has been accompanied by controversy. Cultural relativists argue that a rights-based approach is neo-colonial, advancing as universal norms that are highly influenced by western values and not appropriate for application everywhere. Other opponents argue that by definition rights are not the responsibility of development organizations, pointing to the futility of trying to enforce them in an international development context. Proponents of a rights-based approach argue that the link to rights provides for a clarity of principles and goals in development work, which draws from a range of international instruments, treaties, and conventions that are near universal in that they have been supported and agreed upon by the majority of countries. As such the approach is said to provide an authoritative set of international standards against which processes and outcomes can be judged. Proponents also pay particular attention to issues of discrimination and unequal treatment by actively seeking to include the most marginal and vulnerable groups in the development process, hence addressing issues of deprivation and exclusion. Unlike poverty reduction strategies, however, which target particular 'vulnerable groups', a rights-based approach makes no assumptions about who is the most disadvantaged or marginal, although particular identity-based rights are promoted, such as children's rights and women's rights. The key elements of a rights-based approach are outlined in Table 3.2.

In terms of linking human rights and poverty, the work of Amartya Sen has been influential once again. His conceptualization of poverty – as the denial of basic opportunities and choices fundamental to humanity – has an obvious relevance both to economic and social rights and to civil and political rights. The notion of human development, as the enhancement of a person's capabilities and freedom, has much in common with a human rights perspective. However, a key difference is that unlike human development, a human rights perspective also implies that individuals have claims on the conduct of others. Linking Sen's understanding of human develop-

Table 3.2   Key elements of a rights-based approach

Elements	Features
An express linkage to rights	■ The objectives of development are framed in terms of particular rights, as legally enforceable entitlements. ■ This is seen to give added weight to development goals.
A high level of accountability	■ A central focus on raising levels of accountability in the development process by identifying claim holders (and their entitlements) and corresponding duty-holders (and their obligations). ■ In this way, development moves from the realm of charity to obligation. ■ Obligation is seen to include both positive obligations, to protect, promote, and provide, as well as negative obligations, to abstain from violations. ■ Not only the state but the full range of development actors are held accountable and subject to rights-based standards, including local organizations and authorities, private companies, aid donors, and international institutions. ■ As rights are legally enforceable, such an approach encourages the development of a more rigorous framework for monitoring implementation and sanction.
An explicit focus on capabilities and empowerment	■ The focus is on empowerment and capabilities rather than welfare and need, on users with rights rather than beneficiaries of aid.
A high level of participation	■ Rights come with responsibility and the approach is premised on the understanding that development can only be achieved with a high level of meaningful (not formal or ceremonial) participation from affected communities.

Source: Beall, Lewis, and Sutherland, 2003

ment to the notion of human rights powerfully ties the process of development to the 'idea that others have duties to facilitate or enhance human development' (Moser and Norton, 2001). The rights-based approach has been elaborated in some detail here because one of the local funds profiled in this book, the Manusher Jonno fund in Bangladesh, was designed according to this framework.

Corporate social responsibility

Recognizing responsibilities alongside rights has brought the private sector into the frame, with increasing consideration being given to Corporate Social Responsibility (CSR) as a dimension of social and development policy. Corporations are an enduring feature of the development environment and are ascendant in the context of globalized economic and technological change. Few would contest that corporations, especially certain transnational corporations, are extremely powerful entities (Hutton, 1997; Korten, 1995). CSR is premised on the view that this power cannot be taken for granted and must be accounted for because it is invariably society rather than corporations that bear the costs of creating corporate wealth. Hence, it is asserted that corporations have to take responsibility for the consequences of their decisions, both intentional and unintentional, that they should operate with popular consent, and that they should put something back into society to make up for what they extract, both in terms of human and resource costs. At base, CSR is about finding alternative arrangements for distributing the allocation of social costs more broadly across social institutions (Segel, 2004). Corporations and their managers are increasingly subject to public pressure to play an active role in society and are explicitly regarded by some as critical actors in determining societal welfare (Balabanis et al., 1998: 25).

Galbraith (1998: 31) sees CSR as an obligation, arguing that corporations have responsibilities beyond maximizing shareholder interests, that there is a wider range of stakeholders in the activities of corporations and that operating a corporation is a privilege and not a right. However, there are objections to the idea that corporations have social obligations. Milton Friedman is perhaps the most consistently quoted opponent, arguing that CSR undermines the basic tenets of capitalism and free society and that the only responsibility of business is to increase its profits (Friedman, 1988). Hence, there are ideological issues about whether CSR is necessary or even good. Between these two perspectives – that corporations have obligations to society and that they have no obligations beyond their bottom lines – there are a number of intermediate positions. One such position is that corporations invest in self-interested CSR initiatives for pragmatic or expedient reasons. These might relate to maintaining or improving the corporation's profile vis-à-vis competitors, or could be associated with their long term interests. What is significant is that these debates are occurring globally. CSR is an important additional indicator of how approaches to social policy have become interconnected on an international level, with societies everywhere increasingly expecting that business should be conducted with greater sensitivity to social needs.

Debating and establishing responsibility is one thing; ensuring something is done about it is quite another. There are moral dilemmas about where the mandate for enforcing CSR comes from (Wempe, 1998). One difficulty is that the conditions of accumulation are continually transforming so that it is not always easy to pin responsibility on contemporary organizations for deeds committed in the past. Even in the present there are issues about who determines responsibility and how it is expressed. A further problem is that CSR remains of marginal concern to the majority of corporate organizations operating within the orthodoxy of Western capitalism (Gray et al., 1987: 1).

Some manifestations of CSR relating to employment practices and corporate governance can be monitored through such practices as social audits and social, environmental; and ethnical reporting; although measurement can be problematic (Gray et al., 1987: 12). Other manifestations of CSR are more difficult to monitor. For example, various forms of social investment are undertaken, from oil companies supporting the local communities in the environs of their drilling sites, to philanthropic gestures such as donations to worthy causes. However, they are uncoordinated and serendipitous, beyond which is the vexed issue of regulation. For the most part this takes the form of voluntary self-regulation by corporations themselves. Nevertheless, external stakeholders can and do organize themselves in response to the activities of corporations, whether it be in the form of environmental activism, advocating for ethical investment, or organizing around issue-based concerns. These increased pressures for negotiation and external regulation can take the form of public opinion and media commentary, government legislation and guidelines, or professional codes and standards. It is often negative public opinion that propels corporations towards self-regulation.

CSR and local funds most commonly come together around three critical mechanisms. The first relates to philanthropic efforts on the part of corporations or private sector donors, concerned to reach the poor and ameliorate their conditions in some way, including through educational opportunities. This type of funding is sometimes characterized as 'guilt money' or, if it is associated with a named fund, 'aggrandizement money'. Nevertheless, it can play an important role and progressive foundations, such as the Ford and Rockerfeller Foundations, started in just this way. The second critical mechanism for CSR initiatives relates to the fact that corporations tend to have more sympathy for an enterprise approach to social development than to anything that smacks of a 'hand out'. Hence they are more likely to be in favour of a challenge fund than a social fund model of support. Third, when corporations or businesses of any kind are interested in socially oriented public–private partnerships, it is usually the case that there is a spin-off of some sort for the corporation. For example, their involvement in area-based development projects can usually be explained by the fact that they are contractors in the area. This can be seen, for instance, in relation to the AGETIPS in Francophone West Africa discussed in Chapter Five and the New Life for Paddington project that is profiled in Chapter Eight. For all the good that such forms of local funds undoubtedly do, they are no substitute for nationally or regionally coordinated social policy. Ultimately, they rest on the whim of entrepreneurs and their consciences, they are seriously affected by external factors such as profit margins and the stock market, and invariably they do not coordinate with complementary or similar efforts being undertaken by governments, NGOs, or international agencies. The answer lies not in discouraging such initiatives but encouraging them towards greater consultation, coordination, or partnership.

INSTITUTIONS FOR SOCIAL POLICY AND DEVELOPMENT

The rise to prominence in international development cooperation of the rights paradigm and the focus on CSR paralleled wider debates about the appropriate organizations and institutional mechanisms for advancing social development. It also followed in the wake of a prior concern with community participation and participatory development, and coincided with the interest of international development agencies in public sector reform, democracy promotion, and partnership, as discussed in the previous chapter. Here, the issue of participation is elaborated upon in a little more detail, given its centrality to social development in particular.

Although community development and participation has a long pedigree in development policy and planning, from the mid-1980s development practice was particularly influenced by 'bottom up' and participatory approaches (Chambers, 1996, 1997). The impulse came from a number of directions, including those concerned with community development and empowerment, deriving from ideas of communitarianism (Etzioni, 1993) and populist approaches to development (Kitching, 1982). Radical populism was especially influential in informing grassroots participatory development strategies and social movements. However, participatory approaches soon became central to the mainstream development agenda too, such that by the early 1990s many international development agencies and most NGOs emphasized the importance of participation in a fashion Mohan and Stokke (2000: 252) have identified as a 'liberal and populist approach to local empowerment'. In this arena a tension often existed between democratizing goals and a more neoliberal approach to participation, which was less concerned with empowerment and more with increased efficiency. In the latter case, participatory approaches were advanced not to increase people's voice but as a way of harnessing their energy towards predetermined development goals, usually at the implementation stage. Under such circumstances, participatory approaches could mean little more than extracting the unpaid time and energy of ordinary men and women, adding the obligation of participation to their already onerous roles and responsibilities (Moser, 1993). Even if such instrumentalist uses are not made of participatory approaches, there is always the danger that in community participation communities are cast as homogeneous and are seen as bound by common interests, ignoring all differences within them, whether based, for example, on class, ethnicity, age, gender, or other social cleavages.

More recently, participation has been considered more in relation to democracy promotion. There are two broad types of democracy: representative democracy, whereby elected officials represent the interests and views of citizens within the framework of the rule of law; and direct or participatory democracy in which citizens are more directly involved in decision-making processes. The size, complexity, and diversity of contemporary societies are thought to make direct democracy unworkable. Indeed, except in the case of referenda, direct democracy is not commonly practiced within modern national political systems (Abrahamsen, 2000). However, it is thought to be more effective at local level where citizens can engage more easily in collective decisions, and where it is hoped they will develop a greater sense of civic identity and ownership over the decisions of which they are a part. This engagement can take the form of consultation and discussion, in which case it is deliberative democracy, or can involve actual decision-making and a more thorough-going democratization of local institutions, in which case it is participatory democracy.

Participation in the context of local funds, therefore, need not necessarily be linked to democracy and is not necessarily an indicator of good practice. It depends on the design and implementation of the funds and the purposes for which participation is marshalled. For instance, participation can be used to discern the needs and priorities of intended beneficiaries, through participatory rapid appraisal (PRA) or participatory poverty assessments (PPAs). These techniques can be useful in ensuring wider involvement and discussion about the design and implementation of local funds, although some have remained uncomfortable with such techniques, arguing that they 'have proved compatible with top-down planning systems, and have not necessarily heralded changes in prevailing institutional practices of development' (Mosse, 2001: 17). It is also important to understand the motivations for participation within the practice of local funds and to distinguish between participation as a means by which to influence decisions and participation as control over a deliverable or a service. For example, there are different imperatives at work when participation informs internal relationships within an organization or partnership and when it is used to define external relationships, such as those between agencies providing services and users of those services. A related point is that participation might occur within the context of solidaristic relationships – for instance within the context of kinship groups, communities, or associations, or between agents and clients. In the latter case it may be more concerned with accountability mechanisms although in both cases hierarchical relationships may be involved. In the end, whether participation in the delivery of local funds or other forms of social development is a good thing or not depends on whether it occurs in the presence or absence of a democratic governance agenda.

CONCLUSION

The proliferation of local funds has to be understood within the context of evolving frameworks for social policy and development. This chapter has described these and shown how local funds are variously associated with different approaches, particularly those that have emerged in the post-welfare state era and that involve institutional relationships and arrangements that are very different from pure public sector delivery. In the chapters that follow, examples are provided of local funds that have been designed along the lines of some of the approaches to social policy and development discussed here. In all cases the funds provide opportunities for time-bound and sometimes space-bound activities that by definition are limited. Local funds are also very variable both in goals and outcomes, reflecting how they are embedded in or respond to national and local political contexts. In other words, local funds are often condemned when it is not the funding mechanism itself but the overarching policy paradigm in which they function that is the problem. The importance of the broader policy terrain of local funds becomes clearer in Part II, which traces and explores the development of different funds in various contexts. The success of local funds also depends on matters of practice, discussed in the third section of this book, which in turn relate to the preparedness of organizations and partners to make the adaptations necessary for working in ways that are more flexible and accommodating of partners with different contributions and constraints.

PART II

LOCAL FUNDS AND LESSONS FROM PRACTICE

CHAPTER FOUR

From social funds to local funds in Mexico and their gender impact

INTRODUCTION

The history of local funds in Mexico is particularly interesting because although – as in many other contexts – they developed out of social funds, both need to be understood against the background of a far more comprehensive attempt towards a national social policy with universal reach. This chapter traces the history of social protection strategies in Mexico and how they evolved in the wake of shifts in the country's political economy. In particular it pays attention to how gender issues were addressed in the context of changing policies and programmes. Despite the rich debate on the impact of social funds on disadvantaged people in Mexico and elsewhere, and the growing salience of local funds for poverty reduction and improved local governance, very little work has been undertaken on the differential impact of these funds on women and men. This is despite extensive research having been conducted by feminist scholars and gender and development specialists on the gender impact of SAPs (Beneria, 1991; Cornia et al., 1987; Chant, 1996, 1994; Elson, 1989, 1991; Kanji, 1995; Moser, 1989, 1992, 1996) and more generally on the poverty reduction impact of policy, programmes, and projects on women (Beall, 1998; Jackson, 1996; Kabeer, 1994). Although some attention has been paid to the gender dimensions of social policy and social funds in Mexico (Tacher and Mondragon, 1997), there is virtually nothing written on how the shift from social funds to local funds has affected women's access to services, governance processes, and decision-making, or how it has responded to their gender interests. This is also more generally the case. This chapter reflects on these issues, drawing on the experience of Mexico. It analyses 15 years of policy experience in which funds of various kinds have been deployed with the aim both of alleviating poverty and improving governance, reflecting in particular on whether or not successive funds have benefited women.

Mexico has a comparatively successful history of employing social funds as a means of cushioning the harsh social effects of SAPs. During the 1980s under the *Programa Nacional de Solidaridad* (National Programme for Solidarity) (Pronasol), this strategy became the hallmark of Mexican social policy at a time when macro-economic policy dictated the country's fast track integration into a free market economy, exemplified by Mexico's membership of the North America Free Trade Agreement (NAFTA). Initially, Pronasol was not intended to become a comprehensive solution to all social problems but was rather a short-term mechanism to protect the needy and indigent. It was designed to do this by providing short-term relief through basic social services to those most affected by economic adjustment. However, Pronasol grew in importance, far outstripping early expectations for the programme. Between 1991 and 1992 Pronasol's budget increased from US\$1.6 billion to US\$2.1 billion and investment in Pronasol as a percentage of Gross Domestic Product (GDP) grew from 0.45 per cent in 1989 to 2.5 in 1994 (Sedesol, 1994).

The chapter begins by examining the structural adjustment process out of which Pronasol emerged and the programme's relationship with *Mujeres en Solidaridad* (Women in Solidarity), which was a specific fund established to target poor women in both rural and urban areas of Mexico.

The second part of the chapter covers the period from the collapse of the Mexican economy in December 1994 through the ensuing political turmoil, including the period of the *Zapatista* uprising in the Southern (and poorest) state of Chiapas and the weakening of the 70-year-old national ruling party, *Partido Revolucionario Institucional* (Institutional Revolutionary Party) (PRI), which was defeated in 2000 by the *Partido Acción Nacional* (National Action Party) (PAN) with Vincente Fox being sworn in as President. Former PRI President Zedillo (1994–2000) had already dismantled Pronasol as the focus of policy changed. However, the Fox Presidency sought to improve the efficiency and effectiveness of social policy by reaching those most in need, increasing transparency and reducing clientelism. Fox decentralized many of the funds to the local level and established targeting criteria for them. Importantly for present purposes, funds previously channelled to *Solidaridad* were pooled with the new *Programa Nacional de Educación, Salud y Alimentación* (National Program for Education, Health and Food) (*Progresa*), the aim of which was to extend basic education, health, and food security to the poorest of the poor. This policy trajectory shadowed the World Bank's three-pronged approach to poverty reduction discussed in Chapter One – economic growth, human development, and social safety nets – and reflected Mexico's increasing turn towards the development agendas of the international financing IFIs. However, as the present chapter demonstrates, during this phase funds for women in the social sector virtually disappeared.

The third section deals with the contemporary period. At the beginning of the twenty-first century in Mexico, with the new government in place and with democratic consolidation underway, local funds continue to play an important role in the country's social development. Following patterns observable elsewhere and in line with the post-Washington Consensus discussed in Chapter Two, they are also increasingly concerned with governance. The character of contemporary local funds in Mexico is therefore a far cry from the centralized and monolithic social funds model that characterized Pronasol. Today, local funds with goals of enhancing governance include several stakeholders beyond the scope of government. Large NGOs and philanthropic foundations, as well as multilateral agencies, have all promoted funds aimed at creating conditions for improved local governance. Moreover, many of these funds implicitly or explicitly address gender concerns ranging from increasing the proportion of women in leadership to addressing issues related to women's rights, such as violence against women.

The chapter concludes by arguing that the shift from social funds to local funds with a governance focus has been positive in that it has ensured that resources get closer to the local level where people need them most. However, they get closer to some local people than others and women often appear to be excluded from the process. Despite the fact that gender sensitive language has been integrated into local funds, implementation remains a serious problem with the most disadvantaged women still not benefiting as readily as men.

STRUCTURAL ADJUSTMENT AND WOMEN IN MEXICO

Following the oil price shocks of the early 1970s and mounting external debts as the decade progressed, Mexico – along with a number of other countries in the late 1970s and early 1980s – had to implement a series of economic stabilization measures and SAPs. Occurring under the auspices of President de la Madrid's 'Austerity Programme', the IMF-style adjustment strategies launched Mexico into a process of economic restructuring that had a profound effect on the country's economic and social landscape (Beneria, 1991; Chant, 1996). The restructuring process continued into the 1990s under the PRI governments of President Carlos Salinas (1988–94) and then President Ernesto Zedillo (1994–2000). Some economic recovery was apparent in the early 1990s, during which time Mexico came to be regarded by the World Bank (1993) as one of the most successful adjusting countries. As Martin Feldstein (1987: 23) pointed out at a conference on world economic restructuring, '[C]urrent changes in Mexico are part of a process of economic restructuring that will modify and wake up the entire world.' In this he was correct; but among the policies implemented were massive cuts in government sector spending, especially in the social sector. The effect of this was to increase poverty, a process which was exacerbated by the downward pressure exerted on incomes by wage freezes and rising prices. The initial benefits of structural adjustment reforms were highly concentrated, confined primarily to those engaged in the export sector in a trend consistent with the promotion of export-led growth. Hence the social costs of restructuring the Mexican economy were severe in the short-term, while the new development model proved unlikely in the medium-term to create new jobs or to improve income distribution (Dresser, 1994a).

While typically the Mexican SAPs have been implemented with particularly devastating consequences for the large proportion of the Mexican low-income population, the disparity between price hikes and moribund salaries has affected most social classes. Nevertheless, all indicators seem to suggest that the debt crisis and subsequent adjustment policies have intensified social inequalities, even though severe problems did exist in Mexico before the crisis erupted (Beneria, 1991). Internationally, several in-depth studies have since analysed the effects of adjustment on the most vulnerable and its gender differentiated impact, confirming that disadvantaged women and children have suffered disproportionately in the process (Cornia et al., 1987; Beneria, 1991; Elson, 1991, 1989; Kanji, 1995; Moser, 1996, 1992, 1989). These patterns have also been observed in Mexico (Chant, 1991, 1992, 1996). It was in this context that Pronasol was launched on 1 December 1998 as the major programme aimed at alleviating the negative effects of restructuring on the poor. It received substantial publicity but in the end was inadequate to the task of providing a safety net for growing numbers of poor people (Chant, 1996). In the same year *Mujeres en Solidaridad* was set up as part of Pronasol, with the aim of meeting the needs of disadvantaged and impoverished rural and urban women.

Solidaridad faced a social and political context characterized by hierarchical gender relations, the absence of women's rights, and where their political voice was not heard (Correia and Katz, 2001; Cunningham and Cos-Montiel, 2003). Women were, and remain, under considerable pressure from husbands and families to stay in the home as mothers and housewives (Chant, 1996), and despite the emergence of new trends in family arrangements as a result of the pressure on women to work, there is still strong pressure on women to marry and have children (Beneria and Roldan, 1987; Chant, 1991). In their search for paid work, women do not always find jobs commensurate with their education. Moreover, they find themselves competing with men in a labour market already suffering from over-supply. Women are usually situated in the lowest paid and least prestigious employment; but whatever their employment, since they tend to be viewed as working to supplement their husband's wages, employers also accord them lower remuneration. In this environment, women are often to be found undertaking informal income-generating activities that revolve around the making and selling of foodstuffs such as 'tortillas' or around other domestic skills such as sewing and laundry, which they can combine with child care (Arizpe, 1982). The burdens of child care for working women were exacerbated by the fact that most women resided in nuclear households where men tend to dominate decision-making, especially in nuclear units where wives had few personal resources on which to draw. Furthermore, cultural norms of masculinity (*machismo*) limited male involvement in housework and child care (Chant, 1996; Beneria, 1991). Nevertheless, when pointing to solutions for dealing with the economic crisis in Mexico, the role of the Mexican family was held up as one of the main pillars of support, without recognizing the increased burden on women (Beneria, 1991). This reputation was well deserved; low-income urban Mexican women have historically faced poverty with determination, tackling not only the day-to-day demands but also the associated cultural, social, and political dimensions of their condition (Massolo, 1992, Tacher and Mondragon, 1997). Foweraker and Craig (1990) pointed out at the time that women played a key role in the organization of low-income neighbourhoods. They developed reciprocal relations of mutual support, and female mobilization continues to be a notable dimension of contemporary urban struggles. Moreover, women have been and continue to be critical in challenges to the state and as a result have achieved important improvements in their *colonias populares* (impoverished neighbourhoods) (Massolo, 1992).

GENDER RELATIONS AND WOMEN'S POSITION IN MEXICO

It is important to say something about gender relations in Mexico in order to demonstrate why gender sensitive practice and the inclusion of women in development policy and practice are important. In comparison to other Latin American countries, Mexico has made significant progress in terms of addressing gender issues. Gender gaps in education are not very substantial and maternal mortality rates have declined significantly (from 33.0 in 1992 to 19.4 deaths per 1 000 live births in 1997), as have fertility levels (from 4.3 in 1980 to 3.2 in 1990) (Conmujer, 1999). However, much remains to be done. A study prepared for the Government of Mexico in 2000 notes that poverty and inequalities persist, particularly with regard to disparities across regions and ethnic groups. Moreover, poverty affects men and women differently, in that men and women from the same socio-economic environment encounter different opportunities and restrictions in gaining access to employment, income, and assets. Analysis also shows that the gender division of labour within the family has hardly changed since the 1950s in spite of the critical role women play in Mexican society (Conmujer, 2000). Indeed, a recent study on migrant farm workers in Mexico showed that adult women and girls still carry out much of the domestic work, despite their increasing involvement in paid work. Some young boys, although willing to participate in domestic chores, are usually discouraged by their mothers for fear that their masculinity may be jeopardized, leading to their social rejection (Cos-Montiel, 2001). As a result, many programmes intent on supporting women and challenging gender relations revert to working within the context of traditional gender stereotypes.

Concern with these issues is not the preserve of radical feminists. A series of gender focused studies conducted by the World Bank (Correia and Katz, 2001) on education, labour market participation and earnings, microenterprise development, and communal land reform or *ejido* (communal land plots) in Mexico, demonstrates that gender roles – in particular women's domestic responsibilities and the expectation that men will provide the primary source of household income – have a significant impact on the acquisition of human capital and the differential abilities of men and women to participate in the economy. For example, women's labour force participation – although the fastest growing in Latin America, almost doubling between 1970 and 1990 – still sees women comprising only 35 per cent of the labour force. However, the labour force participation of men has also declined, and along with it their status within their families and their self-esteem. Men, perceived as the main income earners, have experienced a loss of self-confidence. Among the youth, this has led to drug abuse, alcoholism, and violence. Public services and institutions have not yet devised adequate responses to these new employment patterns and changes in family structure.

Both men and women are victims of violence but there are indications that violence among men, particularly young men, is increasing. Existing evidence on interpersonal violence shows that women and children are more likely to become victims inside the home, while young men are more likely to become victims outside of the home (Cunningham and Cos-Montiel, 2003). While it is difficult to assess the magnitude of violence in Mexico, particularly domestic and sexual violence, it is a trend that continues and is a worrying dimension of Mexican society. In 1996, of the total victims treated at the *Centro de Apoyo a la Violencia Intrafamiliar* (Support Centre for Inter-family Violence) (CAVI) 89 per cent were women, of which 86 per cent were adults (Conmujer, 1999). Inequalities between men and women and unfair expectations regarding their gender roles are pervasive, and remain sources of conflict in the family and the community. Moreover, they hinder social and economic development in Mexico. Violence compounds poverty and lack of equity, which are the main problems in Mexico today affecting women and children, who remain particularly vulnerable (World Bank, 2000; Conmujer, 2000; Presidencia de la Republica, 2001). Particularly worrying is the recent serial murder of over 300 women in the Northern border city of Ciudad Juarez, a case which has attracted widespread international attention but has seen few solutions, despite endless promises from the federal and local governments to enhance measures to stop this massive violence.

Although progress in education, health standards, and female participation in the labour force are important, there are substantial variations by region and by virtue of differentiation among the poor. Fertility rates among rural, uneducated women are double that of women in urban areas (4.1 versus 2.4 children per woman), as are those in poor states such as Chiapas as compared to Mexico City or Nuevo Leon (Conmujer, 1999).

PRONASOL: THE GOLDEN ERA OF SOCIAL FUNDS IN MEXICO

In his November 1993 State of the Nation address, President Salinas announced that government spending on social projects had risen by 85 per cent in real terms between 1989 and 1993. Spending for education rose by 90 per cent; for health by 79 per cent; and for the environment, urban development, and water supply by 65 per cent (Presidencia de la República, 1993). Much of that social spending was channelled through Pronasol, which is arguably the most widely known poverty relief programme ever implemented in Mexico. Pronasol comprised an umbrella organization established by Salinas in December 1988 to promote improved health, education, nutrition, housing, employment, and infrastructure, and it also developed other productive projects to benefit those living in extreme poverty. Salinas claimed that Pronasol marked a departure from previous policies of broad universal subsidies, high levels of unfocused government spending, and heavy state intervention in the economy. The short-lived programme (it lasted only one presidential term from 1989 to 1994) was aimed at improving public service provision and human development indicators.

Salinas designed Pronasol to achieve the dual objectives of making social spending more cost-effective and of fostering greater community involvement and initiative in local development projects (Sedesol, 1994; SHCP, 1991). The main themes of Pronasol included the promotion of grassroots participation and a reduction in bureaucracy (at least in theory), as well as the promise of immediate results. The federal government provided financing and raw materials for improving basic community services, although community members were required to conceive the projects and perform the work. Its resources represented, on average, 1.18 per cent of the GDP each year. To gain some idea of how significant such an amount could be for the poor, it can be compared to the poverty gap during those years. According to Wodon (1999) if it had been possible for Pronasol funds to be targeted perfectly as monetary transfers to the most desperately poor, around a third of Mexico's poverty could have been alleviated with funds that, by order of magnitude, were larger than any other social funds.

The stated goal of Pronasol was to mitigate the effects of structural adjustment among the poor, and towards this end it promoted active citizen participation in a similar fashion to poverty funds elsewhere in Latin America, such as the Social Emergency Fund in Bolivia, FIDES in Venezuela, or FONCODES in Peru. Approximately 250 000 grassroots Pronasol committees were formed and designed projects in collaboration with government staff to address the community needs they identified (Sedesol, 1994). The committees mobilized and organized community members, evaluated proposed public works, and supervised implementation. The government then disbursed funds to the committees to finance public works projects or to complement regional development programmes. The latter fell within three strategic areas: social services, production, and regional development. Committees obtained matching funds from state and municipal governments in order to qualify for Pronasol, and this system of match funding served to multiply the economic scale and the potential positive impact of the programme.

Despite its alleged goals and wide reach, most accounts of Pronasol stress that the programme also had political goals (Díaz-Cayeros and Magaloni, 2003; Dresser, 1994a; Kaufman and Trejo, 1996). In particular, it has become commonly accepted that it was used to try and recover the lost legitimacy of the PRI and President Carlos Salinas de Gortari, following the tainted 1988 election in which the system of vote tallying crashed and the opposition claimed that a massive electoral fraud had been carried out. Critics contend that despite some achievements, Pronasol was little more than a politicized repackaging of traditional welfare and public works projects that served to ameliorate rather than address the root causes of poverty in Mexico (Dresser, 1991, 1994; Kaufman and Trejo, 1996). From this perspective, Pronasol's *raison d'être* was to enable Salinas and his supporters to build new political linkages with autonomous low-income interest groups, thereby revitalizing the PRI in the run up to future elections. Critics have also maintained that resources often did not reach those in extreme poverty. As Dresser (1994b) has argued, Pronasol provided state elites with the political conditions necessary to advance and sustain a neo-liberal political economy in Mexico.

Two fundamental criticisms dogged Pronasol from beginning to end: first, that it was not an effective mechanism in the war on poverty in Mexico, sacrificing social criteria in favour of political imperatives; and, second, that the logic of the programme was clientelistic and authoritarian. By redefining beneficiaries of the old state corporatist coalition as beneficiaries of Pronasol, the programme contributed towards rebuilding new constituencies for the state. Kaufman and Trejo (1996) have convincingly shown that in spite of its decentralized structure and the incorporation of state and municipal authorities into the selection of projects to be funded by Pronasol, the programme's system for the allocation of funds was not one based on local choice. Rather it was determined by bureaucrats in Mexico City and delegates of the Social Development Ministry (Sedesol) in each state, all of whom were accountable to the Minister and the President. In other words, Pronasol's objectives and the allocation of its funds were determined by the centre and not in the regions.

WITHIN AND WITHOUT: WOMEN IN SOLIDARITY

In December 1988 a programme for the Integration of Women into Development was created, supporting income-generating projects such as small enterprises, farm-based activities, bakeries, mills, and soup kitchens. From the programme's title it is easy to see that it was underpinned by a Women in Development (WID) discourse, which claimed that women should be integrated into development, usually by means of increasing their income through small income generating projects. In 1989 the programme changed its name to *Mujeres en Solidaridad* (Women in Solidarity) and was incorporated under the Pronasol umbrella. However, its approach remained very much the same, the objective being to improve the economic and social situation of impoverished rural and urban women. Though worthy, it failed to engage with wider gender concerns.

The target group was women living in those regions that exhibited high levels of malnutrition, as well as poor health, housing, and education levels, and the programme aimed to increase their earnings through income generating projects (Sedesol, 1994). Under *Mujeres en Solidaridad* women organized themselves into committees that defined, promoted, and carried out different projects. It formed an umbrella federation of approximately 3 500 organized women's committees that was in charge of planning, executing, and evaluating the projects carried out. It is worth noting that out of the total number of committees created, 65 per cent were among highly marginalized women (Consejo Consultivo del Programa Nacional de Solidaridad, 1994).

Activities were undertaken with both the private and social sectors, and were coordinated by representatives of federal, state, and local governments as well as by the *Mujeres en Solidaridad* grassroots committees. An agreement between a local government and an interested women's committee had to be established for the committee to be eligible to receive Pronasol funds. However, as with the rest of Pronasol, the authorized budget was established at the centralized level and set annually by the Ministry of Finance. The most common types of urban social programme carried out under the *Mujeres en Solidaridad* umbrella related to housing, water supply, and sanitation and the provision of basic infrastructure such as the construction of drainage. Men and women in the community dug the ditches and carried the electricity poles, pipes, wires, and cement on their backs or with their mules in order to contribute to the securing of prioritized public services. Women's productive activities included the establishment of *tortillerias* (places where *tortillas* are made and sold), sewing shops, provision stores, soup kitchens, and bakeries (Sedesol, 1994). However, while the programme addressed many of the felt needs of disadvantaged women, it did little to tackle the broader dimensions of gender inequality, and although thousands of productive projects mushroomed across the country they were largely unsustainable. Usually under-funded, without adequate training, and limited to very low profit activities, after a couple of years of operation women's groups were often abandoned or forced to downsize. Moreover, without relief from their other responsibilities, for most women income-generating projects represented an extra burden. Sometimes they also increased women's problems by creating tensions with men in the household.

Díaz-Callero and Magaloni (2003) argue that the social impact of Pronasol was fairly limited. The timing of expenditure responded to the federal electoral cycle and the allocation of funds was determined by the partisan identity and electoral contests of local executives. Specific funds were earmarked for clientelist purposes and funds were targeted in order to compensate for electoral uncertainty or according to the partisan loyalty of municipalities. Nevertheless, in its heyday Pronasol was considered to be a highly successful programme. Even after its demise various development agencies, including the OECD and the World Bank, have called for the merits of the programme to be revived. For all its shortcomings, Pronasol remains a benchmark and a yardstick against which future social policy interventions will be measured, offering both positive and negative lessons. This holds for *Mujeres en Solidaridad* too. Although the programme did not solve women's immediate problems in a sustainable way, nor directly address asymmetrical gender relations in Mexico more generally, it has to be said that Pronasol opened a space for women to participate actively in Mexico's broader social and political arenas.

SOCIAL FUNDS TO LOCAL FUNDS: PROGRESSIVE OPPORTUNITIES FOR A NEW CENTURY?

Following the political scandal and the financial crisis of December 1994, President Ernesto Zedillo restructured Pronasol. He was swift to change the programme's name because it was widely identified with the now unpopular Salinas. In 1995 he renamed it the *Alianza para el Bienestar* (Alliance for Well-being). He decentralized many of the funds to the local level and established targeting criteria for them. This meant he abandoned the universalist principles of Pronasol. *Alianza para el Bienestar* was divided in three main programmes: *Progresa*, Decentralized Funds for Social Infrastructure and a Fund for Productive Projects. Importantly, funds previously channelled to *Solidaridad* were pooled into *Progresa*, the aim of which was to provide education, health, and food to the poorest of the poor (SHCP, 1998). Through targeting the government tried to increase the effectiveness of its social policy by reaching those most in need. The restructuring process also involved strengthening the powers and responsibilities of state and municipal governments to allocate resources, while simultaneously reducing those of the presidency. In 1998 Zedillo transferred a substantial part of former Pronasol's resources to local governments, the timing of which coincided with the 1995 Fourth United Nations Conference on Women in Beijing. Thereafter the Mexican government followed the guidelines of the Action Plan from the Beijing Conference and sought to mainstream gender across all sector policies. The language of the Beijing Conference began to take root in Mexican policy discourse and terms such as 'gender mainstreaming', 'empowerment', and 'social rights' became integral to subsequent policy, programme, and project rhetoric, while different ministries were encouraged to address gender needs and issues throughout their practical initiatives. It was in this context that women's issues were to be addressed in the development of local funds, which contrary to the experience of social funds, were expected to provide greater opportunity for consultation and collaboration with women's groups.

Progresa changed its name to *Oportunidades* under the Fox administration, where it served as the flagship of Mexican social policy in the late 1990s through to the beginning of the new century and it remains the principal anti-poverty programme of the Mexican government at this time. The aim of *Progresa-Oportunidades* is to help poor families in rural and urban communities invest in human capital by improving the education, health, and nutrition of their children, by providing cash transfers to households linked to regular school attendance and health clinic visits (World Bank, 2004a; SHCP, 1998; Sedesol, 2004). Operating in poor rural areas since 1997 the programme but has recently expanded to cover urban areas as well, with the number of families benefiting from it now surpassing four million (Sedesol, 2004). *Progresa-Oportunidades* currently represents nearly half of Mexico's federal annual anti-poverty budget (ibid.). Families are chosen through the analysis of socio-economic information held at central government level, gathered by way of household surveys conducted in geographically targeted areas that contain high levels of disadvantage.

Combining targeting with a decentralized approach constituted a significant change in Mexican social policy. First, through *Oportunidades* it shifted from a massive social funds programme with near universal reach to more modest targeted interventions aimed at building up the human capital of poor families. Second, through the Decentralized Funds for Social Infrastructure, resources began to be decentralized to state and municipal governments. Together, the effect has been to limit resources available for organized communities because although the government has local funds, they are subject to the parameters of targeting and have strict eligibility criteria that now have to be met by local groups. This in turn has had a negative impact on those without financial and human resources – often including women, who are lacking skills and have less experience in fulfilling the terms of complicated application processes and meeting technical project requirements. This result is confirmed by similar experiences elsewhere, reported in the more general development literature (Kabeer, 1994, 1998; Mayoux, 1995). Insistence on citizen participation can lead to a bias in the selection of projects in favour of groups with greater potential for collective action. A common consequence is that the less formally organized – and here too women are over-represented – are excluded as they do not have the time or capacity to organize or press for public projects.

ProGenero: A NEW ERA FOR WOMEN?

The evidence from Mexico clearly suggests that targeted funds channelled through central interventions are not guaranteed to reach women, let alone the poorest amongst them. Under Fox's administration, *Alianza para el Bienestar* has switched to *Contigo*, a broad social policy umbrella strategy, of which *Progresa-Oportunidades* is the main component. *Contigo* has opened new spaces for channelling funds to civil society and grass roots organizations, which represents a remarkable change in the otherwise reluctant Mexican State, which once regarded civil organizations as a political threat. And, as noted before, when resources were provided this was on a very clientelistic basis. Although this is by all means a step forward in governance terms, the *Contigo* Strategy leaves little by way of resources that can be channelled directly to women in local level communities. However, *Contigo* does have two instruments that can potentially provide funds to local women groups. The first is a fund that grants resources to large NGOs working on gender issues that is available for project implementation. It is intended to reach grassroots groups and – in theory at least – to advance an empowerment approach. However, even here it has been shown that funds channelled through NGOs do not necessarily reach the most disadvantaged women (Cos-Montiel, 2003). The second is a programme targeting women-headed households that aims to support disadvantaged women household heads (or groups of such women) residing in impoverished neighbourhoods. It supports actions that aim to develop their capabilities, improve their work performance, and integrate them into income-generating activities. While successful in reaching women, targeting women-headed households is a controversial strategy in terms of reaching the poorest women. As Chant (1997) has argued for the case of Mexico and elsewhere, women household headship constitutes an unreliable proxy for poverty. Nevertheless, the programme does support women household heads through awareness raising and leadership training, and more immediately by providing child care facilities for children under six while women are working or being trained (Sedesol, 2004). Although the programme recognizes that poor leadership and the burden of housework and child care inhibit women from realizing their potential and participating in public life, implementation remains a serious problem.

A lot of energy and hope has been invested recently in *ProGenero* (Gender Equity Project), an innovative World Bank sponsored gender-focused local funds project that includes among its goals those of social security and social inclusion (World Bank, 2000). The aim is to increase women's access to government sponsored social programmes as well as to build local governance conditions that are gender sensitive and conducive to participation by women (Sedesol, 2004; World Bank, 2000). However, its sponsorship by the World Bank raised many eyebrows in the Mexican women's movement, which for many years has been critical of the World Bank's macro-economic policy recommendations for Mexico. To gain the support of the women's movement and legitimacy in its eyes, in 1999 a group of government-based gender advocates pooled together inputs from Mexican women's organizations, the experiences of staff from the World Bank working on women's issues, and strong leadership from committed government officials, to create ownership of the project among this diverse group.

In terms of what *ProGenero* does, it aims to facilitate the mutual learning and piloting of community-based initiatives to promote gender equity and improved access to government-supported income generation pro-grammes in the context of Mexico's strategy for poverty reduction and social sustainability (World Bank, 2000). Its main thrust is a community-based gender and development initiative that seeks to improve equity in opportunities for men and women, social accord, and inclusive governance through the promotion of community-based actions. *ProGenero* also aims to support basic needs and human capital development by building on the positive impact of recent changes achieved through poverty reduction pro-grammes, while at the same time promoting gender equity and increasing social awareness about gender, development, and women's participation in governance. In other words, the successful implementation of *ProGenero* is designed to move beyond separate programmes for women and to improve the well-being of both poor men and women while at the same time increasing gender equity and tackling discrimination against women.

Designed as an innovative learning experience, the project includes the piloting of different approaches to promoting gender equity across different regions of the country. A review of some of the activities supported by the project, drawn from detailed monitoring and evaluation, shows a consider-able shift in mindset in terms of how to improve the condition of Mexican women. *ProGenero* has introduced a much greater emphasis on leadership training and capacity-building in order to strengthen the civic participation of women. This emphasis is aimed at promoting their participation in both the public and private sectors, raising awareness among male leaders of changing gender roles in Mexican society and providing role models for younger women. Eligible candidates have included leaders from both com-munity and peasant organizations, as well as small business-women and women working in health and education projects, municipalities, or local parents' associations. The shift from social to local funds is also evident in the demand-driven *Convive* Programme, the aim of which is to enhance community life through the fostering of peaceful interaction and toler-ance in community relations. This is done by providing small grants through competitive challenge fund mechanisms to successful grassroots organizations that come up with appropriate and feasible projects.

Despite the enthusiasm of gender advocates in government and the sup-port of World Bank staff, the project nevertheless faced fierce opposition from the departing Minister of Social Development. This was also the case with the new Social Development Minister under the Fox administration. As a result *ProGenero* was eventually transferred to the National Gender Machinery, which does not have the status of a ministry, where it is cur-rently being implemented. Although it is too early to fully assess its impact, the mid-term review is positive about the support provided to community-based initiatives through the small competitive grants fund, *Convive*. This is now successfully operating in 35 small cities, with groups representing a range of socio-economic and cultural backgrounds, including 24 groups that include significant indigenous population membership. Under imple-mentation now are 70 projects that are directly benefiting 1 431 people (979 women and 452 men). In terms of capacity-building on gender equity among community leaders, so far 163 women and 59 men have received training across 22 communities. The sums are comparatively small and coverage limited. However, the focus is appropriate as experience elsewhere suggests that if attention to women's priorities is to be sustainable, women require support to develop their own capabilities in order to press for entitlements on their own account (World Bank, 2004b).

WIDENING THE FIELD: A NEW ERA FOR LOCAL FUNDS?

Accompanying the government's downsizing of social sector spending and social protection interventions in Mexico, it seems that a number of new non-governmental actors are taking over and filling some of the gaps left behind. For example, the Ford Foundation has funded a number of different initiatives based on a local funds model that include a focus on governance. One is *Semillas,* which gives small grants to women's income generating programmes while at the same time developing other skills that strengthen women's participation in public life. It provides training through workshops on diverse topics ranging from developing competence in computer literacy and new technologies to human rights and women's leadership. Another is *Comaletzin,* an indigenous women's project which trains community leaders to improve their skills in local governance and increase their bargaining power in the context of negotiations with local and federal authorities. Recognizing the reluctance on the part of women to put themselves into the public realm, the project sought to address some of the root causes of women's passivity. It identified domestic violence as one the main obstacles to their full participation in society, as well as the fact that sometimes women have to drop out of organizations and collective activities due to pressure from their partners. Even among the project staff it has been reported that violence from their male partners has increased since they started working for the organization. The perception of husbands is often that gender-related work is 'breaking up families'. However, women have gradually gained confidence and participate more, although efforts to integrate men into mixed or men-only workshops on interpersonal violence have so far been resoundingly unsuccessful.

Interestingly, such projects often experience difficulties working with the national gender machinery and its offices at a local level. Consequently they have decided to continue working primarily at the community level where they face less obstruction and have been more effective. Training of members of grassroots organizations in management skills has enabled them to deal with local authorities, and now they are better able to prepare grant proposals or complain to local officials about service delivery. This has been welcomed by government employees who take them more seriously now that they have 'become more professional'. The fact that women are increasing their capacity as community leaders and feel more self-confident means that their work has become much more politicized, and they are trying to find formal channels to connect local issues with wider political ones. It is often this dimension of their progress that government departments, including the national gender machinery, find most threatening; and in this regard it is disappointing that they have not been able to elicit sustained support from the national gender bureaucratic structures.

Despite much progress in the context of women-focused initiatives, it has been less evident in the wider range of local funds projects concerned with local governance and funded by non-governmental organizations and foundations. Women are very much under-represented as agents of change in those projects that are not specifically targeted towards them. This can be clearly seen, for example, in the well-funded bi-national community foundations programme supported by Ford Foundation on the US–Mexico Border (see Box 4.1).

Box 4.1 The US–Mexico border: community foundations as agents of change

The border between the United States of America and Mexico spans 2 000 miles, touching four US and six Mexican states. The region's population is growing rapidly, from nearly 10 million today to an estimated 20 million by the year 2020 (Presidencia de la República, 2001). Communities on both sides of the border are struggling with inadequate social services and infrastructure, low wages, and high unemployment. Rapid, unplanned growth is causing environmental crises, with water shortages and air and water pollution. Mexican border cities are increasingly unable to fulfil expanding demands for basic health care, housing, and public services. US border counties have some of the worst poverty rates in the nation. At the same time, the massive flow of migrants from Mexico crossing the border under dangerous conditions has resulted in significant human rights abuses.

In 1995 Susan Beresford, President of the Ford Foundation, announced her interest in creating a US$10 million fund to promote cross-border philanthropy. She subsequently set aside US$3 million toward the creation of the US–Mexico Border Philanthropy Partnership. The NGO *Synergos* identified 14 US and seven Mexican diverse community foundations operating along the border with varying levels of development. All had the potential to play a critical role in their communities:

- acting as community-based grant makers, matching resources with local needs
- strengthening the capacity of NGOs and CBOs serving the local communities
- bringing together representatives of the public, private, and non-profit sectors in action-oriented partnerships
- connecting local efforts to national and international networks

> ■ expanding local foundation grant making through permanently endowed funds
> ■ providing a voice for local disenfranchised citizens and communities.
>
> Long-term cross-border partnerships were underpinned by three main objectives: building and strengthening the leadership and institutional resources of border organizations; rooting development efforts in local participation and social capital; and encouraging cross-border collaboration that would improve the quality of life.
>
> The partnership also sets out strategies to assist border community foundations in capacity building through (a) bi-annual 'Learning Communities' to share best practices; (b) inter-foundation exchanges; (c) bridge building between diverse community segments and between the foundations and members of other societal sectors; and (d) technical assistance in fundraising and grant making. However, in the words of an advocate involved in the project's design, 'Women are poorly represented, particularly at the decision making level' (Parra, 2004). For example, Ciudad Juarez, which is one of the most impoverished cities on the border and desperately in need of improvements to conditions of governance, exhibits one of the most horrific gender violence problems in Mexico, both in the public and the private domains and including the murder of more than 300 women since 1988. However, despite this reputation the situation has not been acknowledged as a problem of any relevance to women's participation in partnership activities, let alone local governance. This gives rise to the question: can the initiative advance inclusive governance without addressing the massive prevalence of violence against women?

Another recent intervention funded by the Kellogg's Foundation has established a project in which distant communities can share information through the Internet on the prices of commodities so they can get a fairer price for their products. The system can also be used when they want to know about local election results. Unfortunately, however, this is another example of a small funds project in which women do not benefit equally – for instance, by learning about other groups of women and their initiatives, thereby increasing their relative status and sense of empowerment. These two examples suggest that mainstreaming gender does not happen automatically and is best advanced by programmes and projects designed in ways that include a gender focus, where explicit attention to women's participation and gender sensitivity is required.

CONCLUSIONS: ARE LOCAL FUNDS GOOD FOR WOMEN?

The case of Mexico highlights very well some of the dilemmas associated with social funds and local funds and, most particularly, the tensions that emerge when trying to combine poverty reduction and governance enhancing goals. There is no doubt that poverty and social exclusion go hand-in-hand with lack of participation in decision-making and political exclusion, and the Mexican story confirms that tackling social disadvantage requires recognizing and addressing both sides of this equation. Nevertheless, the history of social and gender policy in Mexico reveals this to be extremely difficult in practice. If there is any single lesson to be learned from the Mexican example presented here it is that instruments for addressing poverty and material deprivation, and instruments addressing social and political exclusion need to be coordinated and finessed rather than entangled and confused. With regard to women and enhancing gender equity, the situation becomes even more complex: gender subordination needs to be factored in as a goal of policy that recognizes it as related to, but not synonymous with, the dynamics of poverty and social exclusion (Beall, 1998; Jackson, 1996). So what does the Mexican experience offer us by way of example in terms of implementing programmes that address these multiple goals, and how constrained is practice by macro-economic and national political forces?

The universal coverage sought by Pronasol and *Solidaridad* did have some significant success in addressing social disadvantage, and they also improved the well-being and enhanced the potential of many women. *Solidaridad* had the additional effect of increasing *women's* expectations and the demands they made of government. However, as this chapter has shown, in implementation the programme – which was based on a social funds model – gave rise to a mushrooming of myriad unconnected projects that were abandoned when they became impossible to coordinate or sustain. Although Pronasol was accused of being over-centralized it was nevertheless a linchpin of governance strategies in Mexico at the time. Alongside addressing social protection, there were efforts at redefining state functions and capacity and improving relations with society (Dresser, 1991). Through *Solidaridad* progress was undoubtedly made in terms of increasing the gender awareness of local authorities and women's participation in programmes and projects, but their role in decision-making remained fairly limited. To the extent that women's needs and interests were addressed, this was invariably in relation to their responsibilities as mothers and wives rather than their rights as producers or citizens.

Progresa-Oportunidades should ideally have risen to this challenge, and indeed has sought to do so through its attempt to mainstream gender in its support for local funds and local governance. However, the shift towards economic neoliberalism, combined with widely experienced difficulties associated with efficient and effective targeting, has meant that it is not very clear as to whether the most materially deprived are being reached. While the targeting of deprived groups such as indigenous people is relatively straightforward, as is the targeting of women-headed households, it is likely that many of the non-indigenous poor and women in poor male-headed households still lose out. Nevertheless, political liberalization in

Mexico has given rise to an increased focus on improving local participation and governance and has contributed to reducing clientelism through increased transparency. Here local funds do appear to be having a positive impact. However, during this period, funds for women in the social sector virtually disappeared due both to the redesign of social funds and the impact of the Beijing Conference and its message on mainstreaming gender. While gender became part of all sectoral policies and many ministries tried to address gender through various frameworks and tools, it took *ProGenero*, the World Bank sponsored 'Gender Equity Project', to help keep women's concerns alive in policy discourse and programming practice, something that would have been impossible to achieve without dialogue and coordination with the organized women's movement in Mexico.

With a new government that seeks to consolidate democracy in Mexico, the new century has seen local funds for governance beginning to play an extremely important role in the country's social development. With few remnants of the macro-level and monolithic social funds that characterized Pronasol, local funds for local governance are having a positive impact as resources get closer to the people who need them most. While they are not sufficient to provide universal coverage for the country's poorest and most deprived people, they are proving to be an effective mechanism for leveraging involvement and resources from a wide range of stakeholders, achieving buy-in and reach beyond the scope of government. As the last section of the chapter demonstrates, NGOs, foundations, and international agencies are involved in supporting and promoting funds that are attempting to create conditions for inclusive and responsive local governance. Moreover, many of these funds implicitly or explicitly address gender concerns ranging from increasing women's leadership to addressing women's rights and ending gender-based violence. Nevertheless, there are limits to the way in which women's issues are addressed, and in some of the projects without an explicit gender focus insufficient attention is paid to issues such as power, eligibility, and fairness – including disparities between women and men – in relation to gaining access to local funds. Despite the fact that gender sensitive language has been integrated into the policy frameworks within which local funds are situated, implementation remains a problem. As under Pronasol and *Solidaridad*, many of the most disadvantaged women still fail to benefit equitably from social development initiatives in Mexico, while problems of transparency remain an issue.

If the issues of poverty reduction and gender equity are not conflated then it can be fairly convincingly argued that in Mexico local funds are proving more effective for addressing women's subordination, if not their or their families' poverty, than the much larger social funds Pronasol Programme. However not all local funds for governance automatically benefit women, and indeed the scramble for resources can be more desperate and vicious at the local level than the competition for resources at higher levels of government, with women often being those who are first to lose out (Beall, 2004). It is important, therefore, that the design of local funds programmes includes a gender perspective, with mechanisms to ensure that it is carried through into implementation, monitoring, and evaluation. The presence of gender sensitive advocacy NGOs, acting as a bridge between government and the most disadvantaged and politically illiterate groups, can be helpful, although it is also the case that the NGOs that are sufficiently professional to comply with the bureaucratic procedures of grant making organizations can sometimes lose sight of their *raison d'être*. Hence NGOs can be important partners in the engagement with state institutions, but not alternatives to them.

The inclusion of a specific gender perspective is important, particularly in mainstream programmes and projects, as evidenced by the example of the cross-border initiative funded by the Ford Foundation, described above. Equally important is the involvement of women's organizations alongside other partners. However, neither strategy automatically gives rise to positive gender outcomes or greater equity more generally. In the presence of scarce funding opportunities competition can be fierce, and sometimes an organization's survival depends on successful bidding, something that can override the priorities of clients and beneficiaries – a phenomenon from which women's organizations are not immune. Nor does the inclusion of a gender perspective in programme design necessarily mean that positive gender outcomes will arise. Experience from South Africa suggests that interventions that do not include a focus on women and gender relations in design can achieve such a focus during the course of implementation if the political and policy conditions for women's participation and empowerment are favourable (Beall and Todes, 2004).

In the case of Mexico, the political opportunities for women's involvement have ebbed and flowed. *Solidaridad* clearly played a part in raising awareness, while *ProGenero* brought the issue of women and governance firmly back into the frame. In combination with grassroots and politically organized women working on the ground, it appears that opportunities are increasing for channelling support to community level women's groups in projects that are oriented towards the exercise of rights and the development of organizational and leadership skills. These initiatives are critical in creating conditions of governance that are more inclusive, and they are at the crux of local funds for local governance. However, if governance is about broader social justice, then on their own these initiatives are insufficient. Local funds do not and cannot single-handedly address the needs of all poor and socially disadvantaged people because by definition they are selective on the basis of area, identity, or some other criteria. Hence they are not a replacement for the broader objectives of Pronasol or *Progresa-Oportunidades* but a supplement to them. Second, if as a democratic country Mexico aims to create conditions for social justice and gender equity on a national basis, then ways need to be found to make efforts at including women in local governance more coherent with efforts on behalf of women at national level. This requires that serious attention be paid to the role and location of the national gender machinery and its accountability both to national and local level development and democracy. Gender inclusive local funds for democracy and development are a necessary but not sufficient condition for improving well-being in Mexico and ensuring gender justice.

CHAPTER FIVE

Local funds as an aid instrument: examples from multilateral aid programmes

INTRODUCTION

International agencies command an array of instruments for providing development assistance, ranging from full interest-bearing loans, to concession-based finance, tied aid, unconditional grants, and charity. Decisions as to what kind of assistance to provide, where to direct it, and how to deliver it are based on factors such as the priorities and capabilities of recipient countries, what donors want out of the process, what is being done by other donors, the private sector and NGOs, as well as changing trends and fashions in development thinking and practice. It is sometimes difficult to gauge the suitability of an aid instrument for supporting a particular objective and to achieve a balance of interventions at different levels – for example at the macro, sub-national, or local levels. Local funds should never be seen or assessed in isolation from the broader political, policy, and aid contexts. This chapter traces the evolution of aid policy and practice from projects and programmes, to macro-level policies accompanied by conditionalities such as SAPs, through to the current mechanism of DBS as a macro-level aid instrument. Against this broader background discussion of the meaning and delivery of development aid, this chapter profiles three local funding mechanisms used as aid instruments by multilateral donors. The first two are in Africa, one with a primarily rural focus and the other with a primarily urban focus.

The first profile is of the primarily urban-focused AGETIPs, which are the executing agencies for funds for public works that operate across many francophone African countries, particularly in West Africa. The World Bank and the ILO fund AGETIPs, with the latter providing support to capacity-building, learning, and dissemination of the model, and to the international association of AGETIPs called AFRICATIP. AGETIPs developed as a form of social funds but some also have the characteristics of more recent local funds, as is the case with the fund reviewed here, *L'Agence d'Exécution des Travaux Urbains (à haute intensité de main-d'oeuvre)* (AGETUR), which is an urban-focused labour-intensive public works programme operating in Cotonou in Benin with a strong emphasis on partnership, notably with the private sector. Against the background of a brief discussion of the evolution and strengths and weaknesses of AGETIPs, the following section describes the workings of AGETUR, its institutional relationships, and its agility in reaching poor people. AGETUR is reviewed primarily in terms of implementation challenges and practice, with consideration being given to whether the experience of AGETUR supports the reputation gained by AGETIPs for getting funds swiftly and simply to where they are needed most and, whether it creates sustainable livelihoods or risk management.

The second large local funding mechanism profiled is the primarily rural-focused United Nations Capital Development Fund (UNCDF), which was initially established in 1966 by the United Nations Development Programme (UNDP) group as a special purpose fund for small-scale investment in rural areas of the poorest countries and which has increasingly taken on, and indeed influenced, some of the key features of local funds. Although focused at the local level, the Fund is resourced through voluntary contributions by Member States of the UN and through co-financing arrangements with national governments, other international development organizations, and the private sector. The UNCDF has a poverty reduction focus which is pursued through two trajectories, Local Development Programmes (LDPs) and micro-credit initiatives. In terms of the latter, the UNCDF is involved with the identification, formulation, and management of micro-finance programmes in rural areas; the development and delivery of new micro-finance 'products'; capacity-building and technical advice around these activities; and the dissemination of 'best practices' in micro-finance. The LDPs, which are pursued in close collaboration with UNDP, provide grants and technical assistance for the democratization of development planning and financing, and decentralization, including the transfer of power from central to local government and from local authorities to community-based organizations and individual citizens. The idea behind the LDPs is to give elected officials the resources to invest, while at the same time opening up the planning processes so that local people can have a say in the decisions that affect their lives. In addition to working with local authorities, therefore, the LDPs work with NGOs and civil society to develop the checks and balances to keep local governments accountable, through regular dialogue and a climate of engagement. The focus on the UNCDF here is on the recent experience of its LDP in Mozambique. It is reviewed primarily in terms of policy impact and whether it has impacted on poverty reduction and influenced the conduct of governance.

The third example of support by a multilateral development agency to small projects with a focus on participation and governance is the United Nations Development Programme's Local Initiative Facility for Urban Environment (LIFE), which was an international programme operating across five regions and 12 countries. Using small projects as 'policy experiments' (Rondinelli, 1992), the programme aimed to influence environmental policy through demonstration effect, partnership, and policy dialogue. It provided small grants to local organizations to implement participatory environmental projects in local neighbourhoods that would bring together various partners in collaborative efforts. It was hoped that these would spread through the transfer of ideas and experience, generating further local-level and community-based initiatives and in turn leading to policy dialogue and influence. The programme is assessed here in terms of the strengths and weaknesses of global initiatives aimed at improving well-being and governance through small-scale interventions and funds, and, whether local-level initiatives can influence policy and practice at the national and international levels.

THE MEANING OF AID

Aid is an emotive concept, and a controversial issue for both donor and recipient countries, not least because it is variously conceived. Almost by definition aid is normative, infused with ideology and with more or less obvious strings attached. For example, if aid is used to promote economic growth and/or political reform in less developed countries, a certain type of growth – based on neoliberal principles – and a certain type of political reform – based on Western multi-party democracy – is assumed. Donor governments are usually averse to giving aid to countries or groups that are antagonistic towards them and bilateral development cooperation often involves industrialized countries giving aid to countries that share their political persuasion or that they wish to influence. The first development decade followed the American President Harry S Truman's explicit anti-communist agenda. Very much concerned with promoting the American view of freedom and economic growth, this persisted well beyond the 1950s, as did the fact that aid flows were closely associated with the Cold War and competition with the Soviet Bloc for territorial bases. By contrast, in the 1970s and 1980s the social democratic government of Sweden saw its SIDA giving aid primarily to developing countries with a socialist or social democratic persuasion, such as Tanzania, Nicaragua, and Mozambique. In the case of apartheid South Africa, moreover, SIDA supported the African National Congress (ANC) during its exile, and funded South African NGOs rather than the apartheid government.

Nevertheless, there are some broadly accepted definitions of aid. For example, the Development Assistance Committee (DAC) of the Organization for Economic Cooperation and Development (OECD, 1985: 171) defines what it calls Overseas Development Assistance (ODA) as resources transferred on concessional financial terms, with the promotion of the economic development and welfare of developing countries as the main declared objectives. This would include grants and soft loans, with a grant element of at least 25 per cent. Aid has been extended with differing emphases on economic development and on welfare. There is an argument that aid should not be used instrumentally but should rather be motivated by altruism and involve the transfer of resources in an act of charity. This is the position of most NGOs, while DFID's former Secretary of State for Development, Clare Short, argued that British taxpayers should view the proportion of their taxes spent on aid in the same way. However, this constituted a sea change from earlier approaches on the part of the British government, which like many other bilateral agencies practiced tied aid – the practice by which donors tied their development financing to the provision of goods and services by companies and other institutions in the donor country – a practice which is now thought to seriously undermine the effectiveness and poverty reducing impact of aid (Burnell, 1997).

Defining aid means deciding what should and should not be included when calculating aid and when comparing the performances of different countries. This is controversial. For example, should tied aid count as aid or not? Sometimes direct corporate investment has been included in bilateral aid calculations alongside government-to-government aid. The case can also be made for including trade arrangements as instruments of aid, if there are concessional terms of trade. This was more evident in the past – for example in the European Union's Lomé Conventions on Europe's trade with the African, Caribbean and Pacific (ACP) countries or in trade arrangements between Commonwealth countries. It is less evident, however, under the more recent World Trade Organisation (WTO) regimen. In the past there were strong arguments against including military aid alongside development aid, although more recently aid and security agendas are becoming increasingly enmeshed. Another dilemma is whether or not the activities of the IFIs – such as the IMF and the World Bank should be counted as aid. Since 1972 the DAC of the OECD has stipulated that concessional financial resource flows should have a grant element of at least 25 per cent if a loan is to qualify as development assistance (OECD, 1996). This would mean that the World Bank's soft-finance facility known as the International Development Association (IDA) qualifies as aid, but that of the International Bank of Reconstruction and Development (IBRD), which was set up not as an aid instrument but to promote the international flow of capital and economic development, does not. The IDA loans, known as 'credits', are made available only to the poorest countries, are without interest except for an administrative fee, and repayment is delayed until after a ten-year grace period (Thomas and Allen, 2000: 205).

In practice it is difficult to leave the IFIs out of a discussion on aid because they so profoundly influence the development context. Bilateral aid and private investment often follow endorsement of a country's macroeconomic policy by the IMF and the World Bank and countries at odds with these institutions find it difficult to raise resources from elsewhere. Moreover, although it is a bank, the World Bank is also a not-for-profit organization, offering soft finance and providing in-kind development assistance through advice and technical cooperation to borrowing countries. In this context, aid is undoubtedly used to promote a particular development trajectory towards economic growth and poverty reduction. As such, it is replete with conditionality, understood as the promotion of actions by donor pressure that a recipient government would not otherwise agree with. As discussed in Chapter Two, the most widespread forms of conditionality were the IMF and World Bank structural adjustment packages. It is now generally agreed, however, that on its own, conditional programme aid has proved to be fairly ineffective (Mosley, Harrigan and Toye, 1991; Ranis, 1997). More recently, the thrust of aid conditionality is to link resources to pro-poor growth strategies. Initiated by a number of bilateral agencies, emphasizing a poverty focus in government-to-government aid from the early 1990s onwards, it is now integral to the agendas of the IFIs too. The World Bank notably requires the development of Poverty Reduction Strategy Papers (PRSPs) as a condition of IDA financing and as a recipient country's part of the aid bargain.

HOW AID IS DELIVERED

For most of the post-war period, the development project was the principal vehicle by which concessional loans and grant aid were channelled to developing countries. Projects were considered to be the most efficient way to deliver capital investment and alongside this lay a conviction that projects, with their own separate accounting and administrative arrangements, provided the most risk free way of guaranteeing to taxpayers that aid funding was not being wasted. The focus on projects was driven by the belief that lack of investment was a constraint on development, and project planning was promoted by the international agencies, primarily the World Bank, with the aim of channelling investment resources in manageable packages for the achievement of efficient results (Baum, 1982). Characteristics of projects are that they are time-bound, most typically by a five-year project cycle; they are location-bound, usually being associated with a defined place or area-based development, and, they benefit from having specific and manageable objectives, for example to support particular sectoral activities or levels of intervention. Projects are characterized, too, by a limited budget and a limited set of actors and relationships. Evaluations undertaken in the 1980s and 1990s exposed a litany of problems related to the project approach, both from the perspective of donors and recipients.

The most obvious limitation of projects was that no matter how effectively they were managed the external environment or context was bound to impinge upon their success and if economic conditions were difficult, as they were for many developing countries from the early 1970s onwards, then projects were going to be compromised. Moreover, in a volatile and complex economic climate, project identification and appraisal became more difficult. Other problems, such as weak states, poor markets, and ineffective CSOs heightened these difficulties, which had already been exacerbated in many countries by the institutional climate. Under such conditions – and because of the rigidity of the five-year planning and implementation cycle – projects could not respond quickly to economic shocks and institutional change.

Other problems were associated with the project approach itself. First, for countries with big aid programmes and a large number of donors, the transaction costs of managing and accounting for multiple projects were high. In interviews conducted with government officials, many reported that over 50 per cent of their time, if not more, was spent servicing the reporting needs of donors. Second, the returns were often unsatisfactory, particularly if donor governments tied procurement to their own national contractors and suppliers. A third problem was a lack of predictability in funding, related to the limited project cycle and uncertainty over whether further phases would be supported. Fourth, projects tended to have their own project management structures, which often duplicated or under-mined government systems, compromising their effectiveness. This was particularly the case if project accounting eclipsed the usual structures of democratic accountability in a country. The World Bank (1998) in its *Aid Effectiveness* report put the issue as follows:

> Aid agencies have a long history of trying to 'cocoon' their projects using freestanding technical assistance, independent project implementation units, and foreign experts – rather than trying to improve the institutional environment for service provision [. . .] They have neither improved services in the short run not led to institutional changes in the long run.

Moreover, projects did not prove to be effective financial management instruments. Corruption was as rife within them as without and econo-mists were concerned about fungibility. As Moseley et al. (1991: 29) have explained, 'if aid finances a project the recipient government would have undertaken anyway, then the aid money is actually financing some other, unidentified project which the aid agency does not know about and might not like'. Taken together, these arguments provided a devastating critique of projects that went beyond a call for better project design. Still, although less fashionable, projects remain an important means of delivering and administering development assistance today – though they are less often undertaken directly by donors or their consultants.

The waning of projects was accompanied by a preference for programme aid, understood as general financial assistance to a government's budget and balance of payments (Foster and Fozzard, 2000). The shift from project to programme aid in the 1980s was very much about donors seeking a seat at the policy table. With projects, conditionality was confined to project efficiency and performance and in any case, project funds were too small to give international agencies much clout. With programme-lending, not only were the stakes higher, but the process was more closely linked to pol-icy dialogue (Moseley et al., 1991: 32). It was in this context that the SAPs of the 1980s were pushed, despite resistance from recipient governments, into the neoliberal economic agenda of which they were a part. Just as proj-ects had come to be criticized, so too did programme-lending, most frequently for the adoption of a 'one-size-fits-all' approach to macro-economic reform across countries with very different histories, economies, and institutional contexts. As discussed in Chapter Two, this gave rise in the 1990s to the 'good governance' agenda, a preoccupation with 'getting the institutions right' and aid resources being made available for institutional reform. Technical at first, ultimately the governance agenda began to incorporate democracy goals as well, and aid was used to encourage political reform (Burnell, 2000).

There were doubts as to the desirability and effectiveness of linking aid and political conditionality. In the first place, it is often the least aid-dependent countries that have the most robust democracies – India, for example. In the second place, aid can undermine some of the fundamental premises of democracy – such as transparency and accountability – by virtue of the conditions it imposes, with policy priorities being agreed with donors in opaque negotiation processes outside of reference to national legislatures. A third objection is that if democracy is foisted upon a country from the outside, it can be argued that this is not real democracy. It was in response to such criticisms that some development agencies attempted a shift towards DBS, whereby a government and donor together establish an agreed set of priorities and reforms, and donor funds are channelled directly to a partner government that uses its own allocation, procurement and accounting systems. DBS first took the form of Sector Wide Approaches (SWAps), which referred to financial aid earmarked for a discrete sector, or sectors, with conditionality relating only to those sectors.

The defining characteristic of a SWAp is that all available funding for a sector supports

> [. . .] a single sector policy and expenditure programme, under Government leadership, adopting common approaches across the sector, and progressing towards relying on Government procedures to disburse and account for all funds.
>
> (Brown et al., 2000: 7)

For example, in its first White Paper on international development, DFID (1997) committed itself as far as possible to support government actions and institutions:

> Where we have confidence in the policies and budgetary allocation process and in the capacity for effective implementation in the partner government, we will consider moving away from supporting specific projects to providing resources more strategically in support of sector-wide programmes or the economy as a whole.

SWAps overcame some of the problems of conditionality, for instance, the number of different donors setting different and sometimes contradictory conditions, diminished (Foster, 2000). It was hoped that the process of policy dialogue, particularly in the context of donor coordination, would allow for donor influence without disrupting or displacing government institutions. Some recipient countries welcomed the accompanying reduction in the transaction cost of aid but others felt threatened. For example, in South Africa the Ministry of Health has resisted donor coordination within the sector – in relation to pressure on the government regarding HIV/AIDS, for instance. SWAps came to be accompanied by General Budget Support (GBS), which is support to national budgets, usually through ministries of finance, delivered in the context of longer-term donor commitments and in fewer instalments. It is thought to provide more reliable funding flows that facilitate both longer-term planning and shorter-term flexibility in the face of context-specific problems. This is discussed in more detail in the following chapter. Here, we turn attention to the multilateral local funds programmes that are closer to the remit of SWAps.

FRANCOPHONE AFRICAN AGETIPS AND AGETUR IN BENIN

As discussed in Chapter Three, people's livelihoods are multifaceted and involve a range of assets that they use to survive and to guard against risk. Principal among the assets they employ is their own labour (Amis, 1995; Moser, 1998). Indeed, when very poor people are asked what they most want from government, donors, or NGOs they invariably ask for jobs. With this in mind, AGETIPs should be well placed to address this critical aspect of people's risk management or livelihood strategies. In 1989, the social funds agency, *Agence d'Execution de Travaux d'Intéret Public* (Public Works and Employment Agency) was set up in Senegal and since then the model has been generalized to a number of countries in francophone Africa, such as Benin, Burkina Faso, Chad, The Gambia, Madagascar, Mali, Mauritania, Niger, Senegal, and Togo. They operate under the name *Agences d'Exécution de Travaux d'Intérêt Public pour l'Emploi*, with the same acronym (AGETIPs). AGETIPs are delegated contract management agencies for public works. While in typical social funds the social funds agency selects eligible sub-projects and channels funds to them, AGETIPs, in addition to performing both of these functions, also prepare and execute the elected sub-projects on behalf of the sponsoring agency, which surrenders authority for the execution of the sub-project to the AGETIP management until delivery of the completed works.

AGETIPs have a number of critical features. First, the typical AGETIP is a dual agent, with responsibilities for providing infrastructure and for implementing projects – including the procurement of materials, the supervision of works, and so on. They are set up as national executing agencies for these activities on a competitive basis but in the form of private not-for-profit NGOs. They were set up in this way because government agencies were not well equipped procedurally to deal with small entrepreneurs and community contractors who need regular and timely payment if they are to stay in business and deliver on employment intensive operations. AGETIPs were able to absorb the high transaction costs involved and most have developed considerable contract management expertise by using relatively simple systems and procedures. Indeed, some of them are now sufficiently large and experienced to take on a coordination role and have delegated execution authority. Second, AGETIPs are concerned with poverty allevia- tion and social protection through employment-intensive programmes for public work, usually infrastructure. Third, they use the private sector for labour-based urban infrastructure projects, sometimes seeking out small- sized and community contractors, or affording a mechanism for participa- tion (so that communities can propose projects). Fourth, AGETIPs are seen to promote sound development practice by using local labour and materi- als. Indeed, the ILO has worked to transfer lessons on the technical, social, and economic benefits of this approach not only to other countries but to government ministries. Fifth, because of the rapid spread of AGETIPs since the establishment of the pioneering agency in Senegal, they are regarded as classic demonstration projects and a good example of 'learning by doing'. In sum, enthusiasts see AGETIPs as multi-purpose agencies that involve the private sector in poverty reduction through the provision of employ- ment and infrastructure, that promote community participation, and that offer the prospect of building up competitive small and medium-sized entrepreneurs in local construction industries.

Detractors of AGETIPs point out that they are still highly dependent on external funding – and therefore unsustainable – and also that they suffer many of the problems associated with social funds, as outlined in Chapter One. Second, they are said to put in motion a substitution effect, whereby governments are allowed to abdicate their responsibility for social protec- tion and poverty reduction because the AGETIPs are thought to take care of these areas. A third problem is that because AGETIPs operate outside the restrictive bureaucratic environment of government, often for very under- standable reasons, they can undermine ministries of public works as the main employers of labour for infrastructure programmes. This could potentially harm long-term relations with politicians and government offi- cials, and compromise government structures. It is perhaps for this reason that recently AGETIPs are more often focused on the execution of public works, while municipalities are reclaiming responsibility for the selection of the projects. Lastly, because AGETIPs are agencies that recruit private contractors and are often run by people drawn from the private sector, they are open to accusations of patronage and malfeasance, particularly in countries where there are strong personal networks among the business community. It is for this reason that oversight and procedures have to be firmly executed. For the smaller contractors, who are less well equipped to take on and follow through on complicated project management tools, this can difficult, laying much of the responsibility on the AGETIPs themselves, which in turn have to be squeaky clean.

The AGETUR in Benin was established in 1990 as a legally-constituted NGO, charged with contracting, overseeing, and managing individual projects concerned with delivering urban infrastructure and services. It employs labour-intensive strategies that provide an income to poor people.

The agency is also concerned with the development of small and medium-sized contractors as well as community contracting. Works carried out through AGETUR are financed by various IFIs, such as the World Bank, the European Union, the French Agency for Development, the African Development Bank, the West African Development Bank, the Canadian Agency for International Development, Swiss Cooperation, DANIDA, and the International Development Association, along with contributions from the Benin government as well as local neighbourhood associations. Hence, AGETUR is highly reliant on external donor funding even though it is contracted to the government and forms part of Benin's poverty reduction strategies. The country has a number of policies and programmes meant to reduce poverty, including the Social Action Programme, ILO support to the informal sector, labour intensive Urban Works Programmes, and projects financed through social funds. What binds most initiatives is their focus on either employment creation or assistance to micro-enterprises.

Benin is a small, elongated country located in West Africa between Nigeria and Togo, with Burkino Faso and Niger to its north. During the colonial era it was called Dahomy after the West African kingdom that arose in the fifteenth century, and it achieved its independence from the French in 1960, following which it experienced over a decade of political instability including a series of military *coup d'etats* that came to an end in 1972. It has a population of around seven million people and the unenviable reputation of being one of the ten poorest countries in the world (UNDP, 1998: 7). Social indicators are dire, with a life expectancy of 53 years and one of the lowest literacy rates in Africa. Unemployment is high because of an ailing economy and underemployment is also a serious problem. The rural sector is the backbone of the economy – making up 37 per cent of the country's GNP (UNDP, 1998: 9) – and is based on subsistence agriculture, cotton production, and regional trade. Cotton production represents the vast bulk of total exports and provides most of the waged employment. Hopes of attracting foreign investment through the processing of food and agricultural products and tourism are only slowly being realized. At present, 90 per cent of the country's population is involved either in agriculture or informal sector activities. Representative government was achieved in the late 1980s and democratic reforms were adopted in 1990. Accompanying the end of the one-party system was a new development strategy based on a free-market economy. Nevertheless, the private sector remains weak in Benin, the social situation is still precarious, and poverty remains a burning issue. Moreover, despite an agreement with the World Bank to introduce decentralization into government, this has not yet been realized, not least because of a long history of centralized government and the slow pace of institutional change.

Benin has two main cities, Porto-Novo, the official capital, and Cotonou, the seat of government and economic capital of the country. The urban population is growing at 4 per cent per annum, which is a higher rate than total population growth, largely due to rural urban migration. Cotonou has a population of about 800 000, just over 10 per cent of the national population, and is better off than most parts of the country. For example, in 1996 the average annual *per capita* income of Cotonou was nearly double that of rural areas and higher than the national average (UNDP, 1997: 202). However, the average annual *per capita* income of poor urban households was below that of rural areas. Hence, the city witnesses a high degree of inequality. It is situated along the coastal belt stretching between Lake Nokoué and the sea, and grew out of a cluster of fishing villages to become first a trading post and then a commercial centre. It is located on a site divided by the Cotonou Lagoon, with the two sides of the city linked by two bridges. Today a typical French colonial town, Cotonou is affected by serious flooding during the wet season, which particularly affects the informal settlements on the city's periphery and the unplanned occupation of its suburbs. Urban development in Benin comes under the Project of Urban Rehabilitation and Management (PRGU), which was set up to rehabilitate urban amenities, such as hospitals and schools, and to improve the urban environment and land use. This was in response to Porto-Novo and Cotonou failing to cope with the demands arising out of urbanization. PRGU focused from the outset on poverty alleviation, which was to be through remunerated employment for the jobless and the provision of basic infrastructure and services to poor urban communities. The two were linked through a focus on labour intensive construction or maintenance – of roads and drains for example, and of amenities such as markets, schools, and health centres. Two operational agencies act as project managers on behalf of the government. The first is the *Society d'Etudes Régionales d'Habitat et d'Amenagement Urbain* (SERHAU-SEM), which carries out all pre-implementation studies for planned projects under the programme and assists the municipalities of Cotonou and Porto-Novo. The second is AGETUR.

AGETUR was created in October 1990 with the overriding objective of providing an income to large numbers of people negatively affected by Benin's first SAP, while at the same time improving the infrastructure of Cotonou and Porto-Novo. The agency is in charge of executing government works contracts, largely concerned with road and sewerage construction. Work is carried out through small and medium local enterprises, who are invited to tender for contracts and who are assessed in part on the basis of the number of skilled and unskilled labourers they employ. Although contracted to the government, which identifies the project and holds AGETUR to account, the organization is specifically sponsored by donor agencies. AGETUR works in tandem with the *Centre de Promotion et d'Encadrement des Petites et Moyennes Enterprises* (CEPEPE), which was set up with UNDP funding to build the capacity of local enterprises. Unlike some AGETIPs, AGETUR does not work in isolation from the government. It has support from SERHAU-SEM, which is engaged in the identification of priority areas for investment through a range of research activities, including community-level research. It also has support from CEPEPE, which plays

an essential role in the capacity-building of the small and medium enterprise sector, and which is critical to the execution of AGETUR projects
(Fanou and Grant, 2000). Within AGETUR itself, the relatively small staff of
26 people are all Beninese. Before the establishment of the agency, all construction works in Benin were researched and designed by overseas companies. Now, local companies bid for major public works programmes
alongside international ones, evidence itself that the development of
AGETUR has enhanced local professional and entrepreneurial capacity.

In reviewing what AGETUR has achieved, in the first four years of its existence an average of six billion Benin francs was spent on projects (US$1
was the equivalent of about 768 francs at the time) with only a quarter of
funds received being allocated to AGETUR salaries. Thus operating costs,
while not among the lowest, were not disproportionately high. Moreover, it
seems that AGETUR has escaped the worst excesses of malfeasance with
the agency's director having the reputation of being one of the few local
organizational heads that 'does not automatically receive ten per cent of all
work profits' (Fanou and Grant, 2000: 35). The 189 government contracts
won by AGETUR between 1990 and 1994 as part of the PRGU translated
into 650 000 person hours or the equivalent of 600 permanent jobs per year.
In subsequent years performance improved fairly consistently, with 5 713
jobs created between 1995 and 1999. In addition, the agency has been regularly commissioned to undertake work directly by donors, giving rise to
further job creation opportunities. Not all of the projects tendered for have
been capital projects. AGETUR also allocates contracts to local firms for
maintenance works and services such as waste management, suggesting a
level of sustainability in the contracting and employment of some of the
activities they oversee.

What are these jobs worth and what is their contribution to sustainable
livelihoods? Contractors do employ some permanent employees. These are
usually for jobs requiring a level of trust, such as tallymen and watchmen
and the incumbents are highly dependent on the enterprise in one way or
another. They may be indebted to the contractors or owe loyalty on other
bases. However, for the most part jobs are temporary and essentially manual in nature, hence, it is only very low-income people that take them up.
Evaluative research shows that the people who avail themselves of jobs on
AGETUR projects are those with large families, who generally report poor
access to health care and low school attendance on the part of their children. They are all men, mainly of the marginalized Fon and Adja ethnic
groups and most are rural migrants to the cities. As workers they live in
makeshift shelters in marginal settlements and lead fairly unstable lives,
often engaging in criminal activities, substance abuse, and fighting
amongst themselves (Fanou and Grant, 2000: 35). In terms of the employ-
ment-creation element of AGETUR's goals, it was designed to target the
poorest by keeping wages sufficiently low so as not to attract the better-off
to the projects. In this they have been successful and the work opportunities appear to operate primarily as emergency funds or reception funds for

migrants to the cities. In other words, they provide a safety net level of income for very poor people rather than sustainable jobs with viable wages that could support a worker, or a worker and his or her dependants. It seems, therefore, that AGETUR is better at providing a social safety net for the most needy than sustainable livelihoods and risk management for a large number of poor people.

Nevertheless, AGETUR has been more successful in terms of enterprise development. Since its inception in 1990, the organization has used a total of 107 small and medium enterprises to execute its projects, alongside a larger number of sub-contractors who work with the enterprises that win the actual contracts. This suggests that the tendering process works fairly well and that there is a relatively wide spread of contractors benefiting. Indeed, 69 different enterprises worked for AGETUR in 1999 alone. Community development projects are also part of its brief and might involve the construction of a local health centre, main and feeder roads, pavements, and drains. Community projects have also included waste collection, market gardening and environmental protection activities as job-creating spin-offs from area upgrading. Under the PRGU, AGETUR has clearly been successful in infrastructure development, including in low-income neighbourhoods (Fanou and Grant, 2000).

In assessing whether AGETUR has been successful in terms of poverty reduction, the results are mixed. It is undoubtedly the case that in an infrastructure-poor country, the two main cities have not found it easy to keep up with basic infrastructure and service provision, either to meet the needs of a growing urban population or to develop an infrastructure such that the cities could become competitive. Hence AGETUR fulfils an important role in terms of provision. Moreover, the issue of maintenance appears to be well taken care of. What is more difficult to discern is whether the quality of the infrastructure will stand the test of time. It can often be the case that labour-intensive strategies are more expensive and less reliable than capital-intensive approaches. For example, machine-tarred roads are cheaper than those laid through manual labour. A focus on employment creation can become even more expensive if there is poor or inexperienced workmanship, or an absence of good quality control. With the information available there was no way of assessing this in the case of AGETUR but it is an important issue to bear in mind when local funds are used to support small contractors and low-paid workers in construction and infrastructure provision.

THE UNITED NATIONS CAPITAL DEVELOPMENT FUND (UNCDF) IN MOZAMBIQUE

The UNCDF focuses on building the productive capacity and self-reliance of poor households and communities and as such it is informed by a livelihoods approach. It seeks to achieve its poverty reduction goals in direct partnership with local authorities and community organizations and through consultative and decentralized participatory processes. The UNCDF uses seed capital to develop local institutional capacities in planning and financial management by coupling technical assistance with real resource management responsibilities. The aim here is one of subsidiarity, that is, ensuring that decision-making responsibilities rest with organizations as close as possible to those affected by the decisions made. However, although its activities are primarily focused at the local level, the UNCDF has ambitions beyond it. Through piloting small-scale but innovative approaches it is able to demonstrate success to governments and other partners with a view to promoting policy change or replicating initiatives more widely. It is in this context that the experience of the UNCDF's Local Development Programme in Mozambique needs to be assessed.

Mozambique gained its independence from Portugal in 1975. A prolonged civil war ensued, hindering the country's development. The fighting ended following a peace settlement negotiated by the United Nations in 1992. However, ongoing and severe drought as well as heavy flooding in 1999 and 2000 hindered economic recovery. Since the multi-party elections of 1994 and ensuing political stability, and in the wake of the implementation of macro-economic reform since the late 1980s, there has been increased foreign investment and a dramatically improved growth rate. Nevertheless, the country is still very aid-dependent and has crippling social indicators, including a life expectancy of around 31 years. Hence, undertaking a LDP in Mozambique is challenging, not least because the country remains extremely poor and has not fully recovered from the ravages of war and natural disasters.

In addition, the decentralization process is not well advanced, making local institutional reform more difficult. Mozambique is a unitary state with ten provinces and 128 districts. Politically, each national agency reports to the prime minister and president, while at provincial level governors are appointed as representatives of the central state, to whom provincial line agencies are politically subordinate, with centrally appointed district administrators below them. Technically, central ministries have provincial and district representations. Hence, all accountability channels are directed upwards (Jackson, 2002: 8 cited in UNCDF, 2003: 13). Indeed, a World Bank comparative study of decentralization across 30 African countries, which graded experience of decentralization into high, moderate, low, or none, classified Mozambique's experience as low (Ndegwa, 2002). This is hardly surprising given the country's long history of centralization, both during the colonial period and under early FRELIMO rule, and the fact that development has been focused on economic recovery and reconstruction following the transition from first anti-colonial and then a 16-year civil war between supporters of the ruling FRELIMO government and the rebel RENAMO movement.

Jackson (2002 cited in UNCDF, 2003) has argued that the credibility and legitimacy of the central Mozambique government rests upon three pillars.

The first is its agreement with the international community to subscribe to the prevailing macro-economic orthodoxies and public sector reform along the lines of new public management. Second, the government developed an understanding with the urban intelligentsia and civil society that Mozambique would have a free press, openness, and a socially progressive and secular society. Third, the settlement between the government and the RENAMO leadership is one where the opposition party enjoys privileges in return for a level of quiescence. All these constituencies operate in the Maputo metropolitan area, which suggests particular marginalization of rural district and local governments (UNCDF, 2003: 11). From 1994, an experiment with decentralization was conducted when the National Ministry of Planning and Finance (MPF) launched a fiscal decentralization initiative through the mechanism of a block investment grant to provincial governments to be distributed across line agencies and the departments of district administrators. However, this went into reverse in 1998 with the introduction of donor-supported SWAps, which led to a re-centralization of line agency programmes (ibid.: 14).

In was in this context that the UNCDF supported a LDP in Nampula, one of Mozambique's most northerly provinces with 18 districts and a population of three million people. In the independent Programme Impact Assessment (PIA), the programme was assessed in terms of policy impact, replication, and sustainability, as well as poverty reduction impact. The field research focusing on the poverty reduction impact of the LDP was undertaken in the Mecuburi district of Nampula Province. Mecuburi has a relatively low population density with about 120 000 people, many of whom were affected by major population upheavals and displacement during the civil war. Access to safe water and sanitation is a problem and most houses are of informal construction. The infrastructure is basic, the district roads needing repair and rehabilitation, and the tertiary roads being simply impassable. Social infrastructure is also basic and the district has no secondary school. A LDF had already been operational for a number of years in Mecuburi, supporting a range of economic and social infrastructural projects, distributed across the most disadvantaged areas of the district. Examples included the sinking of wells, the construction of primary schools, health posts, and housing for key personnel such as teachers and nurses. Support to economic infrastructure included the construction of two markets and the rehabilitation of the road between Mecuburi town and Namina.

In terms of local policy impact, a District Development Fund (FDD) was created in Nampula, which reinforced the discretionary budget of the province for public investment and transfer to district governments. Usually provincial directorates manage such funds, but the Nampula Provincial Government now transfers discretionary funds to district administrations to the tune of 5 per cent of its budget. It is prevented from transferring more than this by limited capacity at the district level, including low qualification levels and the lack of a legal framework for planning and fiscal management. Nevertheless, it has been demonstrated that it is possible to rely on districts as a locus for planning and financing and for the district government to be the main government actor in district development. Moreover, the elaboration of the District Development Plan (PDD), and other plans, was carried out alongside systematic community consultation – although community inputs did not always systematically find their way into the articulation of objectives and decisions about priority actions. The independent PIA identified the need for improved data on local conditions and relationships and for capacity-building – both for officials and community representatives – in order to facilitate improved communication between communities and district authorities, so problems expressed by the community could be better integrated into the decision-making processes. The PIA also recommended that current practice should be reversed so that projects could be defined by communities (UNCDF, 2003: 32–6). Problems were also identified with ongoing monitoring and evaluation, as most projects were implemented without much oversight or follow-up.

In terms of replication the LDP has had quite good policy impact, particularly on other donors. With the Nampula project now in its second phase (2002–5) the main systems and processes for district planning are established. They have been taken up or worked with by a range of donors – Norwegian, German, Irish, Swiss, and British development cooperation, for example as well as the World Bank Decentralization Programme – both in Nampula and through extension of the programme to the province of Cabo Delgao. Taken together, there has been a significant impact on national and local government institutions as well as IDAs. Hence it is argued in the PIA that the UNCDF has 'exerted a strong impression on the policy landscape of contemporary Mozambique' (ibid., 2003: 45), with evidence of replication and leverage of resources from different sources, and growing commitment on the part of the state, despite there not yet being a formal national decentralization policy.

There are several aspects of the enabling environment that threaten the long-term sustainability of decentralization and the accompanying financing innovations introduced by the LDP. With regard to the new institutional arrangements and participatory processes, it is not clear whether without external support and funding incentives the inverted vertical relationships between district and provincial levels, and community and district levels – and the accompanying participatory approach – could be sustained in the short-to-medium term. Much depends on the retention of district and provincial government staff trained by the project and the sustainability of the physical infrastructure provided by the project.

The impact of the LDP on poverty reduction is both difficult to measure and controversial. The impact assessment was undertaken in Mecuburi district and, from a survey of 200 questionnaires and 30 focus group discussions, the following was found in relation to perceptions of whether infrastructure was benefiting the poor:

- The provision or improvement of roads was beneficial to the area but did not have a direct impact on the poorest.
- Schools were very clearly an important direct form of pro-poor infrastructure.
- The provision of health centres emerged as a very strong form of pro-poor infrastructure.
- The provision of wells and other forms of safe water supply was critical.
- The provision of markets was potentially beneficial but not immediately a pro-poor form of infrastructure.

On the whole, 88 per cent of survey respondents reported their overall household income and food consumption had improved since the advent of the LDP, although this was more marked among male respondents (92 per cent and 91 per cent) than female household heads (68 per cent and 67 per cent). However, 'question marks must be raised about the level of community involvement in decision-making at the planning stage of projects' even though local communities offered useful inputs (UNCDF, 2003: 73–4). The UNCDF continues to address such shortcomings in its programming and to innovate and take risks. As an agency with a strong presence and a good reputation in Mozambique, deservedly based on its achievements, it has a solid foundation on which to build. However, the PIA reports that it is currently losing its edge and status as a policy innovator (ibid., 2003: 85). If UNCDF is losing its strategic position it is in part because more and more agencies operating in Mozambique are seeing the value of engagement with the provincial and district levels and a focus on institution building. Because of operational problems within the UNCDF in Mozambique other agencies such as the World Bank, which are building on the foundations it has laid, may well end up doing it better and ultimately taking the credit.

LOCAL INITIATIVE FACILITY FOR URBAN ENVIRONMENT (LIFE)

In 1990 the UNDP took on the mission of Sustainable Human Development (SHD). This agenda included poverty elimination, gender equity, employment creation, environmental improvement, and sound governance. Based on the concept of SHD, UNDP launched LIFE as a global pilot programme at the Earth Summit in Rio de Janeiro in 1992. Using environmental deprivation as an entry point for achieving SHD, its primary goal was to promote and demonstrate local-to-local dialogue and participatory community-based solutions to environmental dilemmas in poor areas and to help influence policy. Within this broad goal the programme had three further aims, which were to:

- demonstrate local solutions to urban environmental problems and strengthen institutional capacities and collaborations through small-scale projects involving CBOs, NGOs and local authorities at the neighbourhood, city and country levels;

■ facilitate policy dialogue based on local initiatives;
■ promote the exchange of successful approaches and innovations at the sub-regional, regional and inter-regional levels.

The LIFE programme was initially piloted in 12 countries from five developing regions, with seven chosen in Phase One and five added in Phase Two (see Table 5.1).

UNDP LIFE developed a three-stage approach to local–local dialogue – 'upstream–downstream–upstream' – with small projects designed, implemented, and operated by local CBOs, NGOs, and local authorities at its core. The first 'upstreaming' stage began with the development of a national policy framework and strategic approach to identifying and prioritizing urban environmental objectives. The second stage is to move 'downstream' to select and provide small grants to local organizations to implement participatory environmental projects in poor neighbourhoods. The idea here was to use projects as 'policy experiments' in order to create a setting in which various development partners could be brought together not only to provide deliverables but to initiate policy dialogue. The third stage, then, was to 'upstream' the policy lessons by transferring experience into new initiatives across national, regional, or even global boundaries in a 'local–local dialogue' that became the primary tool and *raison d'être* of the LIFE programme. National and regional networks were formed and developed. Grants were advanced to innovate, to test new methodologies, to document and share successes, to build regional capacity, and to initiate regional, inter-regional and global dialogue on urban environmental issues and participatory and partnership responses (Arrossi, et al., 1994: 157–60).

UNDP LIFE is implemented through small-scale, needs-based projects that deal in some way with environmental problems and that promote women's participation. The maximum limit for funding per project is US$50 000 and the results are ideally to influence local participatory processes and policy dialogue. Initially financial support came from the UNDP itself as well as the governments of Sweden, The Netherlands,

Table 5.1   LIFE pilot countries in the five developing regions

Phases	Asia-Pacific	Africa	Latin America	Arab States	Eastern Europe/ Commonwealth of Independent States
Phase I 1992–3	Thailand Pakistan	Senegal Tanzania	Brazil Jamaica	Egypt	—
Phase II 1993–5	Bangladesh	South Africa	Colombia	Leganon	Kyrgyzstan

Source: LIFE (1999)

Germany, and Denmark. However, at the national level additional funding is elicited from public and private sector organizations, as well as from international donors with a specific interest in a particular country. A successful example of donor and local partnership in a country context is profiled in Box 5.1. At country level the programme is coordinated by National Coordinators who in some cases are located in UNDP country offices but in the majority of cases are based in NGOs that work closely with UNDP. All decisions related to programme strategy, implementation, and management are taken locally by the National Coordinator and the National Selection Committee (renamed the National Steering Committee (NSC) in Phase Two), which in each country comprises multiple stakeholders drawn from among a country's development practitioners and intellectual capital and of which the UNDP country office is only one. NGOs and CBOs are usually the most highly represented, followed by national government.

The NSC structure was set up in order to introduce broad-based accountability into programme management and selection, to facilitate the sharing of expertise and the encouragement of partnerships, and to increase influence. However, NSCs have not been equally effective in all countries. The NSC mandate is wide ranging – providing support, building capacity, monitoring projects, and disseminating information and results – and not all committees had the dynamic leadership and commitment necessary for the task. Moreover, lack of time, travel funds, and investment in those responsible for implementing the projects militated against success. However, in some countries the NSCs were extremely effective, with Jamaica as a particularly successful example in which the NSC led the entire LIFE process. One of the reasons for this success was the recognition that the NSC could not cope with all the functions alone, and the subsequent establishment of a supporting Executive Committee. Other approaches are to create regional committees, and local steering committees in individual project cities.

Box 5.1   The Lebanon Development Marketplace 2005

The Lebanon Development Marketplace (LDM) is an initiative organized by the World Bank Lebanon Office in coordination with the UNDP LIFE programme and *Al Bia Wal Tanmia* magazine. In addition to the influence of UNDP LIFE, it is informed by the World Bank's Development Marketplace (DM), which is an international competition aimed at linking social entrepreneurs with pro-poor development ideas to partners who have the resources to implement them. The DM idea is the World Bank's answer to local funds and is based very much on the challenge fund model. It seeks to give voice to innovative ideas and to provide early stage seed funding. It is seen as a low-cost, low-risk way of identifying ideas that work on the ground, meet urgent needs, and have the potential to be up-scaled.

The LDM is focused on the theme of *Environment: preventing degradation and enhancing sustainability.* The environment in Lebanon is an important national priority, especially given the relatively high level of urbanization in the country. This theme constitutes one of the three pillars of the World Bank Country Assistance Strategy (CAS) for Lebanon over the 2005–8 period, namely 'support for resource and environmental management, *especially as it relates to management of water resources, waste water, and solid waste'.* It also contributes to the fulfilment of two of the eight MDGs – 'Environmental Sustainability' and 'Developing a Global Partnership for Development' – the integration of which into various countries' national strategies and action plans is being supported of by the UN system.

The competition is aimed at supporting community innovations and initiatives to clean up and protect the Lebanese landscape, air, and water. 'Harvesting Youth and Community Ideas for a Better Environment' is a tailor-made country-level competition in the Lebanon, which is open to ideas for initiatives from youth groups, local communities, national NGOs, and academic institutions. The aim of the competition is to raise awareness about environmental degradation; involve the youth and local communities in creative thinking and implementation; and pilot new ideas on the environment which could be scaled up to the national level through a venture capital approach, while diversifying risk and encouraging innovation.

Source: http://www.worldbank.org/WBSITE/EXTERNAL/COUNTRIES/ MENAEXT/LEBANONEXTN/

How successful has LIFE been as a mechanism supporting small-scale projects related to environmental improvement? The evaluation of the first five years (LIFE, 1999) was positive about its success in forming community organizations, even in countries where civil society was not very active, and in some countries the LIFE pilot was the first programme ever to recognize the role of CBOs in development. In all 216 small-scale projects were implemented, helping the formation of new formal groups and strengthening existing organization. The exercise of formulating projects, and managing and implementing them, helped build the capacities of NGOs and CBOs to engage in development activities. There are instances of community groups continuing to pursue larger and more difficult issues, such as land tenure in Jamaica, peace-building processes in Colombia, and the collection of municipal taxes and user fees in Tanzania. The association with UNDP LIFE gave community leaders wider exposure and community groups greater credibility and prestige in their dealings with local authorities. Small-scale projects provided real grounds for building community capacity and demonstrated the potential for community-based initiatives to change the mindsets of both community members and government officials and to create new organizational mechanisms – examples included the creation of the Jamaica National Sanitation Task Force and the passing of a new law in Tanzania requiring local authorities to devote 10 per cent of their revenue to support income-generating activities led by women and youth. In Thailand, several local authorities established community development departments to facilitate popular participation (ibid.: 6).

In terms of poverty reduction, it was demonstrated that small-scale projects reached the poor in most cases and addressed pressing needs such as water supply, drainage, sanitation, and garbage removal, with solid waste management being the most common theme of the projects. It was estimated that the immediate impact on environmental improvement and living conditions in low-income communities directly benefited 1 288 513 people and indirectly more than 5 298 184 (LIFE, 1999: 5). It is notoriously difficult to measure and attribute health benefits, although it is likely that environmental improvements had a positive impact on health. In a number of projects an improved physical environment removed some causes of friction and led to more harmonious relations among neighbours, which can be no bad thing. Some of the projects resulted in the creation of temporary jobs; sometimes participants learnt new skills; while a small number of projects explicitly promoted income-generating activities. Income improvement was not, overall, a particularly successful dimension of LIFE, although admittedly this was not a direct objective of the programme.

In terms of participation and governance issues, it was difficult to sustain an interest in projects that were not relevant to people's immediate needs. An example of a strategically supported project from Thailand was the building of a walkway along a canal. Addressing people's immediate needs, it also had a long-term impact and helped diffuse tension between the local authority and community groups over the canal banks. Similarly, local authorities tended to confine their involvement in the projects solely to fulfil the objectives of the project rather than to build continuous state society relations. However, in a number of countries, such as Pakistan, Tanzania, and Lebanon there was evidence of some local authorities beginning to adopt at least elements of participatory local governance. In answer to the question of whether the LIFE programme promoted 'local–local dialogue' the evaluation team concluded that (LIFE, 1999: 8):

> *Meaningful dialogue was established mainly between CBOs, NGOs in all the pilot countries and with local authorities in some countries [. . .] Dialogue with local authorities and government agencies improved in several countries but not sufficiently to facilitate active involvement of communities and CBOs in participatory governance. In most countries the private sector did not show much interest in engaging in dialogue with NGOs and CBOs. There is a need to make efforts to build shared goals and vision with the private sector.*

In some countries the concept of partnership had more resonance than others, for example in Kygyzstan or in Egypt where, with support from the Frederich Ebert Foundation, several events were organized to bring stakeholders from different sectors together in dialogue. This resulted in the establishment of a national level Partners Group on environmental issues.

In Brazil, the involvement of the private sector was demonstrated through partnership with a private university and in Colombia with private foundations, while in Thailand the Chamber of Commerce was involved. However, private sector involvement in environmental partnerships at the local level has proved to be generally quite difficult.

An important focus of UNDP LIFE was on demonstration, transfer, and policy influencing. For this reason assessment of replication and scaling up was an important dimension of measuring its success. At national level local authorities and government agencies have shown some interest in supporting the replication of small-scale projects. For example, in Egypt the Ministry of Youth announced a grant for the implementation of youth-based environmental improvement projects across the 26 Governorates on the basis of LIFE's example. A similar example of spread can be seen in the example of the Lebanon Development Marketplace 2005 (see Box 5.1). In Thailand, the collaboration of LIFE with the Municipal League of Thailand prompted the introduction of new participatory methods in municipalities across the country. However, after five years there were not a great many instances of scaling up and in most countries projects were formulated and selected without serious thought being given to replication or transferability. As demonstration projects, they were not planned for expansion and hence there was something of a 'disconnect' between the stages of designing and implementing projects and those of influencing policy. Nevertheless, policy dialogue and influence is a slow and gradual process and also one that is inordinately difficult to assess and measure, particularly within the short timeframe of a programme evaluation. Moreover, the geographical and institutional context must necessarily have an impact on learning and spread both within and across countries. The experience of UNDP LIFE has demonstrated that small-scale projects serve a valuable purpose and can create the basis for people to come together and to engage local authorities and sometimes other partners, in this case to work towards improving the local environment. Global documentation and dissemination through Global Technical Support (GTS) drew lessons and recommendations that have had an important influence on thinking and experience not only within the UNDP LIFE network but also beyond. However, the problems of environmental protection, poverty reduction, and state society relations, whether at the level of local governance or in other spheres of governance, are beyond what a circumscribed programme operating at a modest level and scale can handle.

CONCLUSION

This chapter has reviewed some of the challenges of reaching the poorest people and the institutions and levels of government closest to them, through local funds supported by multilateral agencies and implemented largely through sector-wide or single focus approaches. Although the focus has been relatively narrow, the programmes have been wide in their ambitions, relevant to a number of problems ranging from sectoral issues such as urban services or environmental degradation, through to poverty reduction and human development, as well as issues of participation and local governance. The programmes discussed here are also quite large in scale and have been sustained over a significant period and to some fair degree they have been successful. Nevertheless, they have been subject of quite severe criticism too. The AGETIPs have been criticized in the broader context of the condemnation of social funds. AGETUR in Benin is an example of good practice in the context of such interventions but even so, demonstrates evidence of the dilemmas associated with trying to combine a livelihoods approach to poverty reduction alongside goals of public–private partnership.

In both the AGETUR and UNCDF examples, the difficulties associated with trying to combine poverty reduction with governance goals are manifest. In the case of the UNCDF, it has remained solidly committed to local development in the poorest regions of the poorest countries over many decades and has had some important successes, particularly in terms of its risk-taking and innovations in influencing policy and planning more broadly. However, as the brief review of the Mozambique example revealed, success does not always come easily and although poverty reduction was achieved in the Mecuburi District and although institutional change did spread across parts of Nampala Province, the UNCDF proved not necessarily to be the best vehicle for implementation. In the case of UNDP LIFE, the focus on environmental goals alongside those of participatory development and sound governance meant that poverty reduction and income improvement were largely seen as welcome by-products. This helped earn a positive evaluation for the pilot programme and the opportunity for extension in countries and regions where it had success and resonance. In the case of both the UNCDF and UNDP LIFE, there are real questions as to whether a UN agency is the right vehicle for implementing such programmes. Local funds need to be agile and flexible and it is often the case that international development agencies – particularly those with the bureaucratic approaches characteristic of UN offices – give rise to problems of rigidity and the ossification of projects, rather than facilitating the adaptation, learning, transfer, and spread required of 'projects as policy experiments' (Rondinelli, 1992).

CHAPTER SIX

Small funds and direct budget support: innovative examples from bilateral aid

INTRODUCTION

The previous chapter highlighted three local funds programmes, financed by multilateral development agencies and implemented within the context of sector-wide approaches to aid delivery. This chapter continues the discussion on aid mechanisms through a critical look at DBS, whereby donors coordinate themselves to channel resources directly to recipient governments using their own structures and procedures. It makes the case for continued support to the local level, despite all the potential problems associated with small funds. It also highlights the potential of local funds for the promotion of democracy within the context of DBS. This is especially important where DBS takes the form of GBS, which refers to financial assistance as a contribution to the national budget and is generally what is understood by DBS today. To make its case, the chapter reviews two examples of local funds programmes. The first is the Commonwealth Education Fund (CEF), which deals with a single sector, education. It operates out of the United Kingdom under the Chairmanship of Sir Edward George, the Governor of the Bank of England. It constitutes collaboration between three leading UK development agencies, which perform the task of international coordination. They are ActionAid (the lead agency), Oxfam, and Save the Children (SCF) and they work closely with the British Government – the DFID and the Treasury – as well as the private sector. The CEF operates across 17 Commonwealth countries with the aim of raising the profile of the MDGs on education throughout the Commonwealth and of building support across society for the achievement of these.

The second programme reviewed is the Foundation for Civil Society (FCS) in Tanzania. It was established in the context of the trend towards GBS, in order to provide a support mechanism for CSOs wanting to engage more effectively in poverty reduction efforts and advocacy. It grew out of the Civil Society Programme (CSP), which was a project originally designed, managed, and funded by DFID until, after two years, in January 2003 DFID transformed it into an independent Tanzanian not-for-profit organization, while remaining one of its principal funding bodies. The FCS is discussed in this chapter as an innovative but not unproblematic approach to civil society assistance in the context of GBS.

THE STRENGTHS AND LIMITATIONS OF DIRECT BUDGET SUPPORT

DFID's most recent White Paper (DFID, 2000) described DBS as an aid instrument for 'providing financial support directly to recipient Government budgets using their own systems'. Donors in favour of DBS see it as the most appropriate vehicle through which development assistance should be delivered. In the face of mounting criticism of aid and conditionality, an important motivation for moving towards DBS is said to be the empowerment of recipient governments and an encouragement for them to take greater control and ownership of their country's national development. A further advantage is that because DBS works through a government's own systems, public administration and government effectiveness can be supported at the same time.

It is argued that DBS reinforces rather than undermines a government's accountability towards its own citizens, particularly when donor strategy is both to encourage a strong poverty-focus and to promote effective state machinery through support to public sector reform. As discussed in the previous chapter, DBS can be provided through Sector Wide Approaches (SWAps), whereby financial aid is earmarked for discrete sectors and channelled through existing sectoral mechanisms. Increasingly, however, the preferred mechanism is GBS, where funds are channelled through the Ministry of Finance and where national governments make decisions about the allocation of resources, within the context of a framework negotiated with donors.

With GBS, therefore, conditionality is supposed to be limited only to negotiations over policy measures related to overall budget priorities. Usually this means GBS recipients need to demonstrate a strong focus on poverty reduction and human development. It is in this context that the PRSPs, which aid recipient countries are required to produce by the IFIs and bilateral donors, become very important. They are negotiated between governments and donors as a policy framework to inform what is deemed to be a government's own poverty reduction strategy. In practice, most donors remain attached to conditionality although the effect of GBS has been to see the focus shift from a preoccupation with particular policy or expenditure items towards a more general concern with overall policy direction. The direction being promoted is integration into the global economy through increased trade, with foreign direct investment being presented as the best route out of poverty for developing countries. Hence, while DBS might seem like aid with a lighter touch, in reality the pressure is considerable. As one international development worker concerned with local funds put it:

> *DBS is about more conditionality not less. It is very intimidating to have all the donors around a table with a single message. There is a massive concentration of power amongst the donors who have more power now than they ever did in the 1980s. This is very problematic when you see them at work and observe how the*

US or the World Bank can influence other international players. It is a problem to have all the power in the Ministry of Finance as well. In the end governments feel more accountable to the donors than citizens.

While it is probably too early to assess the impact of GBS there are a number of contradictions associated with it that can already be identified. In the first place, GBS strengthens the hand of central governments in a policy context where for the last decade or more international development has promoted decentralization, as demonstrated in Chapter Two. Another contradiction is that from the donor's perspective DBS is a high-risk way of delivering aid. This is particularly the case under difficult conditions or in complex institutional contexts, and there will always be recalcitrant countries that prove to be difficult development partners. Under such circumstances accountability to domestic taxpayers in terms of how aid resources are spent is less straightforward, while ensuring that conditions are met remains problematic.

Hall and Dirie (2002: 1) have argued that 'donors will always be obliged to maintain complex and expensive parallel mechanisms to verify the achievement of national development targets'. Consequently, it is likely that efforts to ensure mechanisms for accountability to donors and the scrutiny of national development will remain demanding. An interesting dilemma here is that the modalities for measuring performance, monitoring progress, and for evaluating outputs have been developed under historically different conditions and the tools of development management remain strongly associated with project and programme aid. This poses a challenge for successfully tracking the impact of aid effectiveness under changing circumstances of delivery, particularly where resources are channelled exclusively to central government. It is in this context that government accountability to citizens becomes an important dimension of DBS and an important measure of its success. As one interviewee argued, '[I]f you have strong civil society actors who understand the issues and can make the case, they are effective in public debate. This should be an indicator for judging if a country is doing well.'

International development agencies maintain some measure of conditionality in their relations with governments, for example, through the negotiation of PRSPs. Alternatively, they provide support to neglected groups or areas through support to partnerships, NGOs, and CSOs operating at the local level. This is either through some element of project aid or, as is more frequent now, through support to local funds. The latter are premised on the assumption that if GBS does no good then at least it does no harm. However, it may actually undermine local processes and institutions by bypassing local governance structures such as municipal and rural councils, NGOs, CBOs, and private sector organizations. A prudent approach is thus to continue embracing a wider and more flexible range of aid delivery instruments alongside DBS, particularly mechanisms for strengthening local institutional engagement. As Hall and Dirie (2002: 1) put the case: '[T]his does not mean that there is no place for DBS; only that other instruments will always be needed to support private sector growth, local government reform and robust civil society.'

DBS is also unable to guide planning and implementation processes, especially at sub-national administrative levels. Consequently meso-level development instruments are best concentrated at the sub-national level, with a focus on improving the status and effectiveness of district and local governments through developing their financial, management, and service coordination capacities; through strengthening institutional and organizational structures across all sectors at district and local level, and through strengthening district and local democratic practices. Hall and Dirie argue that in this way, organizations at these levels are likely to become more effective development partners and better participants in poverty reduction strategies. As such, micro-level instruments are important for ensuring that non-state actors and groups are better able to engage in local and national governance. This is recognized in the United Kingdom, for example, through funds such as the Community Empowerment Fund that are earmarked for use by the voluntary and community sectors in partnership with the government and other organizations. These are discussed in more detail in Chapter Eight on challenge funds.

Local funds and efforts targeted at the local or community level are by no means new types of aid instruments, particularly with regard to NGO involvement. Nor are they without their problems. Like projects, if local funds are not located and understood within broader national, regional, and institutional contexts they can represent a waste of time and resources, or can falter for reasons beyond immediate control. However, an international fund manager interviewed struck a useful chord when he said: 'These small funds have their problems, make no mistake, but we should not throw out the baby with the bath water.' Indeed, the value of local funds, both for appropriate poverty reduction and as a trigger for developing and maintaining democratic processes at the local level, is increasingly being factored in as a component part of a broader suite of aid instruments. Within this context, DBS and local funds are not mutually exclusive and under some circumstances can be mutually reinforcing. Particularly in contexts where the national state is weak, local funds can be an effective way of meeting development targets and of ensuring that governance and democracy goals are not neglected.

ENHANCING VOICE IN EDUCATION: THE COMMONWEALTH EDUCATION FUND

In 2000 the United Nations General Assembly approved the MDGs, discussed in Chapter Three. Among these were ensuring that by 2015 all the world's children would be receiving a good quality basic education and that by 2005 there would be full equality of access to education for girls and boys. The latter goal is nowhere near to having been achieved and it is currently estimated that the first goal will be missed by a wide margin, with 75 million children remaining out of school by the target date for the MDGs. With this grim reality in mind, the CEF was set up to raise the profile of the MDGs on education and to build support for their achievement across the Commonwealth. Designed to support the education sector, the CEF is also informed by a concern with governance and democracy. It sees poverty reduction and human development as unequivocally political issues and is underpinned by three critical ideas about development (CEF, 2002):

- without good governance and democracy, developing countries will stay poor
- without universal free primary education, democracy cannot flourish, and
- without an active and informed society, committed to schooling for all, universal free primary education will not be achieved.

Aimed at setting up national networks and coalitions concerned with education, strategies in all the countries where the CEF is operative are designed to support activities that derive from three broad criteria:

- strengthening civil society participation in the design and implementation of national and local education plans and frameworks
- enabling local communities to monitor government spending on education both at the national and local levels
- supporting documentation, learning, and sharing on innovations that have proved effective in extending quality education provision to all children, especially girls, as well as the most vulnerable and disadvantaged, for example street children, former child soldiers, and nomadic children.

Emanating out of the Treasury, the CEF was launched by the Chancellor of the Exchequer, Gordon Brown, in March 2002 to mark the Queen's Golden Jubilee. The Fund received £10 million in start-up money from the Government through DFID. Initially conceived as a small funds programme of finite duration that would run to the end of 2005 (linked to the gender equity target), the time frame for spending has already been extended to 2007 and the Chairman, Sir Edward George, is aiming to extend the Fund's life by raising a further £10 million, which the Chancellor has pledged to match pound-for-pound, making the fund potentially worth £30 million (CEF, 2002). Associated with the great and the good, the Oversight Committee of the CEF includes prominent British individuals such as the Nobel Prize winning economist, Amartya Sen, business leaders such as Digby Jones, Director General of the Confederation of British Industry (CBI) and Sir Winston Cox, the Deputy Secretary General of the Commonwealth. Three leading UK development NGOs manage the Fund – ActionAid, Oxfam, and Save the Children – with ActionAid as the lead agency on the basis of its long-standing reputation as a leader in the field of education.

The CEF operates across 17 of the 54 Commonwealth member countries, all of which are developing countries or face resource constraints in relation to the provision of education. In Africa the Commonwealth countries involved are Cameroon, Gambia, Ghana, Kenya, Lesotho, Malawi, Mozambique, Nigeria, Sierra Leone, Tanzania, Uganda, Zambia, and Zimbabwe. In South Asia they are Bangladesh, India, Pakistan, and Sri Lanka. Briefing meetings were held with Ministers of Finance from the 17 countries during the Commonwealth Finance Ministers' meeting in London in October 2002, also attended by all the Central Bankers and James Wolfensohn, President of the World Bank. The High Commissioners or Ambassadors of all 17 countries also attended dinners at the Bank of England to be fully briefed, while business leaders from across the world have been invited to breakfasts, lunches, and dinners at the Bank of England to seek their support. Through such initiatives, remarkable momentum was built up for the CEF within quite a short space of time.

In the early planning stages, the assumption was made that the International Management Committee (IMC) of the three UK agencies would centrally control the Fund. However, ActionAid felt that while a collaborative approach worked in the UK, this was not automatic at country level. Indeed, both international and national NGOs competed amongst themselves for funds and were not used to cooperating. Hence, the challenge was to foster collaboration in the Commonwealth countries themselves. As a result the IMC exercises very light oversight, confined to ensuring that the three broad criteria of the Fund are respected and adhered to and that the money is used for coalition building and not service delivery. Moreover, rather than having all the countries competing, the IMC has divided up the money according to the size of the population. For example, £1.7 million has gone to India with its extremely large population, while only £150 000 has gone to the Gambia, which has a population of just one million, with most countries getting between £450 000 and £750 000. Fourteen of the 17 countries are now implementing fully agreed strategies, leaving only Pakistan, Zimbabwe and The Gambia to finalize their plans and significant achievements from CEF are beginning to be seen in a number of countries.

A different UK agency took the lead in each country, depending on where each had the most experience or reputation. If, for example, the lead organization were Oxfam their country office would be responsible for appointing a national coordinator and devising a viable fund. This would be done in consultation with ActionAid and SCF as well as other in-country stakeholders. The role of the national coordinators was to draw up plans for working on the ground with local NGOs, CBOs, parents' organizations, faith-based organizations, businesses, and CSOs, with the idea of raising awareness on the fundamental importance of education and particularly primary education in their societies. Given that the aim of the CEF is to develop national coalitions on education, the countries that have experienced most success have been those where it was able to build on prior momentum. Typically, this has derived from two trajectories. National initiatives linked to the Global Campaign for Education have provided an important impetus in some countries. In others, the CEF networks have been built on existing civil society coalitions with experience in advocacy and organizing around policy issues. In Kenya, according to one CEF interviewee 'the CEF did not go into virgin territory but built on existing coalition-building history which actually influenced the design of the CEF'. Here civil society organizations mobilized around education issues linked the call for increased education spending to the Cancel the Debt Coalition. They also did an inventory of the costs for parents of educating children. This made a considerable impression on the opposition movement and when it ultimately became the first post-Moi government one of its early decisions was 'to get rid of user charges and within a week one million more children went into school'. Although this raised new challenges such as large class sizes the coalition generated energy and debate in the education sector and 'regular dialogue with the Ministry of Education'.

Inevitably progress varies across different countries and in most it has taken some time to build the CEF itself, and the national coalitions it aims to support. In countries where the process is most advanced, the coalitions have moved beyond mobilization towards commissioning research for evidence-based advocacy and budget tracking. In Kenya, for example, the point has been reached where communities are holding education authorities to account, within the context of a decentralization process that sees education as the responsibility of both national and district level governments. The Coordinator of the CEF Secretariat explained the situation as follows:

> People are talking about the national education budget and saying where is it; why are we paying the teachers; why are we paying for services; why are we paying for infrastructure? [. . .] The budget of the schools is the district budget and this is where the engagement is happening, in District Education Management Committees or School Management Committees at the district level, and people are becoming aware of budget levels and lines and how they are used [. . .] CEF has brought education debates out of the smoky rooms of policy dialogue to where it is debated openly among parents, even children, to the point where people are engaging with it and there is a groundswell of public opinion on education.

However, not all countries' national coalitions are similarly advanced and the original timeframe for establishing the CEF was probably unrealistic given that three agencies had to be convened and their activities harmonized across 17 countries. Staff had to be recruited and strategies developed before any funds could be dispersed. Moreover, the planning period and the introduction and implementation of the CEF among CSOs took a long time. As the programme moved to the grassroots level it was accompanied by a careful process of wide consultation, capacity-building, and participation, important in terms of familiarizing a wide range of stakeholders with a new way of working. The approach has paid off, with CEF partners increasingly becoming recognized as the political voice of civil society in relation to education in many countries. Moreover, the good practices of many CEF partners are feeding into local and national level policy processes through their membership of government education policy and planning committees. For example, in Uganda, Nigeria, Kenya, Bangladesh, India, Ghana, and Zambia, CEF partners are members of such committees both at the local and national levels, where they share with decision-makers insights from their research and practice (CEF, 2004a: 2).

CEF is also promoting shared learning among CSOs in a number of ways; for example through national and regional workshops, annual review, and reflection processes at the country level, involving a range of partners and other stakeholders, as well as through support to capacity-building and networks and coalitions, such as the two regional networks in Africa – the Africa Network Campaign on Education for All (ANCEFA) and the PAMOJA Africa Reflect Network. PAMOJA is an Africa-wide participatory education and development initiative established in 2002 by African Reflect practitioners to facilitate learning, sharing, and the continuing evolution of Reflect practices in Africa. It focuses primarily on links between adult literacy and access to basic education for children, and the facilitation of budget-tracking skills and other areas of capacity at the community level. While CEF has served to advance such networks, it has also to be borne in mind that the success of CEF was built on existing energy and networks, generated by organizations and NGOs concerned with education. Indeed, one of the triumphs of CEF is that it took into account the views and experience of those seasoned in educational campaigning and fed these into the design.

A recent management report (CEF, 2004b: 2–3) provides the following examples of success in a number of African countries:

- CEF Uganda, through its partners, has placed the education of hundreds of thousands of internally displaced children in the North of Uganda on the government's agenda for the first time, securing an immediate emergency response from the EU and UNICEF.
- CEF in Zambia has set up an Education For All Forum, which for the first time guarantees a space for civil society to feed into government policy on education. This Forum is currently joining forces with the Ministry of Education to campaign for more teachers, in order to meet the education targets despite the IMF recommendation that the Government of Zambia cannot recruit more teachers due to their ongoing economic reform process.
- In Kenya, a CEF partner, Cancel Debt For the Child Campaign (CADEC), initiated and submitted new and innovative legislative Bills in Parliament, which have been adopted by one of the political parties committing to sponsor the motion in Parliament as soon as it reopens in March 2004. This legislative motion and Public Debts Management Bill was presented to Parliament for debate through the parliamentary

support group. If enacted it will become a new legislation and regulatory Act to check government borrowing and spending which will redirect all cancelled debts to education and health, among other social services. Capacity-building activities on budget tracking and advocacy have led to increased awareness, knowledge, and skills at the community level, opening up new avenues for lobbying local leaders, bureaucrats, and other policy makers. Notable examples are the women's lobby group of Kajiado trained by DUPOTO, who have approached the Minister of Education demanding a slot in the district and local authority Education Bursary Committees, because they have realized that they have a stake in education.

■ In Ghana, district level coalitions on education have been formed in every single district – opening up discussion on education between local organizations and local government so that tailor-made responses can be found to the different education challenges in different regions of the country. The CEF is also supporting the resuscitation of the national coalition on education – Ghana National Education Campaign Coalition (GNECC) – which had been experiencing structural challenges.

■ In Nigeria, the Civil Society Campaign for Education (CSACEFA) has been invited to play a leading role in developing the country's Education For All (EFA) plan. The EFA plan is the government's main policy for the delivery of free Universal Basic Education (the first nine years of school) to all Nigerian children. CSACEFA also inputted into two legislative bills, specifically the Universal Basic Education and Child's Rights Bills, on the terms of the enforceability of the provisions of the law and the constitution of monitoring and supervisory boards.

CEF success has also extended to Asia. Improved working relationships have developed between civil society and government education departments in Sri Lanka and India. In the Indian state of Tamil Nadu, CEF has helped create a model for including disabled children in mainstream schools, which is now influencing policy and practice in many other states in India. Also, through the Joyful Learning Centres in Hyderabad and other Indian states, access to primary education is being made possible for children from poor rural and urban families, most of them girls and former drop-outs. CEF, through the collaboration of the Global Campaign on Education, is bringing all the different key stakeholders and players from civil society in the education sector to work in a more coordinated manner as opposed to their previously individualistic approach. It is hoped that a national education coalition will emerge from all the efforts. The most progress in Asia has been made by the CEF in Bangladesh where, building on the experience in East Africa, the coalition has involved university research departments, some of which have themselves joined the coalition, in a process of educational budget-tracking.

Box 6.1 The institutional and policy context for developing the CEF in Nigeria

In April 2000 at the World Education Forum in Dakar, Ghana, the Dakar Framework of Action was developed, with six goals for achieving Education For All by 2015. One of the distinctive features was the recognition of the role of civil society in developing partnerships with governments for ensuring that the commitments made at Dakar were met. The roles of civil society in helping to shape pro-poor policy, in planning and implementation, as well as in monitoring and evaluation were recognized as being critical to enabling the achievement of the EFA goals. Even before the Dakar meeting, ActionAid-Nigeria was at the forefront of promoting civil society participation in education policy and planning processes in Nigeria. It was also instrumental in developing a strong national coalition on education – the CSACEFA – which emerged as a strong network and 'voice' on education policy issues and holding the government to account in Nigeria. This history meant that the CEF in Nigeria was able to build on a strategic foundation and programme of work.

Nigeria is a signatory of the 1990 Jomtien Declaration on education and the 2000 Dakar World Education Forum goals. Nigeria is also a signatory to the Universal Declaration on Human Rights and the African Charter on Human and Peoples' Rights – two international conventions that further oblige the state to treat education as a basic human right. Moreover, the country's policy on the achievement of the EFA goals is clear. In 1977, the National Policy on Education (NPE) introduced the Universal Primary Education scheme, which was, however, a colossal failure - among other reasons, due to inadequate planning and infrastructure, poorly qualified teachers and limited learning materials, and the fact that political commitment and funds were not forthcoming. In 1999, the Nigerian Government launched Universal Basic Education to re-invigorate the education sector, encouraging closer involvement of communities and civil society as well as linking basic education to anti-poverty strategies. All these intentions, however, remain largely on paper, apart from the appointment of a key civil society activist as National EFA Coordinator.

It is against this background that the CEF saw an urgent need to strengthen capacity amongst civil society actors for engaging on EFA. Among the strategies adopted to strengthen the policy capacities of civil society representatives in Nigeria and to support civil society involvement in the governance of education, are: funding networks relevant to education; conducting research on issues that provide an evidence base to advocacy activities; raising debates on universal basic education; producing copies of education legislation in accessible and user friendly formats; and organizing meetings to discuss them. CEF resources are also used to strengthen the structures and capacity of education CSOs because this way of working is new and part of the aim is to strengthen partners. As the Coordinator of the CEF Secretariat said of the CEF in Nigeria: 'You cannot demand accountability from government and not be transparent yourself so it is important funds are spent on organizational learning.'

Sources: ActionAid-Nigeria, 2002 and interviews with the Coordinator of the CEF Secretariat.

For all its successes, the CEF is not without is weaknesses and is unlikely to escape the problems that beset all small funds, no matter how well-designed or implemented. In getting the CEF going in countries where the experience of advocacy and policy dialogue is less familiar, it has been difficult to get international and national NGOs, and other partner organizations to give up their fixation on service delivery and to embrace the more challenging agenda of advocacy and influencing policy as well. This has been exacerbated by the drive to spend money. A problem that was neither unanticipated nor one that is exclusive to the CEF is that of potential under-spend on projects, particularly in the early phases. With the bulk of funds destined for the projects themselves, spending on organizational costs such as start up, management, capacity-building, and institutional learning cannot and does not absorb a high proportion of such funds. Additionally, particularly when fund-raising proceeds apace, this can outstrip the capacity to absorb and distribute resources for new projects. In the case of the CEF, of the original £10 million only £2.5 million had been spent after two years. With fundraising from the corporate sector (for example Zurich, Vitabiotics, Citigroup, Cadburys, ICICI, and others), alongside matching funds from the Treasury, it is estimated that a further £5 million will be raised by March 2005 (not £20 million as originally hoped) (CEF, 2004a: 1). The projected scaled-down expectation may be a blessing because even with an accelerated rate of spending, it is difficult for CSOs to absorb and utilize large amounts of money within a tight time frame. As the Chair of the CEF Management Committee put it: '£10 million is a huge amount of money for coalition building, campaigning and advocacy work. You can spend £30 million easily on service delivery but not on advocacy.'

To be fair, this was anticipated by DFID and the CEF contract states in relation to the other vexed issue of social funds, that of sustainability:

> *Concerns have been expressed about the capacity of the civil society in focal countries to absorb significant amounts of new funding in this time frame and to demonstrate the impacts required. Therefore the agencies and DFID will consult in the later stages of the funding period to consider how best to apply any unspent funds, for example by extending the duration of CEF or using all or some of such funds to capitalize national coalitions and thereby help to ensure their longer term sustainability.*   *(cited in CEF, 2004b)*

The understanding is that any monies left over at the end of the CEF will devolve to the country level, so long as the in-country DFID people are in agreement. In such cases the future could take a number of forms. For example, the CEF Management anticipates that a number of bilateral agencies as well as multilateral agencies such as UNICEF and UNESCO will be interested in sustaining a strategic engagement with civil society on education:

> *This will echo the shift in the way such donors support governments – away from individual 'projectized support' to strategic engagement, sector-wide planning and*

> *budget support. The CEF is playing an important role in showing how this strategic engagement can be achieved – and how civil society capacity can be built to engage constructively in policy dialogue on education.*   *(CEF, 2004a: 3)*

The original contract saw sustainability at country level being attained through the 'capitalization' of national coalitions on basic education with remaining CEF funds, aimed at guaranteeing a continuity of their work and an independence of their voice. Building on CEF experience and links they would be encouraged to use this base of funding to leverage further resources from other donors and sectors. A second anticipated model would be to nationalize the CEF, converting it into a national 'Civil Society Education Fund', which would manage remaining funds under the over-sight of in-country DFID offices. Further funds could also be raised from this base under the trusteeship of an inter-agency committee that would be free of political or particular donor ties. However, the CEF management recognizes that other options might arise through the negotiation and con-sultation process as it unfolds in different country contexts. The important issue to recognize is that national coalitions or inter-agency committees can easily become accountable upwards towards the donors and lose their accountability downwards, hence compromising their own political voice or that of their associates. Critical in seeking ways forward, therefore, is a technical design that accommodates rather than undermines processes that are transparent, accountable, and democratic.

Beyond national sustainability, the CEF is concerned with maintaining the alliances that have been built up at international level both prior to and during the CEF, and to share the CEF experience with other countries. Although remaining CEF funds will not be used for this, the network is con-sidering the possibility of developing a global civil society education fund, linked to the Global Campaign for Education (GCE), with which the CEF already has strong links. There are also relationships with regional coali-tions that will require nurturing and developing. For example, the CEF, in collaboration with ANCEFA and the GCE, convened a workshop on educa-tion during the Commonwealth Heads of State meeting in Abuja, Nigeria in 2004. In attendance at the meeting were civil society groups from Uganda, Mozambique, Senegal, Niger, Burkina Faso, Malawi, Ghana, Sierra Leone, and Nigeria. A *communiqué* highlighting key education issues was deliv-ered to the Commonwealth Head Governments Meeting (CHOGM) through the Commonwealth People's Forum and although CHOGM was overshadowed by developments in Zimbabwe, it was an opportunity to raise key education issues with a wide constituency (CEF, 2004b).

In regional and international strategies for sustainability, the same ques-tions may arise as those that arise at country-level, about the need to sep-arate fund management from political voice. These considerations are not premature because they are critical for the sector. While the CEF is finite, the issues are not, and the organizations involved in the CEF are concerned with the long-term sustainability of the work. As a recent management report states (CEF, 2004a):

> *We are making an important contribution to changing the way that people and organizations work together around education, not just in Commonwealth countries. We have forged some creative new partnerships and we are already showing the value of these to delivering improvements in education around the world. The need for this work will not end abruptly in 2005. Indeed, this mode of work will need to be sustained through to 2015 if we are to achieve the MDGs. CEF was always seen as a catalyst – a means of building new momentum. CEF itself should not and need not continue, but the work absolutely must!*

The work must continue not least because of DBS and the need for recipient governments to maintain accountability to citizens concerned with the education sector. The Coordinator of the CEF Secretariat explained the link as follows:

> *CEF fits very clearly into the current direction of DBS and the fund captures the other side of the coin. How do you ensure that the money put into DBS gets spent properly? So it is important that accountability should be to the citizens and not to the donors. This is where the funds come in and why there is so much support for them now.*

However, as the Chair of the CEF Management Committee observed, small funds are often operating around big agendas that are highly political:

> *Everyone says you need political will but you do not just need the political will of the party in power. You need the collective will of society so the people in power have no choice but to respond. In a modest way we are playing a part in this.*

ESTABLISHING A NATIONAL LOCAL FUND IN TANZANIA: THE FOUNDATION FOR CIVIL SOCIETY

The Foundation for Civil Society (FCS) is a not-for-profit Tanzanian company governed by an independent Board of Trustees and Council of Members. It was registered in September 2002 and started full operations in January 2003. At the time of writing, the Foundation had been operating as an independent Tanzanian agency for just under two years. In its previous incarnation it was called the CSP, a competitive grant-making mechanism for civil society organizations beginning in 2000, which had been designed, funded, and managed by the DFID. In the transition from the CSP to the FCS, CARE Tanzania was the Management Agent overseeing the grant-making process, TRACE (a Tanzanian training organization) was the Capacity Building Agent providing pre-designed training programmes to applicants and grantees, while the National Evaluator was responsible for the evaluation of grantees as well as developing linkages between the organizations funded by the FCS. TRACE and the national evaluator still fulfil these functions under the management of the Foundation, but CARE has no role in the new Foundation (Wiseman, 2004).

The FCS was designed to constitute a funding mechanism for CSOs in Tanzania engaged in poverty reduction efforts in line with the country's anti-poverty policies and the PRSP, which was endorsed by the Boards of the World Bank and IMF in late November and early December 2000 respectively. The FCS allows donors to add to an aid landscape dominated by GBS, support to CSOs and networks to assist them in participating in policy dialogue on poverty reduction, in order that they are better able to hold the government and private sector to account. The initial reliance of the FCS on DFID is diminishing as it successfully leverages funds from elsewhere and as other donors sit on the Foundation's Board and are represented on its Council of Members. Current funding is committed up to the end of 2005 for a sum of $10.7m, though involved donors – notably the Swiss Agency for Development and Cooperation (SDC), Royal Netherlands Embassy, and Development Cooperation Ireland (DCI) – have expressed commitment to a longer time horizon, while other donors are clamouring to support it – notably the Canadian International Development Agency (CIDA) and the Norwegian Agency for Development (NORAD) (Wiseman, 2004: 4). There is at least one member from each of these agencies on the Board and each of them is represented on the Council of Members. The Canadian International Development Agency (CIDA) and the Norwegian Agency for Development (NORAD) are prospective donors and members of the Council, for which they pay US$100 per year (ibid.).

The thinking behind the FCS was grounded both in a poverty reduction and a governance perspective, thus seeking to combine strategies in much the same way as intended by the multilateral supported local funds in West Africa and Mozambique discussed in Chapter Five. However, the approaches both to poverty reduction and to governance were very different and strongly influenced by progressive international NGO and CSO networks. In this perspective the role of CSOs is critical in allowing the voices of ordinary people to be heard throughout the policy process. CSOs are also considered vital in ensuring that public institutions function in a manner that is transparent and that in holding them to account, citizens are aware and confident of their rights. Further, this perspective sees CBOs as playing an important role in addressing risk and protecting people from vulnerability, not simply through service provision but through advocacy and through providing people with strategies and mechanisms to voice their concerns. A crucial role for CSOs here is to create links between CBOs in order to increase skills levels and to strengthen the impact of advocacy. For example, this perspective very much informs the strategy of ActionAid, the lead agency for the CEF, the case study discussed in the following section. Interestingly in the case of the FCS, DFID and like-minded bilateral donors not only sought to take up and fund this approach but also sought to do so in respect of a local rather than an international or UK-based not-for-profit organization.

Box 6.2   What the Foundation for Civil Society funds

The FCS funds organizations to carry out activities in any of the following areas:

1. Policy

The CSF funds projects that enable civil society to be involved in developing policy; sharing and popularizing policy; monitoring and implementing policy. Examples of activities under the Policy theme include:

- participatory poverty monitoring, which compares and contrasts information on poverty and disseminates the findings widely;
- planning within communities on how specific policy changes affect their livelihoods and how they might respond;
- community participation in setting priorities for national policies;
- raising public awareness on policy issues.

2. Governance

The CSF funds projects that raise awareness of the rights of people and the responsibilities of government; strengthen cooperation between organizations working on rights issues at local and national level; increase access to justice for poor people. Examples of activities under the Governance theme include:

- public meetings on national policies;
- radio programmes on governance issues such as corruption;
- participatory theatre to raise awareness on rights;
- training for civil society and local government leaders on changes in roles and responsibilities under local government reform.

3. Safety nets

The CSF funds projects that broaden the scope of the vulnerable to take part in development through membership of CSOs that include them; activities that reduce vulnerability and promote community responsibility. Examples of activities under the Safety Net theme include:

- establishment of support networks for and with the vulnerable;
- activities that identify innovative solutions for the vulnerable;
- information dissemination on best practices in community managed activities for the vulnerable.

4. Advocacy strengthening

The CSF funds activities that create linkages and learning between organizations; strengthen consortia and networks; develop skills and understanding in policy and governance.

Examples of activities under the Advocacy Strengthening theme include:

■ exchange programmes between advocacy organizations in Tanzania;
■ skills training in policy analysis and advocacy for staff members;
■ establishment of outreach information.

Source: Adapted from Wiseman 2004: 5

In seeking to understand what lay behind DFID's innovative approach to civil society assistance in Tanzania it is important to recognize both value-based and pragmatic motivations, which can each be identified in the following quote from the *Tanzania Country Assistance Plan* (DFID, June 2003–December 2004):

> Organized civil society has a key role to play in stimulating the demand to hold public officials to account and is growing and developing, particularly the indigenous NGO, faith-based and privately owned media sectors . In supporting the development of effective and accountable government, we will bring together our work on supply-side reforms with our work on demand-side capabilities.

Wiseman (2004) has recently reviewed the development of the FCS and has argued that at the time of its development, DFID needed to address internal contradictions in its support to civil society more generally. Support was focused mainly on funding locally based international NGOs and the Department became uncomfortable with this. Seeking to shift policy towards channelling more resources at national civil society organizations, the East African region's DFID's Direct Funding Initiative (DFI) delivered support to CSOs across Uganda, Tanzania, and Kenya. Nevertheless, despite efforts at economies of scale, for example through a region-wide approach, the transaction costs remained high. Moreover, there was an increasing imperative for civil society assistance to mesh with broader policy frameworks and it was in this context that DFID sought a new mechanism to channel funds to the local level in Tanzania. As Wiseman (2004: 6) has argued:

> [. . .] it was increasingly felt that they needed to ensure an effective mechanism was developed to balance the growing focus of funds going directly to government through DBS and the PRSP, with an emphasis on building the voice of Tanzanian civil society to hold the government to account and ensure civil society was participating effectively in the PRS process.

Budget support is of particular significance as an aid instrument for DFID in Tanzania, which is seen as a critical test case of DBS and the PRSP process. DFID's DBS to Tanzania is projected to grow from £62 million in 2003/04 to £78 million by 2005/6, forming around 70 per cent of DFID's overall budget in-country and representing one of the largest amounts going to DBS internationally (DFID, 2003). In this context, the Foundation has a critical role in providing a voice for civil society and ensuring accountability in the use of donor funds. Indeed, DFID's support to the FCS was driven precisely by this hope.

DFID did not always intend that the CSP would become an independent organization but once the programme was into its second year it began exploring, with other donors, possibilities for its future. The Swiss showed an immediate interest and joined a Steering Committee to guide the establishment of the Foundation, with the view to encouraging further civil society funding from other sources on a longer-term basis. This was soon forthcoming as donors recognized the strategic importance of such a support mechanism for their agencies, absorbing relatively few funds from within their overall portfolios. However, while low in financial cost, the FCS has proved to be inordinately costly in terms of time, as for many donor staff involved in the Foundation, it has required more hands-on engagement than other programmes. The Poverty Policy Adviser for DFID in Tanzania, Gerard Howe told Wiseman (2004: 7):

> *For its sum our engagement in the Foundation is completely disproportionate. Although it has been questioned internally at different times, this investment has been deliberate. There is a strong internal belief in the concept and the model – it's been crucial to underpin that with continuity of active support.*

Another staff member in an international agency put it thus '[T]he feeling among staff working in donor agencies that have moved to a budget support agenda, is that there's less opportunity to be in touch with the realities of Tanzania – the Foundation provides that opportunity to some extent' (ibid.).

Donors also find the Foundation a convenient mechanism to channel funds directly to Tanzanian CSOs in such a way that they do not have to take on the management and overseeing of the funding process. However, the Foundation stands to be victim of its own success, as presently it does not have the absorptive capacity to manage the funds it receives. Moreover, there is an anxiety that if pressure to spend takes precedence over a discerning approach to the nature of activities and organizations funded, then as donors rush to fund the Foundation it could develop the potential to lose its strategic edge. Another problem that besets funding bodies such as the FCS is that they become the main or only channel for civil society funding, putting it in a very powerful position and destabilizing the organizational balance within the sector. As Wiseman (2004: 8) has pointed out, the FCS needs to 'build up a strong profile, identity and direction for itself before it can take on further funding but the realities of donors wanting to join the table and approaching with funds while this happens might disrupt that journey'.

From the perspective of the Foundation, it needs to be aware not only of its niche within civil society and development but also of its long-term financing. Although the donors interviewed by Wiseman saw their agencies as likely to fund the FCS for up to ten years, the Foundation has to consider what to do beyond that period. As with the CEF, discussions have ranged across a number of options, including the setting up of an endowment. In Tanzania this is considered to be complicated, although there is precedent elsewhere. For instance, the Freedom Foundation in Bangladesh was set up through an endowment from the Ford Foundation when it extracted itself from direct involvement in the country. However, the policy context in Tanzania makes this difficult, not least because the fiscal arrangements do not encourage corporate philanthropy. For the time being, however, the Foundation's Board remains dominated by donors and a number of Wiseman's (ibid: 10) interviewees brought into question the autonomy and 'Tanzanian-ness' of the Foundation as a result. Critical in countering this was seen to be diversifying the Foundation's Board of Directors so that a stronger Tanzanian identity could grow. Staff and grantees considered it important that the Foundation was a registered Tanzanian CSO and wore this as a badge of pride:

> Staff who had worked under CSP and had remained with the Foundation felt that their sense of ownership and commitment had increased and that this was a significant motivator in their work. For grantees it also demonstrated a longer-term commitment and stability in funding for civil society within a precarious and fast changing funding landscape . . . However . . . when asked where they saw the Foundation in five years time views varied enormously between 'just being a successful funding agency' to becoming a cutting edge civil society forum engaged in connecting organizations of all sizes to national policy debates and processes.

> (Wiseman, 2004: 15)

The direction of accountability – whether to donors or to civil society – will play an important role in determining how Tanzanian the Foundation remains. The nature of the grantees and their projects will be significant in shaping how much of a voice the FCS provides for civil society. There can be a tendency in such funding organizations to avoid party politics and in so doing to avoid small 'p' politics and opportunities for democracy promotion as well. Some of the projects supported by the Foundation are profiled in Box 6.3.

Box 6.3   Profile of some FCS grantees and projects

The Tanzania Youth Aware Trust (TAYOA) was established in 1998. It has a network of 750 volunteers, providing education on HIV/AIDS, entrepreneurship and civic/human rights to youths in Tanzania. It received a grant from CSP in January 2002 for three years under the governance theme for 62 460 000 Tanzanian shillings. The grant was to train 120 young people throughout the country on the conducts of the national assembly, including the key functions of the Prime Minister and National Assembly Speaker. It is hoped that training will equip them with skills in advocacy and lobbying in Parliament, and start opening out democratic processes to be more transparent and accessible to young people.

The Child Concern Consortium was established in 2000 as a membership organization focused on increasing access to quality social services for children and their families. It has received three grants from CSP/Foundation. Initially it received a rolling small grant of 3 450 000 Tanzanian shillings for capacity-building (an area no longer funded by the Foundation) to develop a strategic plan for the organization. Immediately afterwards, they received a medium grant for a one year project to implement a reproductive health and HIV/AIDS prevention programme in schools. Subsequently, they have received a further fund of 103 million Tanzanian shillings for three years to expand this project.

Kimara Peer Educators and Health Promoters Trust Fund was established in 1992 by a group of people affected by HIV/AIDS, with the aims of improving community health through health education, care and counselling. They initially received a grant for 23 205 500 Tanzanian shillings for capacity-building, for training project staff in organizational development, advocacy, lobbying, and resource mobilization among other activities. In October 2003 they received a three-year grant for 103 million Tanzanian shillings under the safety net theme, for their HIV/AIDS community outreach programme, for their orphans and vulnerable children group and for counselling sessions.

Mwanayamala Women's Development Group (MWAWODE) is a small community-based savings, credit, and income generation organization run by a group of women. It has received two small rolling grants. The first was to organize training in setting up and operating a small business. The second was to conduct seminars in six wards on issues of local governance with a mixture of participants from the community including ward leaders and local business people.

Source: Wiseman, 2004: 15–16.

CONCLUSION

The two funds profiled above point to a general awareness, both within the donor community and beyond, that DBS as an aid instrument has limitations and comes with problems. Though DBS certainly does not weaken or duplicate a government's own financial and administrative systems and conditionality may be negotiated, this is debatable and there are few guarantees that recipient governments will not abdicate responsibility for social sector spending and poverty reduction, particularly in relation to excluded groups or marginal regions. Further, public sector reform goes only part of the way towards enhanced delivery and governance, especially at the local level. Local democracy remains critical if lines of accountability are to extend primarily towards citizens. It is here that small funds can play something of a part. Mechanisms for citizen participation are generally quite underdeveloped. Not all CSOs are well prepared for advocacy, let alone participation in policy dialogue. The local funds discussed in this chapter pres-

ent examples of innovative initiatives for enhancing the voice and involvement of ordinary people in development. Is it possible on the basis of this
evidence to argue that democracy can be promoted by aid to small funds,
especially in the context of Direct Budget Support? The case of the CEF
implies that it is. Experience so far also suggests that it is easiest if resources
are channelled towards existing social movements, networks, and coalitions that have their own momentum and *raison d'être* rather than imposing an agenda on them. It can be more difficult when the normative agenda
of small funds starts as some distant person's bright idea.

Community based development and locally targeted funds are not new
and over many years national and international NGOs have struggled to
develop processes and procedures for their effective delivery. It is with this
in mind that in both the examples presented above, DFID as the donor
involved attempted to defer to organizations and consultants with this
experience behind them, for guidance on the design and delivery of the
CEF and the FCS. This also allowed for the different funds to capitalize on
their experience and expertise within the sector as well as existing networks
and coalitions. The CEF has been particularly adept at using such linkages
to better understand the terrain of education politics and policy at different
levels and to strategically locate itself within broader national, regional,
and global processes in relation to institutional contexts. Sometimes, however, it has proved difficult to sustain the advocacy and democracy agenda,
particularly in difficult national contexts. Tanzania is a relatively peaceful
country with comparatively open state–society relations. Under such circumstances it is possible for CSOs to be challenging as is, for example, the
Foundation for Civil Society. This is more difficult in other contexts, as illustrated in the case of Manusher Jonno in Bangladesh, discussed in Chapter
Nine.

Even in the case of the innovative strategies discussed in this chapter,
there are myriad problematic issues to contend with and resolve. These
include issues of sustainability, autonomy from donors' agendas, independence from cooption or manipulation by political parties and governments, as well as issues around accountability, representation, and
legitimacy. The opportunities for taking risks and advancing democracy
through local funds can be undermined by the demands of management,
monitoring, and evaluation processes, which encourage risk aversion, as
well as accountability upwards to donors rather than towards grantees and
partners, or like-minded networks among civil society organizations. The
following chapter explores participatory budgeting, an approach to local
funding that derived not from donors but from municipalities in the South.
It considers the potential in this model for advancing sound governance
and democracy.

CHAPTER SEVEN

Participatory budgeting and local governance: South–North lessons

INTRODUCTION

Social funds are often considered to be most effective when they maintain a distance from government. Participatory Budgeting (PB) constitutes a very different model of funding local governance; one in which citizens or their representatives are encouraged to participate in the budget writing process in concert with local government. In their simplest form, Participatory Budgets (PBs) allow for the formal and organized participation of citizens in the elaboration of government budgets. Citizens are involved in several stages of negotiation on spending priorities by means of delegates elected onto some form of council. Through this process, resources are divided between geographic or priority areas based on a weighting system that combines the subjective preferences of citizens with objective quantitative criteria (Goldfrank and Schneider 2002: 1). PBs have been interpreted as an educative process, as an empowerment process, as a means of increasing transparency and accountability, and as a route towards radicalizing democracy by combining representative and participatory democracy. PB was first developed and refined in Brazil. Seen by many as an exemplary form of development practice, it is spreading regionally in Latin America as well as internationally.

Three objectives, which are not exclusive of one another, have been identified as driving the PB process. The first is administrative, where PB is seen as a way of improving the efficiency of public administration; the second is social, where it is hoped that the PB process will invert investment priorities; and the third is political, where the goal of PB is that of 'democratizing democracy' (Cabannes, 2003: 57). This chapter considers these various interpretations by first tracing the development of PB in Brazil, paying special attention to its development in the cities of Porto Alegre, Recife, and Horizonte. Second, it briefly considers the expansion of the PB model to Western Europe and then considers in more detail the initial steps towards institutionalizing PB, in Salford in the north of England. The chapter concludes by assessing the opportunities and limitations of PB as a means of funding local governance and democratization.

THE POLITICAL CONTEXT IN BRAZIL

In the mid-1970s, the military dictatorship that had been in power in Brazil since 1964 began to weaken in the context of a 'golden era' of popular mobilization (Abers, 1998a: 41). Between 1974 and 1985 Brazil underwent what has been called a 'third wave' of democratization (Mainwaring, 1999), and during the 1980s and 1990s saw a significant re-emergence of civil society (Avritzer 1999: 124) with the organizations involved growing up alongside an emerging discourse of citizenship rights (Baierle 1998: 122). In 1988 a new constitution was drafted with the aim of providing a more enabling environment for democracy. This included improved electoral competition and the formalization of more participatory structures at local level (Cabral and Moura, 1996; Souza, 2000, 2001). At the centre of re-democratization were urban social movements demanding housing and basic services, and a radical trade union movement. It is out of this context that the *Partido Trabalhista* (PT) or Workers Party was established in 1981. Taking care to distance itself from the centralist tendencies of traditional socialist parties, it organized itself at neighbourhood level, in schools and workplaces, with groups at this level electing delegates to zonal, municipal, and regional forums. As Abers (1998a: 42) explains, this 'pyramidal' system was 'to insure bottom-up decision-making in which a large party base rooted in popular movements has direct contact with the top leadership.'

Hence participatory programmes at municipal level were critically associated with the increased presence of leftist parties at local government level, particularly in the PT. The party had 32 mayors in 1988, 53 in 1992, and 115 by 1996, and the popularity of participatory programmes in Brazil had much to do with the political dissemination of this approach by the party's intellectuals and think tanks (Souza, 2000: 9). However, as Souza (2000: 5) has pointed out, participatory policies predated re-democratization in Brazil and even under the military regime a small number of progressive municipalities, usually at the initiative of individual mayors, adopted participatory policies as a way of putting pressure on the federal and state levels of the military government. Nevertheless, re-democratization gave impetus to the spread of participatory programmes, particularly as it occurred in parallel with decentralization efforts seeking to expand public participation in decision-making processes (Melo et al., 2000).

With decentralization, local governments were able to experiment with a range of participatory forms, including community councils for deciding on education, health, and social welfare policies, as well as PB. This was facilitated by the increase in municipal revenues brought about by the 1988 Constitution, and the improvement in the financial situation of many municipalities, not only through state transfers – which in any case were phased in over a five-year period – but also through local governments increasing their own revenue-raising efforts (Souza, 2000: 9). Brazil saw a real process of devolution taking place, including the devolution of fiscal powers, which was a necessary – if not sufficient – factor in ensuring the municipal autonomy that allowed for the development of PB programmes (Melo et al., 2000: 9; Souza 2001: 163). Nevertheless, as Souza (1996) and Tendler (1997) have demonstrated, decentralization does not automatically give rise to positive results, with much depending on the capacity of local government to take on enhanced responsibilities (Davey et al., 1996).

PARTICIPATORY BUDGETING IN THREE CITIES IN BRAZIL

PB is significant as a way of funding local governance because it formalizes the participation of citizens in decision-making processes. This represents a shift from a simple consultation with citizens' representatives over policy towards a formal institutionalization of a rights-based approach to development, which gives rise to a deliberative form of citizen participation (Goldfrank and Schneider 2002; Souza, 2000, 2001). How effective the process is depends on a range of factors including the nature of participation, the way priorities are decided, and the extent of the resources under deliberation. While often impressive, the extent of popular influence should not be exaggerated given that the amount of the budget involved only ever relates to discretionary spending. Hence, the proportion of the budget open for deliberation is typically about 10 to 15 per cent of the whole budget, with the major proportion of the budget earmarked for other purposes (Sousa Santos, 1998). There are differences of opinion as to the efficacy of PB as a means of enhancing governance and democracy, with some arguing that citizen mobilization and engagement have increased dramatically as a result of PB, both among the poor (Elson and Norton, 2002: 64) and the middle classes (Goldfrank and Schneider, 2002: 13) and with others remaining more sceptical or cautious (Souza 2000, 2001). This section reviews the experience of PB in three cities of Brazil, the names of which are commonly associated with the practice – Porto Alegre, Recife, and Belo Horizonte.

Porto Alegre

Porto Alegre is the jewel in the PB crown and is certainly the city that has the reputation for their most successful implementation. With a population of over 1.3 million, the city has experienced rapid urbanization over the last two decades; so in this sense the context has been a challenging one. However, Porto Alegre is an important city economically for the southeastern state of Rio Grande de Sul, and exhibits some of the best social indicators in the country (Sousa Santos, 1998: 465). In 1989 the PT came to power with an explicit goal of 'inverting the priorities' and governing in favour of the poor and marginalized, although it also gained the support of the middle classes due to the impressive results of PB, enabling it to win every election since (Nylen, 2001: 132). Following its first electoral victory, the PT created a number of participatory initiatives, the major one being a creative experiment to engage a large part of the population in the formulation of city budgets (Nylen, 2001: 132). In 1996 the programme was nominated by the UN Summit on Human Settlements as an outstanding 'urban innovation' (Sharma 2000: 33).

Porto Alegre was not without its democratic traditions and boasted a well-organized civil society partly rooted in opposition to the military regime (Souza, 2001: 168). Moreover, contemporary studies show that 34.8 per cent of citizens are members of local associations (Souza, 2001: 168). In 1985 organizations in the city such as trade unions, community organizations, cultural groups, and neighbourhood associations, which by that time had become a powerful social movement, formed the Federation of Neighbourhood Associations of Porto Alegre (UAMPA) (Wampler, 2000: 6). Although heterogeneous and composed of a wide variety of groups, ranging from those with not-in-my-backyard (NIMBY) motivations through to those with clientelist roots and Marxist inclinations, the UAMPA was ultimately defined by its connections with the PT, particularly among the leadership (ibid.). The initiative for PB came from the UAMPA, which succeeded in significantly influencing the final structures and procedures (Avritzer, 2000:9; Goetz and Gaventa, 2001: 45).

The municipality, which retains substantial power over the formulation of budgets, has two main organizations managing the PB process – the Planning Office (GAPLAN) and the Community Relations Office (CRC) – although there is a range of other institutional mechanisms involved (Sousa Santos, 1998: 468). Each year there are two rounds of plenary debates held in each of the 16 regions of the city and on each of the five thematic topics held up for discussion. In the first round of meetings general information about the city budget is presented by government officials, after which citizens draw up their priorities for investment in their neighbourhoods. Representatives are then elected for year-long District Budget Forums, which then negotiate among themselves to agree on district wide priorities (Souza, 2001: 166). The delegates are selected directly by the citizens as individuals, and members of community associations cannot be elected as delegates. Moreover, their election follows a decision on priorities so that they act as representatives but not decision-makers.

At the end of the second round of plenaries two councillors from each region and for each theme are elected, with the rules stating that any one councillor can only be elected once (Sousa Santos, 1998: 472). They, together with representatives of an umbrella organization of neighbourhood communities and the civil servants trade union, form the Council of Participatory Budgeting (COP), which assumes responsibility for revising the budget proposal put forward by GAPLAN in order to include the demands presented by the District Budget Forums. The budget proposal is finally passed on to the legislature, which divides up resources according to a weighting system that combines subjective citizen preferences with objective quantitative criteria (Avritzer, 2000a: 4–5). The structure of the PB process is shown in Figure 7.1. This process has given rise to other

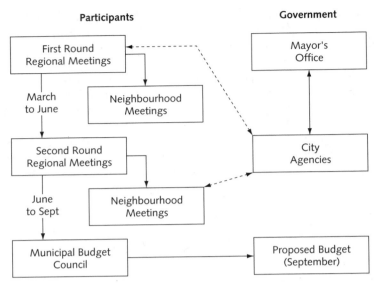

Figure 7.1   Yearly participatory budgeting cycle in Porto Alegre
Source: Drawn from Wampler, 2000: 9

participatory processes such as the *Cidade Constituinte* or Constituent City project, aimed at discussing the future of the city in a broader and longer term perspective than that of PB and designed as a response to criticisms of short-termism in relation to the PB focus and process.

PB in Recife has had more mixed results, and the city is often studied within the context of 'lessons learned'. However, the challenges faced by Recife are perhaps greater than those faced by Porto Alegre. It is a coastal city and is the state capital of the north-eastern state of Pernambuco. The city has a population of 1.8 million and a significant proportion of Brazil's *favela* or informal settlements. This is due in part to the poverty of the city's hinterland, which suffers from a lack of rural employment opportunities and periodic droughts, resulting in a steady stream of rural-to-urban migration. Politics in the city are polarized, with electoral volatility and a high turnover of left and right in executive positions (Melo et al., 2000: 43). Neighbourhood associations proliferated in the 1970s and 1980s, and they continue to press for urban services and land rights (Wampler, 2000: 6). Together they have come to form an active urban social movement with a broader political agenda, which constitutes an important political player in the city and is seen by some as among the strongest social movements in Brazil (Cabral and Moura, 1996: 59).

Recife

In Recife PB started in 1993 but grew out of earlier initiatives, notably the *Prefeitura nos Barrios* (PNB) programme during the late 1980s when the left-wing mayor Jarbas Vasconcelos (1985–9) led the municipal authority and was dependent on the support of low-income communities for his government. When Jarbas Vasconcelos returned to power in 1993, he launched a revival of the PNB under the new name 'participatory budgeting'. By this stage the example of Porto Alegre had permeated throughout Brazil and influenced the set up and design of PB in Recife, which came to develop a hybrid model that gradually incorporated pre-existing community level forums and councils (Melo et al., 2000: 51–3). Recife is interesting from the perspective of PB because there has been political change at local government level and the PT did not dominate the city politically. Otherwise, performance is fairly lacklustre. About 5 per cent of the city's budget is subject to PB (or 9 per cent if related programmes are included), which represents between 15 per cent and 25 per cent of the municipality's capital expenditure. Further, only 80 per cent of the budget is typically implemented within any given year. Nevertheless, PB has resulted in some shifts in expenditure towards social programmes and local infrastructure benefiting the poor (Devas et al., 2001: 34). Moreover, since 1997 Recife has stood out for its focus on the gender dimensions of PB and has carried out a participatory budget with children and the youth (Cabannes, 2003: 31).

PB is organized through six regions and 15 micro-regions of the city. Public meetings are held in each micro-region to discuss broad budgetary options and the resources available, as prepared by city officials. Then 500 delegates are elected at the micro-region level, roughly one per 4 000 citizens, through a combination of individual votes and votes of community associations, in order to prioritize the expenditure options. They are elected for two years and can be re-elected only once. Their election takes place before the definition of priorities, so they are the decision-makers for communities (Melo et al., 2000: 60). Around 30 delegates are then selected to participate in supra-regional meetings that consolidate the priorities in the light of technical feasibility, city-wide needs, and resource availability. From this, the budget is prepared and sent to the legislative chamber for approval (Devas et al., 2001: 34). The General Forum, comprising the mayor, secretaries, technical staff, representatives of the legislature, NGOs, CBOs, councils from the different sectors, and elected delegates, debates priorities, decides lines of action and methods of programming, and evaluates the implementation of plans. The decisions of the General Forum are implemented by the General Coordination Committee, which in addition to operationalizing decisions also monitors progress, disseminates information, and engages in capacity-building. It is supported by Local Coordination Committees that organize activities in each region, including the election of delegates.

The structure of the PB process in Recife is shown in Figure 7.2. Despite problems, particularly in reaching the poorest citizens of Recife, the PB process has extended participation considerably and this has included representatives of low-income communities and groups. While the proportion voting for delegates is very low at 2.3 per cent, 'many thousands of citizens

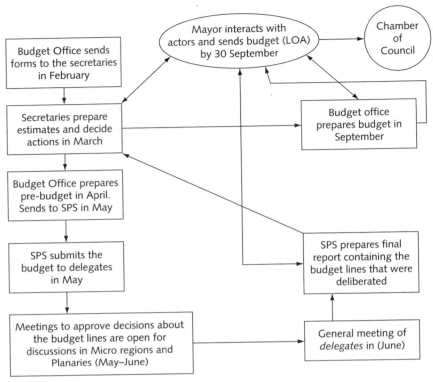

Figure 7.2   The participatory budget process in Recife
Source: Vibe, 2002: 32, drawn from Melo et al., 2000: 65

participate in meetings which establish spending priorities' (Devas et al., 2001: 34). This means local councillors, who feel they have more of a mandate, often challenge the delegates, so that the process is perceived as 'a threat by the local legislature' (ibid.).

Belo Horizonte

Belo Horizonte is noted as a good practice example for the way it links PB with other planning instruments (Cabannes, 2003: 31). It has a population of 2.1 million people and is a modern Brazilian city that was especially built to fulfil its role as the capital of the south-eastern state of Minas Gerais. As an economically important city in one of Brazil's most developed areas, it is the distribution and processing centre of a rich agricultural and mining region and has burgeoning industries and a high rate of urbanization. Belo Horizonte was a latecomer to PB, adopting a programme after Porto Alegre and Recife and being able to learn from the experiences of these and other cities. Although its experiment with PB is well known in Brazil, Belo Horizonte has not gained the same international exposure as Porto Alegre or even Recife. Nevertheless, it has gone further than many other cities in

Brazil in terms of its concentration on participatory efforts in the budget process, bringing into the open issues of poverty, inequality, and uneven power relations (Souza, 2000: 9). As in Porto Alegre, PB was associated with electoral successes by the left (Souza, 2000: 10).

The PB process in Belo Horizonte begins with two rounds of assemblies in each of the city's nine sub-regions and follows a similar pattern to the process in Porto Alegre. Once priorities have been decided upon and the regional delegates have been elected, 'Priorities Caravans' are organized, which involve delegates going on bus tours to make physical checks on the problems indicated as priorities in the sub-regional meetings. Another aim of the caravans is to give delegates a comparative overview of the regions in order to choose priorities that are not too specific or fragmented but that can lead to joined-up responses. The Regional Forum then draws up the list of priorities, and it is here that members of the committee are chosen to be in charge of overseeing the implementation. The final phase is the Municipal Forum in which the PB is formally presented. In 1994 Belo Horizonte also introduced thematic forums – in education, health, environment, social development, and administration – to work with the regional assemblies and with the aim of broadening the issues covered (Souza, 2000: 12). Unlike in Porto Alegre, the forums were more consultative and this led to the thematic forums being replaced by a single forum for housing as a result of pressure from the Homeless Movement, giving rise to a new participatory forum known as the Housing PB. Apart from housing the preferences of local residents in Belo Horizonte are for sewerage, street paving, upgrading of informal settlements, health, and education.

Whereas in 2000, 38.4 per cent of residents of Porto Alegre belonged to some form of civic association, in Belo Horizonte the figure was only 27.7 per cent. Although a much larger proportion of the population was found to be politically aware and 37.3 per cent had some faith in civic associations representing or defending their interests, a large 53.3 per cent did not believe civic associations or politicians would defend their interests (Seltzer, 2000 cited in Souza, 2000: 15). This said, direct participation in PB in Belo Horizonte went up from 28 263 in 1994 to 52 900 in 1995, involving 800 grassroots movements. Delegates are elected from among participants at neighbourhood or micro-level regional meetings, one for every ten participants (Nylen, 2001); and unlike in Porto Alegre, individuals who are members of community associations can be elected as delegates (Souza, 2000: 18). Over 40 per cent of the delegates were found to be women, most between 30 and 40 years of age. Most participants were only basically educated and from the poorest sectors of society, but there were significant participants[T.A.J.1] from middle-income areas and groups. The vast majority, while members of civic or community-based associations of some sort, declared themselves not to be affiliated to any political party (Somarriba and Dulci, 1997 cited in Souza, 2000: 16–17).

In the first year of PB in Belo Horizonte, half of the local resources for investment were allocated according to the decisions taken by PB, although

PB resources only represented 5 per cent of the total budget. Favourable outcomes from the PB have in turn also led to broader participatory processes such as the *Forum da Cidade* or City Forum, which was set up in 1999 to provide a vehicle for wider participation in discussions over the city's Master Plan. It included local officials and was a response to criticisms that PB was too focused on short-term demands (Laranjeira, 1996 cited in Souza, 2000: 22). There has of course been opposition. Resistance came in the main from the powerful agency in charge of the city's public works, SUDECAP, which in turn had strong links with the building industry. This was tempered by changes to the agency's board and the growing popularity of PB, which saw approval from 85 per cent of delegates, and by the identification of problems not with the system itself but with lack of sufficient resources. In 1994 an opinion poll found that PB had the approval of over 67 per cent of Belo Horizonte's population and was the most popular of all local government policies (Pereira, 1996 cited in Souza, 2000: 19). Local councillors are also better disposed towards PB than in many other cities, including Porto Alegre, partly because it is not seen as a PT policy or as the result of mayoral imposition. For many councillors PB is also seen as a way of freeing themselves from clientalist demands on the part of constituents, which they often find impossible to satisfy, while at the same time having some element of discretionary spending through having certain resources that they are allowed to allocate freely. While criticized by the PT, this pragmatic decision won over a broad range of councillors who are unlikely to 'put an end to their well-entrenched politics of personal assistance' (Souza, 2000: 22).

Part of Belo Horitonte's success with regard to PB is that a significant proportion of funds going towards the programme come from revenues raised locally. Belo Horizonte moved from 22nd place to fourth place in terms of revenue collection between 1989 and 1994, with 24 per cent of its increased revenue coming from local sources compared to 11.3 per cent in Porto Alegre and 9.9 per cent in Recife. This demonstrates first, how low taxation was prevalent a feature of clientalist politics under the former military regime, and second, how popularly elected mayors felt able to raise taxes in order to fulfil their electoral commitments. The experience contradicts arguments that when sub-national levels of government enjoy a large proportion of central government transfers, this acts as a disincentive to raise their own revenues (Souza, 2000: 8–9). Belo Horizonte is an interesting model precisely because PB has been largely delinked from a single political party.

LESSONS FROM THE EXPERIENCE OF PARTICIPATORY BUDGETING IN BRAZIL

There is a range of ways in which the benefits and limitations of PB can be evaluated. Some assessments of PB see the benefits of participation in terms of efficiency arguments and the fact that it leads to improvements in policy effectiveness and delivery. Others see PB as leading to the empowerment of marginalized social groups and as addressing the real needs and interests of ordinary citizens. Yet others see PB in terms of broader political goals and as a means of achieving real democracy. The lack of before and after comparative studies means that it is difficult to assess whether popular engagement in PB constitutes a new phenomenon or is part of an ongoing process of citizen involvement in civil society activities that predates the PB programmes, an issue that has important consequences for any assessment of whether governments can be proactive in stimulating citizen engagement and participation.

Beginning with the financial dimensions, in Brazil generally the PB represents between 2 and 10 per cent of the overall implemented municipal budget. In Porto Alegre, 100 per cent of the budget is regarded as participatory, as elected delegates in the PB forum examine and influence the overall budget before it is sent to the *Câmara de Vereadores* or City Council, although the part of the budget discussed in assemblies in which all citizens can participate corresponds to only 10 per cent of overall resources. Porto Alegre is clearly an impressive case. As shown in Table 7.1, the proportion of the budget open for deliberation under the PB programme is far higher in Porto Alegre than in Recife, as is the actual amount of money available. In Porto Alegre all areas of discretionary spending are included in the negotiation process, compared to only 10 per cent in Recife where the PB programme is still used for particularistic political party interests and a parallel clientalist structure (Vibe, 2002). In Belo Horizonte, with its combination of participatory and particularistic structures, PB resources represented only 5 per cent of the total budget. However, in the first year of PB half of the local resources for investment were allocated according to decisions taken by PB, with the amount rising in real terms over successive years (Souza, 2000: 14).

In real terms, the resources coming under discussion within PB processes in Brazil amount to between US$2 and US$36 per capita per year, which gives some idea of the financial importance of participatory budgeting and shows that some real influence can take place over how

Table 7.1 Estimated and actual investments in three Brazilian cities (Year 2002, in % and in US$ million)

No	Municipality	% Investment		
		Estimated	Actual	%
1	Recife	15.87	13.37	84
2	Porto Alegre	10.68	7.7	72
3	Belo Horizonte	18.9	9.03	48

Source: Cabannes (2003)

investments are made in the city (Cabannes, 2003: 50). Moreover, it is reported that the success of PB has led to a reduction in local tax evasion, so that the proportion of funds coming from local sources has increased – and along with it municipal autonomy (ibid.). This is an important efficiency argument that makes PB attractive to local authorities.

The nature of participation and how it is understood forms an important part of the debate. The PB process is primarily an area-based exercise and as such it has been critiqued for excluding particular groups such as women, migrants, ethnic minorities, and so on. In some cities, such as Recife, particular effort has been made to reach identity-based groups, and the whole practice of having thematic committees – for instance on health, education, or housing – that cut across the different areas is one way this has been addressed in Brazil. In terms of the structures and processes involved in promoting popular participation the dominant model in Brazil is that of the Participatory Budget Council, an authority specifically created for the purpose of PB, with variants in its form across the different cities. For example, Porto Alegre's practice of engaging directly with individual citizens may allow for new leaders and groups to emerge, but they might not have clear representative authority. The more flexible approach of Belo Horizonte that allows for delegates to emerge from local associations might be more representative, but only of entrenched and exclusive sectional interests. Nevertheless, pre-existing associations with experience as intermediaries can bring valuable experience to the table (Melo et al., 2000). Recife, which has delegates elected both on an individual and associational basis, has had a limited impact on popular participation and the executive remains firmly in control, setting the agenda and budget priorities. The resistance of local councillors to PB in Recife is reinforced by the fact that the delegates make choices using their own judgement, operating more like councillors themselves (Devas et al., 2001: 34).

It is more difficult to assess the extent of participation. Souza (2000: 24) has argued that for the World Bank and the multilateral community more broadly, the approach to participation is generally 'instrumental and cautious'; and such a perspective is not compatible with a PB programme that, rather than just promoting the voice of citizens in a context where agendas have already been set externally, actually proposes greater autonomy in and control over decision-making on the part of citizens. While the former approach has led to cynicism and fatigue with regard to exhortations to participate in development practice (Cooke and Kothari, 2001), the latter is often dismissed as being dewy eyed and utopian. Sousa Santos (1998: 507) puts the case well in relation to PB in Brazil:

> *Participatory budgets are subjected to a cruel dilemma: they are either conceived of as not working and bound to fail and therefore must be discarded as foolish utopias, or they are conceived of as working and bound to succeed and are adopted by the World Bank, where they are ground, pasteurised and converted into new appendages of conditionality.*

With this in mind it can be argued that the Brazilian experience, as high-lighted across the three cities profiled above, has promoted a wide inclusion of participants in the PB process in ways that go beyond shallow consultation and towards genuine involvement in decision-making. While there is inevitable unevenness, in all three cities there is evidence of reasonable distribution across a range of different income groups, with strong representation of low-income communities and the popular classes (Melo et al., 2000; Sousa Santos, 1998; Souza, 2000, 2001).

In terms of combating clientelist traditions in Brazilian local government, Porto Alegre appears to have been quite successful – more so than Recife. Belo Horizonte's more pragmatic response to the existence of clientelism has perhaps been sensible in the short term, in a context where the process could have easily been disrupted, preventing the growth of the PB programme in the city at all. More broadly, the literature in Brazil has noted the capacity of PB to challenge clientelist patterns of politics (Goldfrank and Schneider, 2002; Souza, 2001) by combating politicians' use of resources to gain or sustain political support (Sousa Santos, 1998: 484). This has both to do with procedures designed to increase transparency having been instituted and with the increased influence on decision-making processes of wide coalitions of progressive actors (Goldfrank and Schneider, 2002: 4–9).

As far as service delivery is concerned, all three cities have shown improved effectiveness, greater control, and better redistributive effects, with a good implementation record too in the case of Porto Alegre (Goetz and Gaventa, 2001: 45). In terms of whether PB reflects the priorities of the poor, there is consensus among most commentators that this has been the case (Abers, 1998a, 1998b; Nylen, 2001; Santos, 1998). Surveys of participants confirm this view although Souza (2000: 27) points out that the evidence is less clear among non-participants, particularly the poorest amongst them. Drawing on evidence from Porto Alegre and Belo Horizonte, she points out that the great majority of poor citizens do not actively participate in the programmes, probably because income and jobs are their priority rather than infrastructure, which is the main focus of PB investment. This suggests, therefore, that while PB might be good for the socially excluded and for marginalized areas, it does not necessarily address chronic poverty.

The limitations of PB coalesce around two main criticisms. The first is that only a small percentage of the budget is dealt with as part of any PB programme. While there are variations across cities, and of the three high-lighted above Porto Alegre is clearly ahead of the field, the proportion of the overall municipal budget remains relatively small. Second, by their very nature PB programmes are short-term exercises, lasting only a year or two; and they are generally focused on neighbourhoods or area-based activities. Hence, they are structurally constrained from being able to engage with issues city-wide. This was particularly evident in Recife (Melo et al., 2000: 91), which, unlike Porto Alegre and Belo Horizonte, has not yet extended participatory processes to the municipal level or city-wide forums. Problems faced in Recife include poor institutionalization, weak executive commitment, and the dual and fragile role of delegates, which have all combined to weaken the potential of the PB programme in the city (Melo et al., 2000: 118). Nevertheless, as Wampler (2000: 16) has pointed out, the Recife case is interesting because a weak executive provides for a more contentious political space in a context where participation is still a learning process. The success of Porto Alegre in extending democracy through its PB programme has been put down to the city's highly organized civil society and history of democratic traditions (Santos, 1998), and this has led to city-wide impact. However, there has been city-wide impact in Belo Horizonte too, despite the fact that it does not have the same political history as Porto Alegre and has lower levels of associationalism.

A real challenge in all three cities was to give up the impulse to remain autonomous from traditional political elites. There were relatively low levels of collective action in the 20-year democratic period prior to the 1964 military coup, and those that did exist were tied into clientelist relations (Abers, 1998b: 515; Avritzer, 2000b: 64). Popular associational activity was further weakened under military rule in all three cities (Avritzer, 2000b: 64; Souza, 2001: 162).When organizational activity did emerge it gave rise to impressive social movements, which emerged out of the factories and *favelas*, often backed by progressive NGOs and those parts of the Catholic Church espousing liberation theology. It reached a peak of mobilization in the early 1980s, with the formation of the UAMPA in 1985 (Wampler, 2000: 5). Together with the forging of new cross-class coalitions that included community leaders, left-leaning activists, and middle-class professionals, this undoubtedly lent support to the development of PB programmes. Although the most combative segments of the movement are now comparatively quiescent and have given into strategies for state-society cooperation (Cabral and Moura 1996: 59), they were fundamental to the ignition of PB. In the most successful case of Porto Alegre, participation was structured through direct citizen participation as a deliberate ploy to break the clientelist features of existing local governance (Melo et al., 2000: 53). There was also a definite strategy on the part of the PT to forge new associational patterns that challenged the pre-existing power structures. This raises questions about the transferability of PB into contexts where CSOs are less robust, where coalitions of interest are more difficult to forge, and where the political conjuncture allows them less influence.

Souza (2000: 23) is convinced that PB encourages participation in highly unequal societies such as Brazil. Moreover, it represents an important step in relation to the state having a role in facilitating citizen participation in policy-making. Problems relate mainly to implementation. For example, even when local governments genuinely seek to implement inclusive participatory decision-making, they are often foiled. There are issues of power in open forums where the better off or more vocal tend to dominate, prohibiting the effective participation of weaker or more marginalized mem-

Table 7.2   The strengths and weaknesses of Participatory Budgeting in Brazil

Strengths of Participatory Budgeting	Weaknesses of Participatory Budgeting
■ Makes representative democracy more open, involving the participation of more segments of civil society ■ Reduces clientelism, populism, patrimonialism, and authoritarianism; increases transparency and changes political culture ■ Stimulates associational life ■ Facilitates a learning process that leads to more active citizenship ■ Inverts priorities away from the better off towards the benefit of the poor ■ Provides a means for balancing ideological concerns about empowerment with pragmatic responses to citizen demands ■ Provides a structure that can carry on beyond a government's term of office ■ Encourages participants to move beyond individualistic concerns to solidaristic perspectives and to see problems in terms of city-wide issues	■ Interaction with the government puts the independence of communities and social movements at risk ■ Forms of clientelism still survive ■ Strength of civil society is uneven and still developing in places ■ Financial and resource limitations limit the scope of PB ■ Communities stop participating once their demands are met ■ Difficulties persist in broadening participation with young people and the middle classes being under-represented ■ Programmes disappoint participants because of the slow pace of public works ■ There are cleavages between political parties and officials ■ PB risks creating a fuzzy boundary between the role of government and civil society ■ Fragmented decisions and short-term demands can jeopardize long-term urban planning

Source: Souza (2000: 31)

bers. There are also issues to do with cooption, whereby government officials can manipulate community groups or delegates. There are sustainability issues too. PB places great demands on the time and energy of participants, and most poor people have little of either to spare. In considering whether PB programmes operate as instruments for increasing democracy, Abers (1998a: 49) argues that 'the policy has clearly opened up the black box of governing to large numbers of ordinary people'. Based on national indicators, Nylen (2001: 28) is more circumspect about the democratic potential of PB on the basis of its redistributive effects within Brazil's asymmetrical power relations. Souza (2000: 28) concludes that PB does have an effect on local democracy by bringing representatives of low-income areas and social groups into the decision-making arena, although she remains reticent on the issue of changing power relations.

SCALING OUT PARTICIPATORY BUDGETING AND THE EUROPEAN EXPERIENCE

PB has been extended to around 250 cities. Although most remain in Brazil, there are initiatives in other Latin American cities – particularly in Peru, Ecuador, Colombia, and the Southern Cone countries, as well as several experiments in European cities that make specific reference to the example of Porto Alegre 'as a paradigmatic and referential city' (Cabannes, 2003: 8). For Europe, Cabannes (2003) shows that while some cities, such as Córdoba in Spain, have replicated the Participatory Budget Council model by having an authority specifically created for the purpose of PB, others have built on existing European structures or organizations such as parish councils or networks of neighbourhood associations, as has been the case in Pieve Emanuele in Italy. Cabannes comes down in favour of 'tailor-made' over 'bolt-on' structures because he believes they are more likely to change the balance of power, whereas integrating PB into existing structures runs the risk of the process becoming 'diluted'.

The majority of PB practices in Europe started between 1998 and 1999, and although there are a number of variations they generally fuse local practices with one of two basic models (Allegretti, 2002):

- the 'democratizing' approach, which is modelled on the experience of Porto Alegre in Brazil and which can be seen in Spain (Rubi and St Feliu de Llobregat) and France (Bobigny, Saint Denis, Morsang sur l'Orge, and Chateau Malabry)
- the 'efficiency' approach, which is more managerial in its aim and form and is based largely on the experience of Christchurch in New Zealand. This has been more influential in Germany and Finland (Hammelinna).

Whether a process can still be called PB when it is an extension of an existing home-grown policy is a question that has concerned those involved with PB in Europe, and it was debated at length in the course of developing a PB model in the UK. The discussion coalesced around the related issue of whether PB constituted a political programme aimed at solving problems of representation, clientelism, and corruption, or whether it was simply a set of tools for more effectively managing community engagement with government.

Local authorities wishing to innovate have to work within the political climate and the political realities in which they find themselves. In the case of Brazil, political backing has been identified as a key factor behind the successful uptake of PB experiences. This is not least because of the important position PB has within the national agenda of the current ruling Workers Party. Alongside the party political dimensions of PB there has been, more generally, a high level of motivation to support participatory political processes that might serve to prevent a return to military rule. However, in Europe similar impulses for adopting a politically driven PB process do not always exist. For example, when the first ideas for PB surfaced in the northwest of England, the Local Authorities in Manchester and Salford were invited to join a fact-finding trip to Porto Alegre. The idea was rejected and two alternate reasons for this were given at the time: some argued that there was little a UK local authority that was successfully regenerating itself could learn about poverty reduction from a Southern country; others made the point that local newspapers might make damaging accusations against councillors wasting taxpayers' money on overseas junkets. Both these responses connected firmly with deliberations on whether a local authority considering PB could or should adopt a 'tailor-made' model from another context or whether instead they should adapt their own existing practice within revised policy frameworks.

An important lesson to be derived from efforts to export a model such as PB to the European context is that local authorities do not only embrace change but also resist it. This acts as a particular constraint when hierarchical or bureaucratic patterns are deeply entrenched, in local authorities that are poorly resourced and across political landscapes that are risk-averse. This does not imply that PB is bound to fail in Europe; on the contrary, if replication gives way to adaptation then home-grown processes can emerge. These might mirror, approximate, or even diverge from the original PB model, but the key issue is that they are appropriate for democratizing context-specific state society relations. Critical to this process is understanding the motivations of local politicians and council officers in wanting to adopt or resist PB. Resistance to PB in Europe is not only based on conservative reaction, but can also derive from the fact that many European cities already have consultative and participatory processes in place at the local level and are resistant to 'reinventing the wheel'. For example, there is an established history of neighbourhood planning and participatory strategic planning. Some of the more creative responses in Europe are those that seek to link such initiatives to the more radical agenda of citizen involvement in budgets.

CONTEXTUAL FACTORS AFFECTING THE TAKE-UP OF PARTICIPATORY BUDGETING IN EUROPE

A few contextual points are worth making in relation to efforts to introduce PB in Europe. The first is the influence of language and culture including political culture. PB was developed in Portuguese-speaking Brazil and has most easily translated to Portuguese-speaking Europe. Moreover, most of the dense technical analysis of PB, such as the work of Giovanni Allegretti in Italy, has happened from within a southern European language context where some of the language barriers have been better traversed. Not surprisingly, therefore, some of the earliest European models of PB have been in Portugal, Spain, and Italy, where national networks reach over to Brazil. European models have tended to come about at the instigation of local mayors who have links with left-leaning international networks, and who in turn have linked these to the European labour and social justice organizations with which they are associated. Examples of this include Saint Feliu de Llobregat near Barcelona, Bobingy near Paris, and Pieve Emanuele in Italy. So links based on shared Latin culture and left-oriented political culture, between Porto Alegre and a number of cities across Europe, have been important – perhaps more important than the Portuguese language connection with Brazil.

Another set of contextual influences relates to networks created by migration to and from Brazil. Porto Alegre has a very diverse population and is unusual in Brazil for having particularly strong Italian and German influences, dating back to early periods of European migration. Often linked with Catholic Christian belief, another conduit for the spread of PB has been through international faith-based networks. The role of liberation theology is evident in PB and has been influential in its transfer to Europe. It was certainly a factor, for example, in the receptiveness to PB of people involved with the CPI in Salford, discussed below, many of who were in faith-based organizations. Indeed, the CPI was underpinned by strong inter-faith partnership, particularly early on in its establishment; and it has been administered under a national UK charity, Church Action on Poverty. Interest in PB on the part of international development agencies and NGOs has also had an effect. An example can be seen in the role played by OXFAM UK, which supported the development of PB in Salford. Networks associated with international development organizations have been particularly important in the UK and have influenced the way in which PB has been taken up.

Focus on Porto Alegre as the home of PB and as the site of its 'purest' application is a point of contention, with some challenging the dogmatic promotion and transplantation of the Porto Alegre model. Even in Brazil it has not always proved possible to graft the fully articulated experience of Porto Alegre onto new contexts and institutional relationships without modification or change. The CPI has advanced what it sees as a more realistic approach, which is to look for and adhere to key principles while at the same time building on contextual circumstances and the 'managerial' culture of the local authority. A further perceived advantage of this approach is that it can avoid what has been an uneven experience in some parts of Europe, where high profile models of PB have stopped abruptly as a result of a change in the political leadership (e.g. Saint Feliu de Llobregat). The more cautious character of local councils in the UK has meant they are more risk-averse and less volatile than some of the European local authorities. However, they also resist change and are harder to influence as a result. In the end only time will tell whether the tailor-made or the bolt-on versions of PB will prevail in the European context.

TOWARDS A FRAMEWORK FOR ANALYSING PARTICIPATORY BUDGETING IN EUROPE

On the European mainland in particular, there has been a growth in transnational networks promoting closer integration and highlighting good practice. This has facilitated a number of direct exchanges between Brazil and Europe and has inspired a number of seminars and residential workshops bringing together participants from all over Europe. One example was a week-long residential training course delivered by Unimondo, the Italian branch of the One World network, in Trento in 2002. A number of Brazilian participants, along with local politicians and activists from more than six European countries, attended to discuss PB. The overall objective was to provide participants with both the theoretical basis and the operative tools necessary for the elaboration and effective adoption of a PB model in their local community. Alongside transnational networks fostering PB as part of local democracy enhancement, run those that see the political foundations of PB as of secondary importance. They are more concerned with its perceived effectiveness in modernizing services and in extending already established consultative or participatory initiatives. Such networks feed into formal regional political processes in Europe. The structural development funds flowing in and out of Brussels through the powerful European Commission carry with them a strong managerial approach that is most commonly associated with the northern European member states such as the UK and Germany. In such a bureaucratic and managerial environment it is difficult to introduce let alone institutionalize systems that will enable a 'service user' perspective or increase the focus on 'citizen voice'. It is this latter approach that has most strongly informed the institutional context for PB in north European cities such as Salford and Berlin.

Another area in which experiences of PB differ across Europe relates to preference for what might be called 'top-down' or 'bottom-up' approaches. Top-down approaches tend to emanate from the centre, which drives the formulation and design of policy. These approaches are not without innovation and because they apply a set of universal principles might even be better at breaking old moulds than bottom-up approaches. In Europe, centrally driven policies include the formulation of a European Constitution and efforts to strengthen the European Parliament. In relation to PB, the highly innovative model developed in Porto Alegre was developed centrally. Bottom-up approaches in Europe are most in evidence with relation to models of participatory governance and initiatives that seek to devolve power and place stress on the role of citizen input within local development boards and new participatory governance structures. In parts of Europe where this experience is well developed and entrenched, there is a strong argument for taking account of and building on this experience rather than reinventing the wheel or creating multiple and competing structures. The contrast between the two approaches is represented in Figure 7.3. Using this framework it is possible to locate a particular PB

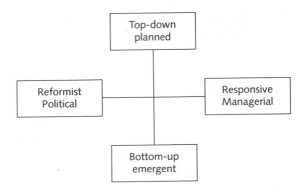

Figure 7.3   Different models of citizen involvement in setting budget priorities in Europe

model on the diagram as a way of identifying and understanding the differences and similarities between the various experiments that have emerged. In the following section we turn to the case of the CPI in the UK, starting by locating it within this framework.

PARTICIPATORY BUDGETING IN THE UNITED KINGDOM

PB UK is being delivered by the CPI, which was established in April 1999 with the active support of Oxfam's UK Poverty Programme and through a 'learning exchange' with the cities of Porto Alegre and Recife in Brazil. The CPI has its own management committee, drawn from community and voluntary sector volunteers and professionals. It receives funding from the National Lottery Community Fund and from a range of charitable and statutory bodies. The overarching goal of the CPI is to enhance the capacity of grassroots activists, community groups, and faith-based projects in disadvantaged communities in Manchester and Salford. Its specific aims include:

- undertaking social, political, and economic analysis of forces which create and sustain poverty and social exclusion within communities and neighbourhoods (Analysis)
- developing proposals for action at local, regional, and national levels to address the needs and issues identified within communities and neighbourhoods (Strategy & Action)
- developing coalitions and networks to engage with the strategies and policies of the major strategic players within neighbourhoods, local authority areas, and the regional and national contexts (Networking & Engagement)
- participating in wider policy debates about poverty, social exclusion, neighbourhood renewal, and urban regeneration, and local democracy at local, regional and national levels (Policy Debate)

- participating in learning and exchange with organizations and community networks with similar aims and methods across the UK and internationally (Sharing Good Practice).

The work that the CPI has been engaged in with community networks in Manchester has been labelled a bottom-up approach and fostered by current government policy in the UK.

In Europe only a highly politicized authority, perhaps with a radical mayor offering strong independent leadership, would be likely to adopt wholesale a tailor-made approach drawn from the Brazilian model. Under pressure the default position of local authorities would be to stick to their own agreed processes rather than to take risks with anything unfamiliar. In the opinion of the CPI, which has been working consistently on developing PB in the UK, there is no evident track record of political willingness and there are few strong independent mayors in Britain who would embrace PB unconditionally. This reality has forced Community Pride to adopt a more 'bolt-on' and pragmatic approach, integrating PB into existing institutional relationships and procedures. This has not been greatly discouraging because it is believed to reduce social isolation and constitute a positive response towards involving people in broader social engagement.

To this end CPI's approach to transferring PB has been described as follows:

- *Building political confidence:* The local authority needs to see PB as resolving some of their problems too, whether it be managing an over-strong bureaucracy, or re-invigorating a difficult democratic situation. Political leaders must feel that PB is not too challenging, and helps them manage their departments.
- *Engaging with existing consultation structures:* Understanding the political context includes joining existing community networks, even when they are run by the local authority. Revenue Budget Consultation is an example of this type of work.
- *Promoting independent networks of community groups and associations:* This needs to happen in order to feed the process with potential participants. It is done both by supporting individual community activists and by feeding in relevant research and liaison expertise, to nurture community networks and define how best to relate to the local authority.
- *Committing to a pilot stu*dy: The study has focused the attention of the local authority for longer than is possible through a one-off seminar or presentation, and seeks to overcome their natural risk-aversion and create a degree of acceptance by managers. The process has been facilitated by interviews with departmental service managers, in order to understand the main challenges from the local authority's point of view. Experience suggests that at least three years working though a pilot study is probably necessary in order to embed PB principles into the working practices of local authorities.

■ *Working to identify a pot of money for PB investment.* The funding should be something extra and should not challenge existing powers and resources, for example, it should not come from an already dedicated pot, such as for salaries. A target might be 1 to 2 per cent of the annual revenue turnover of the authority, and to begin with, maybe even less.

■ *Stressing good branding and marketing.* It is necessary to launch PB with something that says this is a new beginning. A strong annual cycle is promoted and publicized, which links together planning, participation, and democratic processes.

■ *Realizing that it will take time to build participation:* Often word-of-mouth and direct experience are the best ways to motivate people who have become cynical about the value of engaging with the local authority. Budget literacy work is one way CPI has laid down some foundations from which more a participatory approach is possible.

Overall, CPI is designed for the purpose of moving local communities and authorities towards a new level of participation. Once underway it is believed that internal reforms or renewal will inevitably be required to keep participation at a higher level.

Other authorities working hard on promoting citizen engagement and combating social exclusion, such as Bobingy in France or Manchester's own poor relation Salford, have taken a different approach. In Salford, since 2001 the CPI has been in discussion with the City Council about the potential of PB. This has led to a feasibility study and significant interest in the idea of PB across a wide range of agencies in the UK. In a climate of cuts, Salford, like most local authorities in the UK, has little flexibility in terms of its budget. One possibility being considered in taking PB forward is to extend the current system of devolved budgets and to implement a process for setting priorities for action. Existing Community Action Plans (CAPs) provide a loose mechanism for linking local needs to funds, and CPI and Salford City Council are working towards developing greater clarity on this. At community committee level, CAPS set out a range of proposals to be implemented and, for a number of reasons, they could play an important role in developing a PB process in Salford. First, community committees cover nine clear geographical areas. Second, they represent an existing vehicle that could be used to translate local ideas into service delivery. Third, the council is used to working with community committees and with ideas generated from them through action plans, so this area of technical expertise already exists in Salford.

Despite such progress, in Salford consultation is still seen as a way of providing information rather than as a way of involving citizens in decision-making. Hence, part of the need for clarity relates to developing clear and transparent processes for translating findings from communities into service plans. Consultation needs to be nudged away from one-off and one-way exercises towards an ongoing dialogue between Salford citizens and the local authority, so that priorities can be chosen with a clear understanding of the cost implications and trade-offs. Local authority budget development is often viewed as a very technical process, only of interest to City Hall bureaucrats; but Salford has taken a number of important steps to inform local people about its spending plans and if it embraces PB, this could strengthen the Council's budgetary development process in line with its Community Action Planning. This in turn would provide citizens with the opportunity to understand the budgetary process and debate the implications for their areas. It is towards this end that the CPI is working with the local authority and local residents in Salford.

CONCLUSIONS

How replicable is PB, and what are the conditions for the successful construction, duplication, or transfer of the PB experience in Brazil? Some argue that PB is the child of Porto Alegre, born of a particular political and institutional conjuncture and as such it does not travel well (Abers, 2000 cited in Souza, 2000: 26; Santos, 1998). Others see PB as only being adopted and successfully implemented by leftist political parties and see the process being compromised by swings in political power between parties of the left and right. However, the successful experience of Belo Horizonte suggests that these misgivings are misplaced. A clear prior condition, and one that is often missed in approaches to participatory development that are institutionalized within the real world of development practice (Cooke and Kothari, 2001), is that the process needs to be recognized as political. This does not necessarily mean that the process has to be dominated by party politics; indeed these can be more of a hindrance than help. Rather it suggests that the process needs to accommodate conflict and struggle. It also means that PB programmes cannot be regarded simply as administrative interventions that are transplanted from one context to another through a 'cut-and-paste' methodology without taking cognizance of the broader political environment (Vibe, 2002: 51). That said, the discussion of PB in Europe suggests that in addition to the inspirational aspects of PB, some of the technical innovations developed over a number of years in Brazil do have resonance elsewhere and can facilitate greater participation and state society synergy in decision-making.

Whether participation is consultative or instrumental (Cooke and Kothari, 2001) is an important determinant of the success of PB. Goetz and Gaventa (2001), for example, have made the point with regard to participation in general that citizens have a right to be involved in decision-making processes not as 'choosers' but as 'shapers'. Elsewhere I have argued for participatory processes to be promoted not simply to improve efficiency but to reshape power relations and patterns of distribution (Beall 1997b: 952). From this perspective, it is suggested that PB can only be transformative when participation poses a real challenge to underlying structures and relations of power. The most successful examples of PB appear to be those where there is a degree of political will accompanied by a willingness to embrace conflict, in a context where there are sufficiently broad and effective coalitions of interest that are able to negotiate and coordinate a long-term strategic approach. In Porto Alegre, for example, a strategic coalition is in place that has grown out of an organic process of contentious interaction between civil society organizations and formal political structures, with both feeding off the engagement with each other. Moreover, this is made possible by virtue of actors and structures prepared to forge alliances that are committed to the process of change (Alvarez et al., 1998: 15; Evans 2002: 234). In the case of Porto Alegre, it was the state that was particularly important in building the coalition; but different organizations or intermediaries can forge alliances too.

Even when the political conditions are right and processes are well in place, there are a number of challenges that persist across the PB processes reviewed. The first is finding ways of bridging participatory budgeting and broader planning processes. A second and related challenge is that of reconciling the short-term demands of sections of a city's population with more long-term, strategic city-wide imperatives. A third point, related in turn to the first and second challenges, is that when a large proportion of the total budget for investment is subject to PB – such as in Porto Alegre, where it is 100 per cent of the budget – popular demand for housing, services, and secondary infrastructure can inhibit investment in primary infrastructure such as bulk sewers, water treatment plants, or motorways, with adverse impacts on overall human and economic development in the city (Cabannes, 2003: 67).

Most important from the perspective of this book is whether PB can promote enhanced state society engagement and whether it offers a positive example of state generated citizen participation and empowerment. Vibe (2002: 42) suggests that this is the case when there are broad coalitions of interest; for example, as with the PT led coalition in Porto Alegre (Souza, 2001) or as in the case of Recife, where the development of the PB programme was on the basis of a coalition of community associations and political party actors (Melo et al., 2000). With reference to Porto Alegre, Baiocchi (2001) warns that excessive focus on the role of civil society, without recognizing the importance of government in the synergistic processes that characterize state–society relations (Evans, 1996a, 1996b), is a mistake. As Tendler (1997) has also emphasized in reference to the decentralization process in Brazil, the role of government is a crucial factor, and this holds true for PB, both in terms of the state's initial engagement with the progressive coalitions driving the programme, and as a more sustained commitment to the programme on the part of the government (Vibe, 2002: 41). However, PB is likely to have some limitations in this regard. As Sousa Santos (1998: 506) has observed, it is questionable whether PB can be sustained as a destabilizing project due to the fact that 'a destabilizing idea that succeeds in converting itself into a sustainable practice always runs the risk of loosing its destabilizing potential as it succeeds'.

For all these caveats, PB holds interesting lessons and constitutes one of the most important local development strategies coming out of the South to influence policy in the North. The following chapter traces the rise of challenge funds in North America and Europe and how in Britain especially these have been exported in the context of development cooperation. Interestingly, the PB experience has been to pull citizens directly into closer engagement with government, whereas the challenge fund model as it has been developed in and exported from the UK has been to facilitate community-led local partnerships and local democracy through special purpose agencies or intermediary NGOs that engage a range of interests within an overarching project. One of the questions posed across these two chapters is whether PB speaks to local political sovereignty while partnerships speak to elite-dominated community managerialism.

CHAPTER EIGHT

Challenge funds and partnership: North–South lessons

INTRODUCTION

Challenge funds have their origin in industrialized countries, particularly the United States, where they constitute an important part of the funding repertoire of many different organizations. Demand for resources, whether from government agencies, charitable foundations, or private companies, inevitably outstrips the supply of grant funding. Under such circumstances, the challenge fund approach seeks to achieve efficiency and elicit innovation by getting applicants to compete for resources. So, for example, university scholarships might be awarded to the graduate students who submit the most cleverly constructed and cutting-edge research projects. Challenge funds are often underpinned by an element of agenda setting, as illustrated clearly in Box 8.1, with awards going to grantees that tailor their proposals towards the particular concerns or preoccupations of the award-making bodies. In Europe, they have become very much associated with community-led and area-based development strategies. In Britain the challenge fund approach was entrenched through successive strategies supporting urban regeneration.

This chapter critically considers challenge funds and the partnership principle, both in general terms and more specifically through case studies in the context of urban development. The issue of partnerships in the United Kingdom is explored through the experience of one programme in London, New Life for Paddington (NLP). The chapter then turns to the experiences of the City–Community Challenge Fund (C3) – a pilot programme initiated by the UK's DFID and now operating under the financial auspices of UN-Habitat – in the cities of Kampala and Jinja in Uganda. The Ugandan case points to some of the issues that arise when exporting Western models to developing countries in the context of development cooperation. Both cases are instructive in highlighting the advantages and limitations of a challenge fund approach.

Box 8.1 Examples of different kinds of challenge funds

In Canada TVOntario's Lifelong Learning Challenge Fund (LLCF) has been developed to fill critical gaps in the skilled trades labour market. Funded by the Ministry of Training, Colleges & Universities, the LLCF was launched in 2000 as a $5 million project to attract matching funds from private and public participants for the development of new online programmes for the automotive, e-commerce, health, food services, trade, and manufacturing sectors.

In Britain the Department for Transport developed a challenge fund offering small grants to assist with the cost of not-for-profit projects promoting road safety, proposed by organizations other than local authorities. £200 000 per annum was allocated by the government to this challenge fund, for grants of up to £20 000 each. Projects are expected to support Britain's road safety strategy by promoting casualty reduction, for example in relation to child safety, driver attitudes to speed, and improving the safety of vulnerable road users such as cyclists.

In the United States the Ford Foundation, in partnership with the John S. and James L. Knight Foundation, initiated the Challenge Fund for Journalism in September 2003. The aim was to promote diversity in the news media through specific journalism organizations that received support to broaden their base of financial support. They had to raise new funds from individual donors, which were then matched up to the target amount. For example, the National Association of Black Journalists was offered match-funding for projects up to US$50 000 if they could raise funding from non-traditional sources such as individual members, chapters, friends, supporters, communities, and businesses.

The UK's Foreign & Commonwealth Office (FCO) initiated the Climate Change Challenge Fund (CCCF) as a joint initiative between the FCO and the Department of the Environment, Transport and the Regions, in cooperation with DFID and the Department of Trade and Industry. It promotes the use of clean technologies in developing countries and countries with transitional economies, in order to help reduce emissions of 'greenhouse' gases. The scheme funds projects between £10 000 and £50 000 that make use of UK expertise in renewable energy and clean technologies. It aims to raise the profile of UK business and government in developing countries and to help British companies take advantage of the opportunities offered by the need for climate-friendly economic growth.

The Government of India is setting up a City Challenge Fund (CCF) as an incentive based grant facility to support the reform of municipal management, service delivery and local economic reform. It is targeted at cities with populations above 500 000, of which there are 69 – seven metropolitan cities, 20 cities of over one million, and 42 cities between 500 000 and 1 000 000. The choice of cities will be on a competitive basis, taking into account political capacity and commitment to developing and implementing citywide reforms. Central government assistance will be restricted to 75 per cent of the total cost, with the remaining 25 per cent being met by the state government or municipality, which should have an elected body in place in order to access the fund.

CHALLENGE FUNDS IN URBAN AND COMMUNITY DEVELOPMENT IN BRITAIN

The idea of challenge funds is introduced in Chapter One where they are identified as originating in North America and becoming increasingly popular in Europe, especially in the UK. The challenge fund approach came to Britain under Conservative Party rule in the 1990s in the form of City Challenge, which was introduced in 1991. This resulted from lessons learned on visits to the USA by Michael Heseltine, as Secretary of State for the Environment. City Challenge was part of a sustained assault on the traditional post-War form of local government by successive Conservative governments during the 1980s and 1990s. An early implementation of City Challenge took place in Canary Wharf as a response to the grave troubles facing the then Urban Development Corporation and its London Docklands development. In this flagship project, little thought had been given to the reactions or futures of communities in low-income housing in the area and an *ex-post* solution was sought. Bailey (1995: 64) has outlined the critical characteristics of City Challenge in the United Kingdom:

> *The innovative features of the initiative were that deprived neighbourhoods were to be targeted by independent regeneration agencies, using public money and the leverage of private sources set up to prepare and implement action plans over five years. Action plans were required to identify a 'vision' and to specify, with clear targets, both property-related and 'people-orientated' strategies.*

Although it is not absolutely clear that Docklands residents saw their vision realized, this was the approach adopted around Canary Wharf. From the early 1990s, this model came to dominate policy initiatives designed to tackle the problems of urban decay in the UK, leading to the commitment of over £1 billion of public expenditure each year to such schemes (Brennan et al., 1998b: 1). Interventions ranged from quite large area-based programmes, such as Enterprise Zones and Urban Development Corporations, right down to neighbourhood-level and more people-orientated projects such as the Task Force Initiative.

In April 1994 City Challenge gave way to the Single Regeneration Budget Challenge Fund (SRB CF). The SRB combined funds from four government departments, with the aim of simplifying administrations and providing more flexibility in the use of funds. It was administered by de-concentrated regional offices, based on the assumption that strategies should be defined locally rather than nationally, with government establishing the overall guidelines. It also combined 20 previously separate programmes designed to bring about physical, economic, and social regeneration in local areas. The idea was that the combined fund would catalyse further resources from the private, public, and voluntary sectors and would stimulate development through enhancing the competitiveness of local actors. According to Brennen et al. (1998: 2) there were three principal features to the SRB approach:

- Partnership – addressing the complex nature of the regeneration problem through encouraging the interaction of economic, social and physical actors in intersectoral partnerships.
- Competition – partnerships bidding for funds from the SRB CF in the hope that this would lead to innovation and partnership formation.
- 'Hands off' management – local partnerships demonstrating effective management and monitoring arrangements, as these would not be the responsibility of the government, except for period performance reviews.

These three elements, along with the principle that partnerships should leverage private-sector finance of at least double the public sector commitment, have come to critically inform the development of challenge funds not only in the UK but in Britain's international development cooperation as well. However, as is shown below, leveraging private sector resources is not quite so easy in all late-developing countries.

Although it has evolved, by and large this model has persisted in the UK – even if challenge funds and the partnership principle are not without their critics. Bailey (1995: 65) said of the SRB not long after it was set up:

> The ultimate test of its success will be the extent to which it can galvanize local stakeholders, central government departments and the private sector, all of which have very different priorities, to work towards a single set of objectives.

Writing in the UK nearly ten years after Bailey, Sullivan (2004: 194) is similarly cautious:

> While partnerships are many and varied in the local public policy system [. . .] there are significant stresses placed on the realization of the partnership principle in relation to demonstrating shared ownership and accountability.

Not least among the stresses is the fact that in the UK, particularly since the 1980s, local government has operated within the context of successive governments with strong centralizing instincts. Most recently, as the new Labour Prime Minister, Tony Blair (1998: 20–2 cited in Stoker and Wilson, 2004a: 1) laid out the conditions for partnership:

> Where councils embrace [our] agenda of change and show that they can adapt to play a part in modernizing their locality, then they will find their status and powers enhanced. [but] if you are unwilling or unable to work to the modern agenda then the government will have to look to other partners to take on your role.

In the UK, the initiators of partnerships requiring community strategies are most often local authorities. In developing countries the initiative towards partnerships often comes from other sources, usually donors or NGOs. Either way, the partnership agenda is seen as synonymous with the modernization of local governance and local funds are at the heart of this approach.

Bailey (1995: 66) raised another point pertinent to the present analysis of challenge funds in the UK and Uganda and this concerns area-based strategies. Integrated area-based development (IAD) embraces a wide range of practices, adopted through varied institutional forms and across different spatial scales. We saw examples of this approach with the AGETIPS in Benin discussed in Chapter Five. Although IAD has been criticized as a way of targeting poverty, which is usually dispersed across a whole population rather than being concentrated in particular locations, area-based approaches have gained favour in the UK as a response to social exclusion (Glennester et al., 1999). Moreover, area-based strategies are usefully employed as a means of pursuing particular policy objectives. For example, IAD is used to promote economic restructuring and as a means of establishing 'joined up governance' and 'development in the round' (Turok, 1999). Turok outlines five main approaches to urban regeneration: business development, human resource development, physical business infrastructure, neighbourhood development, and the social economy. In developing countries the project approach to delivering basic needs was first advanced by the World Bank in the 1970s, and area-based strategies were followed in slum upgrading and the formalization of shantytowns and informal settlements. By the 1990s IAD had given way to city development strategies that sought to move beyond neighbourhood or area-based approaches to embrace an urban management position. The rationale was that projects were fragmented and did little to address the dysfunctional management of cities (Devas, 1993). This rationale informs some of the criticisms leveled at local funds, which are thought to work for the micro-level but to fail to add up to much at the local level or beyond it. However, IAD has remained important as a way of achieving inter-sectoral coordination and tackling area-based problems, and local funds are often a central part of IAD strategies.

Another criticism that can be applied to IAD and challenge funds alike is their emphasis on 'getting things done' and their preoccupation with targets and outputs. This can lead to designers and implementers losing sight of processes and the need to develop ownership among people living and working in IAD areas. Challenge funds have the additional problem of setting up communities in competition with one another. Authors writing on IAD (Brownill, 2000; Brownill and Darke, 1998; Alsop et al., 2001) also posit that insufficient attention is paid to social development and that the needs of diverse groups are not recognized or addressed. While earlier forms of IAD were dominated by integrated physical development approaches, such as the New Towns in the UK and informal upgrading schemes that were fashionable in international urban development from the 1970s (Van der Hoff and Steinberg, 1993), there is now much greater emphasis on social and economic development. More attention is also paid to local community and stakeholder involvement and to linking up different levels of government and the various agencies involved within in an area (Boyle and Eisenger, 2001).

Participation is seen to be variable due to the power relations among and within the partnership organizations involved in IAD and challenge funds. For example, representatives of communities, often women, are no match for private and public sector representatives who are often from male-dominated establishments that set the organizational culture of partnerships (Brownill, 2000). Bailey (1995: 66) is especially critical of the use of competitive processes to identify 'winners' and 'losers' across or within communities. This has the potential of undermining cooperative behaviour and setting one set of neighbours against another. He is concerned that attention is paid to ensuring an even geographical and political spread across local authority areas rather than to an exclusive focus on the quality of bids. In the context of developing countries, where the extent of deprivation is invariably so much greater and where the majority of people are very badly off, it is to be questioned whether setting up groups and communities in competition with each other is a useful exercise. Nevertheless, for better or worse area-based strategies remain important vehicles for delivering development at the local level and there are good examples to be found (Beall and Todes, 2004). The same applies to challenge funds, as this chapter illustrates.

Box 8.2   The Home Office Challenge Fund and the European Refugee Fund

The Challenge Fund (CF) and the European Refugee Fund (ERF) are both administered by the Home Office and share similar aims. The CF was established in November 2001 to support the implementation of the Home Office's Refugee Integration Strategy and is designed to promote innovative projects that address specific social needs amongst refugee communities. The ERF is a European Union initiative established by the Council of Europe in 2000. It delegates to Member States the power to implement initiatives to support refugees, addressing reception conditions, social and economic integration, and return home if desired. Both funds tackle similar issues, but there are distinctions between them.

The CF is open to voluntary and community-based organizations and public bodies, such as local authorities, primary care trusts, and not-for-profit organizations. Private sector organizations cannot apply for funds directly but can be part of partnerships bids. The fund specifically targets existing smaller voluntary and refugee community-based organizations and pays full project costs for up to 12 months, usually accepting proposals for between £20 000 and £50 000.

The ERF is subject to the same rules on eligibility as the CF – voluntary and community-based organizations and public bodies – with private bodies permitted to be a part of partnership bids. However, here partnerships and consortia of projects access funds most successfully. While no fixed limit is in place, the Home Office states that it anticipates applications to be between £30 000 and £80 000. The ERF generally makes available grants of up to 50 per cent of the project's total costs, thus requiring match-funding, and again for a maximum of 12 months. Because the administrative and management requirements of the ERF are more complex, new organizations or small projects are unlikely to be successful in their applications. Moreover, where there are consortia there must be a lead body identified which will assume legal responsibility for the project.

Both the CF and the ERF are intended to promote the integration of people whose stay in the UK is 'of a lasting and/or stable nature'. Funding is concentrated upon activities that directly benefit refugees in their integration into the life of their communities, that help them attain employment, housing, education, and health care, and that develop social relationships and networks, both within specific ethnic groups and between refugee and host communities. Projects that support refugees to engage fully in UK society, such as language skills and the promotion of knowledge about UK culture and customs are also considered for funding, as are those providing advice on legal rights and support for refugees in the process of considering citizenship.

THE PADDINGTON DEVELOPMENT TRUST AND NEW LIFE FOR PADDINGTON IN LONDON

This case study is of an urban development partnership programme that derives from the challenge fund model and which is being executed in North Paddington, a relatively deprived area falling within the City of Westminster in London in the UK. North Paddington developed as a residential area primarily during the second half of the nineteenth century, with housing varying from very poor dwellings near the canal and the railway to more respectable housing in the neighbourhood known as Queen's Park. The area suffered considerable bomb damage during the Second World War, followed by a period of slum clearance and then construction of high and low rise apartment buildings during the 1950s and 1960s. During the 1970s, demolition and construction gave way to a policy of improving privately owned properties through the establishment of General Improvement Areas and Housing Action Areas, whereby residents were supported to maintain or improve sub-standard housing. By the early 1990s some of the post-War construction was found to be problematic. The tower blocks were demolished and the low-rise blocks were given a facelift. Over the last 15 years policy has shifted so that social and subsidised housing has been developed by housing associations. This has brought many new people into the North Paddington area (PPRU 2001: 3).

In 1965 Paddington was combined with the old boroughs of Marylebone and Westminster to create the new City of Westminster. This fell under the jurisdiction of the Greater London Council from the time of its creation until it was abolished in 1986. Thereafter, its powers devolved to Westminster Council, although a further change came in 2000 with the creation of the new Greater London Authority, when London acquired for the first time a directly elected Mayor and an elected Assembly. There was quite a lot of activity at community-level in this part of London, but following the election of a Conservative government in 1979, the Conservative-controlled Westminster Council labelled many voluntary organizations 'political'. From 1982 Westminster Council was led by Shirley Porter, notorious for her efforts to win votes for the Conservative Party through the sale of council houses, and during the 1980s and early 1990s 'there was a constant and bitter struggle between the Council and many North Paddington groups and residents' (ibid.: 4). From the mid-1990s relations between local organizations and the Council began to slowly improve. In 1996 the North Paddington Society was formed, and over time this evolved into the Paddington Development Trust (PDT), a community-led organization with social objectives formed in 1998 with the specific task of urban regeneration. This coincided with the coming to power of the New Labour government in 1997, which despite some changes in policy direction has remained committed to the partnership principle that is now the dominant feature of challenge funds in the UK.

Since then, the PDT has rapidly expanded into an innovative community-based enterprise, which primarily acts as a Regeneration Company and Accountable Body for public and private sector investment, geared to the creation of social and economic independence for people living in North Westminster. By 2006 PDT will have been directly accountable for £18 000 000 of investment into the area (PDT, 2004). As the Chief Executive of the PDT described the organization: 'In some senses it is a classic NGO but there are not many NGOs around here operating economic development'. The Trust has facilitated a number of new and active partnerships involving public, private, voluntary, social, and community enterprises, which in turn has created a local infrastructure geared towards economic, environmental, and social regeneration in ways that allow disadvantaged people living in Paddington to become economically and socially independent. The Trust operates with four core values: mutuality (sharing benefits within the community); empowerment (creating opportunities for local people); financial self-sufficiency (acquiring an income-generating asset base); and equal opportunities for all communities, which it seeks to achieve through four theme groups focusing on strategic intervention in the local community. These are: Health and community safety; employment and enterprise; young people and education; and building sustainable local capacity.

Since 1999, trends in wider government policy have been moving towards local-level development in the UK, and the PDT – together with partners – has responded to these trends by facilitating the establishment of Neighbourhood Forums in each of the deprived Wards in Paddington – Church St Ward, Queens Park Ward, Westbourne Ward, and Harrow Road Ward. This has been a protracted and careful process, most importantly involving constructing or reconstructing community relations and helping previously excluded communities engage with mainstream public agencies. This in turn has helped the PDT in its goals of bringing mainstream services to previously excluded areas and creating new opportunities for all the people living in Paddington (PDT, 2004: 2). The first of the neighbour-hood management programmes to come into being in Paddington was sit-uated in the Church Street Ward and began with a £3 000 000 grant once it had produced a five- to seven-year plan arising out of a needs assessment and prioritization exercise.

NLP was designed by the PDT and began life in October 1999 as a community-based programme delivering a wide range of services in Paddington. It works together with over 100 local delivery partners, 40 per cent of whom are black and ethnic minority-led organizations, and over the last three years it has implemented over 150 projects across a deprived area of London. Since 2001 the PDT has managed NLP in conjunction with a number of joint working partners: Westminster City Council, Westminster Primary Care Trust, Job Centre Plus, and City of Westminster College. It has expanded rapidly since its formation, primarily through assuming the role of Accountable Body for a £13.5 million SRB programme that commenced in 1999. The SRB award was made to implement the NLP Community Plan, designed to address significant deprivation in four wards within the London Borough of North West Westminster (Queens Park, Harrow Road, Westbourne, and Church Street). Due to be completed in 2006, the SRB budget will be fully committed over the next two years although fund-raising and development planning by the PDT extend to at least 2015.

While the relationship between the Westminster Council and community organizations in North Paddington has greatly improved, it is not close. One interviewee in North Paddington commented as follows:

Most of the senior officers in the Town Hall live in Brighton or Sussex and commute into Westminster every day. Even the junior officers who make the contacts with the community members come into town from Reading or from quite some distance. This is because the remuneration is good but what it does is it distances public services from the management of these poor communities and the same can be said of the developers.

The PDT reports directly with the London Development Agency rather than Westminster Council and does such work under the wing of local gov-ernment, which is the usual UK model. Nevertheless, the PDT serves as an important bridge between City Hall and the people of Paddington and is critical in forging partnerships, even though it maintains an arm's length relationship with government. Indeed, the PDT has an autonomous if con-nected presence in the area both on the ground and through the Great Western Studios and Workspace, which it helped finance. It is here that the PDT offices are located, together with a number of community organiza-tions and enterprises, in a new and modern building constructed on marginal land beneath an elevated road that cuts through Paddington.

In reviewing what the NLP Programme has achieved, the Mid-Programme Review of the PDT (PDT, 2002) points to the programme hav-ing provided investment and impetus 'to enable local people to begin to connect with mainstream services'. Important here has been the production by the PDT of *Paddington People*, a community magazine that focuses on local issues and *www.4paddington.com*, a web site that keeps people informed of the activities and opportunities linked to NLP and provides a range of information on the area. Work accomplished so far has provided a community-based infrastructure delivering on education, jobs, training, youth, health, early years, and community safety. Specific examples include support to the Paddington Refugee Centre, together with the Westminster Refugees Consortia and the Department for Health's local Primary Care Trust; Paddington Youth Connections and Westminster Youth Services; Paddington Enterprise Programme and the Portobello Business Centre; and the Community Policing and Youth Leadership Programme together with the Black Police Association.

The NLP also supports small community groups and increased capacity in resident engagement. This is done through a number of 'community chests' that range in size from £500 up to £6 000, for which people bid. The Trust has funded about 150 of these small projects as the Chief Executive of the PDT explained:

> Projects can be anything from a wide screen TV for an old people's home to support for capacity-building in a small organization giving advice to refugees. We also provide funds for match-funding so you can get a one-off grant from us as a development grant and then a match-funding grant. Some regimes require match-funding and we do not. So people will use the community chest as match-funding to leverage other funds.

The NLP wanted to include projects from £15 000 to £30 000 but Westminster Council rejected this. The NLP view is that scaled-up activities are often more effective and cohesive. One PDT interviewee provided the following example:

> We have many refugee organizations offering similar services to their own groups but the more successful ones operate across groups. If every ethnic minority comes in for their own group, do you fund every new organization or do you try and foster cooperation and integration? So giving lots of money to small groups of people is not always the best solution, especially if you are trying to address diversity and inclusion. You are getting a piecemeal service, which is not good.

However, support for smaller projects is widespread and is not confined to the Council. It was noted that their popularity derives from the 'feel good' they generate but:

> If you go with these small projects like the widescreen TV, there is a positive impact on the quality of some people's lives but strategically you are not having an impact. And eventually the TV set will break. There is no return on the feel good factor.

Though there are some frustrations involved in the smaller community chest funding, there is no sense among the PDT staff that the effort is not worth it. Moreover, there is a long-term and inter-generational focus in their perspective, whether it is with regard to sustainable infrastructure and quality services, or literacy training and youth work. As the Chief Executive of the PDT put it: 'You fund kids at the age of six and within a five-year planning cycle they are 11 and then 16 and then 21. The time element tips very fast in this environment.' He went on to say of the people working on NLP: 'Here everyone knows their patch and cares about it. It has to be like this to have "street cred" and a strategic planning focus'. This is in sharp contrast to the private sector, which although an important partner in Paddington, is not always a willing one. As is demonstrated in Chapter Nine as well, this is a common experience of local funds elsewhere too, with reluctance on the part of the private sector to get involved. In Paddington, developers have to pay a community tax levied by the Council but most are not particularly concerned as to how the money is used. For example, a company in the area put 100 000 square feet of managed office space up for sale and their only concern was that it was sold. According to one of the PDT staff, when they do get involved private sector partners often favour 'feel good' projects and when this happens it works against the PDT planning strategically.

In many ways, NLP is a conventional UK urban development partnership that fits into an evolving policy strategy that has recognized the value of engaging with people at the neighbourhood level. However, not all community initiatives are successful and not all neighbourhoods well organized. Nor is NLP without its problems. However, the experience of North Paddington is interesting and there have been some considerable successes that, above all, derive from community engagement with the process, facilitated by a skilled and dedicated team in the PDT. Particularly impressive has been the way the competence and innovation of the PDT has achieved strategic management in partnership with government agencies and coordination with the private sector, as well as enabling stewardship of multiple community-level organizations and the oversight of their projects. As such it is worth saying something about the Trust's management, staffing, and procedures. Overall responsibility of the management of the PDT rests with Trustees who determine policy and supervise the performance of Trust operations. Trustees are made up of local people including representatives from core funders. The Chief Executive reports regularly to the Board and supervises 15 staff members organized in four teams: Programme Management and Development; Finance; Neighbourhood Renewal; and Youth and Community Development. He also carries out day-to-day management of the PDT on behalf of the Board.

In the Programme Management and Development Department two staff members are entirely devoted to assessing and supporting programmes organized under each of the four themes. They also manage the selection process that takes place through the theme groups, which are made up of representatives of community-based organizations, public sector organizations, and local people. For example, the theme group on Education and Young People might ask for expressions of interest and the theme group will assess these against the strategic criteria for the group. The full proposals go to an appraisal group elected by the theme group that either accepts, rejects, or asks for more information from the group. The theme group has full powers of allocation up to £75 000, after which the proposal goes to the Board. Once a project has been appraised and approved it gets a grant agreement. It has to provide documentation accounting for expenditure, is paper monitored on a quarterly basis and physically monitored annually. For smaller funds especially, the monitoring requirements are minimal and the PDT has opted to be relatively soft in terms of auditing. Despite this, when PDT's programme management systems were extensively audited on behalf of the London Development Agency in 2003, they scored 69 per cent on performance and were rated in the top ten best SRB programme management systems in London (PDT, 2004: 8). In explaining this success the Chief Executive reported that:

> Almost no one has taken advantage yet. There was one, but we recovered. We have been through some crises in community management and have dealt with them without hysteria. So there are learning curves. But it is a robust system. I am a great believer in community enterprise and that you should empower as many people as possible to do what they can. Our real challenge is to bring big money into the neighbourhood against a strategic plan.

Similarly, as shown in Table 8.1, although there is light touch monitoring this does not mean ignoring the evidence-base of progress made. Although significant attention is placed on building confidence, participation, and processes, the PDT can demonstrate tangible and calculable outputs too.

In the final analysis, the success of the PDT derives from firm links into the community, a clear mission, and strong organizational and management principles. However, its sustainability depends as much on factors lying outside its control than on its own track record and performance. Sadly this is often the case for many successful local funds. In the case of NLP, this is a finite programme that may come to an end in 2006 with the conclusion of the SRB award. The PDT has a range of other partnerships and funders and is confident it can continue working until 2015. At present it seems secure, with a community participation approach informing strategies – such as the London Development Agency (LDA) and its Economic Development Strategy, and the Westminster City Partnership's Neighbourhood Renewal Strategy. The PDT is also currently benefiting from government initiatives, such as the Westminster City Council Civic Renewal Strategy (CRS), which incorporates the formation of a Local Strategic Partnership; the current Labour Government's Neighbourhood Renewal Strategy; the formation of Primary Care Trusts by the Department of Health; and a range of community-orientated government initiatives across all departments. All of these initiatives impact on regeneration and renewal in North Paddington and the work of the PDT, which facilitates partnership from the community perspective. At present, public policy is generally geared towards community participation and there are plenty of micro-level actors within the planning framework. However, whether there is 'new life' for the PDT in the longer term will depend very much on the on-going commitment of successive British governments to community-led regeneration and community-led strategies.

CHALLENGE FUNDS AND BRITISH DEVELOPMENT AID

It was enthusiasm over the British experiment with challenge funds and the potential for community-led initiatives in the context of multi-sectoral part-nerships that led the DFID to consider adopting this approach in the context of the UK's aid programmes. As discussed in Chapter Six, DFID has revised its funding instruments. In addition to DBS it has introduced Partnership Programme Agreements with UK-based international NGOs and a suite of four challenge funds – the Business Linkages Challenge Fund (BLCF), the Financial Deepening Challenge Fund (FDCF), the Civil Society Challenge Fund (CSCF), and the Mini Challenge Fund, along with numerous other small country-based funds. Only one is briefly discussed here. The CSCF was set up in July 2000 to replace the Joint Funding Scheme (JFS), which was an instrument by which DFID provided 'matched funding' for projects outside its bilateral country programmes. NGOs could apply to the Scheme for up to 50 per cent of the funding required for a project, and, at the end of the fund-ing period, could apply for further resources to continue the project. Around £37 million annually was distributed through the JFS in its last three years. The CSCF was designed as one of several mechanisms by which DFID sought to both broaden and deepen its engagement with civil society in the UK. This was with a view towards maintaining its links with international organiza-tions such as Oxfam, ActionAid, SCF, and Christian Aid, as well as less wellknown NGOs. DFID also sought to build links with less conventionally funded organizations, such as trade unions, worker organizations, local authorities, and private sector organizations. The CSCF has also moved beyond discrete development projects to attempt to give increased voice to the poor and greater influence over the decision-makers who affect their lives. Hence the CEF discussed in Chapter Six is a typical example of this model, even though it was funded out of the Treasury.

Resources under the CSCF were allocated from April 2000 according to priority themes, with DFID stating that precedence would be given to ini-tiatives in its target themes. These change from time to time but are gener-ally focused on enhancing the capacity of poor, marginalized, or excluded people to participate in public policy formulation at local, national, or international levels and on developing the skills of poor people to interact effectively with decision-makers. The development of skills relevant to budget-tracking in some of the countries where the CEF is more advanced would be a good example of this taking route. While welcoming the CSCF and its approach, some of the more established UK-based NGOs have done so cautiously, because there are more organizations competing for funds through the same channel with only a limited increase in budget allocation. Moreover, whereas under the JFS it was possible to apply for a second *tranche* of funding for a project, there is be a five-year limit on the duration of funding for projects under the CSCF. This is a deliberate feature of the CSCF design, which recognizes that the kind of relationship-building and capacity enhancement envisaged by the Fund take longer than shorter-term projects, but this then is balanced by the need to maintain sufficient funds to attract new applicants.

The re-focusing of DFID's spending in relation to civil society has affected different UK NGOs in different ways. Those that were engaged in mobilization and advocacy work with a wide range of partners have benefited, while those concerned primarily with service delivery have suffered. A number of the larger international NGOs do both, gaining credibility and legitimacy in their policy-influencing work through their detailed knowledge of needs on the ground, derived from their role in service delivery. Hence, there has been quite widespread concern that under the CSCF this will be neglected and that their reach will be limited, by being forced to desert work in areas where local civil society is weak or fragmented. The CSCF has also given rise to greater competition among UK-based NGOs and this has led them having to spend scarce resources on building up and maintaining a high organizational profile. In some cases the challenge fund has led to enhanced cooperation, such as through the CEF, but it can also reduce the potential for inter-NGO cooperation. A further objection that has been raised is that in responding to challenges posed by a constantly changing funding environment, it may become difficult for UK-based NGOs to maintain their own integrity and independence while still securing funding for their work. These problems are not exclusive to international development NGOs and, as with not-for-profit organizations – such as the PDT – operating in the UK, they are diversifying their funding base and exploring new funding partnerships. In the meantime, DFID is seeking to establish the challenge fund model in developing countries themselves. The following section profiles an example of this strategy, in relation to fostering community-led urban development in Uganda.

THE CITY–COMMUNITY CHALLENGE FUND PILOT PROGRAMME IN UGANDA

The C3 was a pilot programme set up by DFID in both Uganda and Zambia in September 2000. It was designed along the lines of community-led area-based urban development and in conception and execution has more in common with UK IAD partnerships such as NLP, than some of the other DFID challenge funds discussed above. Indeed, the primary aim of the C3 programme was very close to that of the PDT: to assist organizations of the urban poor and their representative local authorities to undertake localized initiatives that provide resources for small-scale innovative activities of broad community benefit.

The Infrastructure and Urban Development Division (IUDD) of DFID provided £1 000 000 for a two-year pilot programme, with an extension phase of a further year agreed within this budget, plus a further extension with an increased financial contribution of £300 000 made via UN-Habitat who took over the C3 pilot in 2004. Critical to the C3 model was the development of effective and transferable mechanisms that could channel multiple small-scale funds to such initiatives, within the context of urban development partnerships involving organized communities, CSOs, different levels of government, and the private sector. A secondary aim was to assess the viability of challenge funds, and more specifically the C3 methodology, as a mechanism for international development agencies to reach and empower the urban poor. This aspect is discussed in more detail in relation to the Zambian experience in Chapter Nine. During the pilot phase the Local Government International Bureau (LGIB) was the international programme manager for Uganda. Their local partner was the Uganda Local Authorities Association (ULAA) in Kampala, which now runs C3 in the post-pilot phase, and governance of the programme was through a National Coordination Committee (NCC). C3 was implemented in two cities, Kampala and Jinja.

Uganda is predominantly a rural country, with 85 per cent of its 22 million people living in the countryside. Nevertheless, urbanization in Uganda is on the increase due to population growth and rural–urban migration. A city designed for 600 000 residents, the capital city Kampala is now estimated to have 1.5 million residents, as well as a much larger daytime population who work and do business in the city and who use its infrastructure and facilities. Jinja is the second largest town in Uganda, with a population of over 100 000, which doubles in the daytime. Located at the source of the White Nile, it was founded in 1901 as a colonial administrative centre and became a municipality in 1957. The town is situated close to a major hydro-electric power station and supports a metal founding industry as well as industries associated with processing the produce of the surrounding region, including tobacco production and brewing. Though a much smaller urban centre, Jinja faces its own pressures. The economy of Jinja was devastated by the factory and enterprise closures that followed the flight of Ugandan Asians who were persecuted by Idi Amin and it has not yet fully recovered. This led to high levels of long-term unemployment. In both these contexts assistance to urban areas has become a necessity rather than a luxury.

Another important contextual issue of relevance to C3 is decentralization. Until 1986, government in Uganda was tightly centralized and there was very little role for local-level decision-making, particularly over resource use and allocation. However, local governments thereafter were progressively granted more authority. In 1993 the party of government, the National Resistance Movement (NRM), adopted decentralization as a means to strengthen democracy and improve social service provision in the country. The 1995 Constitution of the Republic of Uganda and the Local

Government Act of 1997 formalized this. Decentralization involved the transfer of administrative fiscal and financial powers from the centre to locally elected district and lower councils that grew out of the Resistance Council system that was first established by the National Resistance Army between 1981 and 1985. This system was based on village councils, which have now been transformed into Local Councils (LCs), the apex being the district (or municipality in the case of cities), with four levels (LC1–4) below them. These councils are constituted by elected representatives, with one third of positions on all local councils being reserved for women, and with over 10 000 women elected to local government in 1998 (Ahikire, 2003: 213). Drawing on Government of Uganda documentation, Kiyaga (2002: 15) identifies the objectives of decentralization in the country as follows:

> This extensive devolution of power is intended to improve service delivery by shifting responsibility for policy implementation to the beneficiaries themselves; to promote good governance by placing emphasis on transparency and accountability in the management of public affairs; to develop, broaden and deepen political and administrative competence at local level; to facilitate democratization by promoting inclusive, representative and gender-sensitive decision-making; and to alleviate poverty through collaborative efforts between central and local governments, development partners, NGOs, CBOs, the private sector and other stakeholders.

However, as pointed out in Chapter Two, there is a lot of well-justified scepticism about the democratic potential of decentralization, or even its capacity to effect enhanced popular participation or improved service delivery. In Africa as elsewhere, decentralization has been seen as a vehicle for increasing public support for central government (Mutizwa-Mangiza and Conyers, 1996) and as an agenda promoted by donors. While in Uganda political expediency may well be part of the decentralization agenda for central government and donors alike, openings nevertheless have been created for those not used to having voice.

It was in this broad context that the C3 pilot programme aimed to assist disadvantaged urban communities address material deprivation and to better leverage resources and institutional support from government at different levels, donors, NGOs, and the private sector. The overall programme was informed by a livelihoods perspective, with livelihood opportunities understood as being comprised not only of direct access to income generation but also access to assets and human development inputs such as education, health care, housing, and services. However, equally important was an emphasis on governance and support to people in urban communities so that they might use the decentralization process more effectively. At the same time it was seen as important to enhance the capacity of local authorities to respond to community-led initiatives and development demands. In Kampala C3 was piloted in Kawempe Division, one of the city's four divisions embracing the most densely settled part of the capital city. Kawempe has an estimated population of over 200 000 and is a mixed income settlement. Infrastructure levels are also mixed, with the area as a whole not connected to the main sewerage system. Within Kawempe there are many informal settlements with poor water supply and sanitation, no drainage, inadequate solid waste collection, and minimal amenities. Formal employment is scarce and the majority of low-income residents work in the informal economy. It was for this reason, and because people's immediate needs were for income, that the C3 programme in Kawempe concentrated at first almost exclusively on micro-credit schemes. This was an important early lesson in terms of the transferability of lessons from the North to the South. In the absence of basic welfare support and social safety nets, it is difficult to get communities engaged in collective action towards the development of what are perceived as less pressing needs such as infrastructure and services.

Nevertheless, this was a problem for the programme as micro-credit was not the intended focus of C3 at all. In Uganda people have experienced numerous different development fashions, one of the more persistent being a propensity on the part of donors and NGOs towards supporting micro-credit credit programmes. From the perspective of the ULAA and the NCC, not only did this deviate from the objectives of C3 but also it was not a particularly original approach, thus undermining one of the principal aims of the pilot – innovation. However, it should not have come as a surprise. When projects are demand-driven people often come up with the ideas they already know about and find it difficult to imagine other possibilities. Moreover, an important principle of C3 was that initiatives were to be community driven and the Local Implementation Unit (LIU) in Kawempe Division strongly lobbied for micro-finance. In this situation, it was difficult for the ULAA and NCC to refuse, despite their misgivings about their own expertise and C3's capacity to manage this project in a specialist and already crowded field. Loans were provided ranging from the equivalent of around £16 to £800. Projects included fish farming, poultry projects, mirror manufacture and framing, broom making, furniture making, charcoal making, and small fresh produce stalls. Beneficiaries remained overwhelmingly individual and the match-funding element that was supposed to take place through onward lending to a new round of beneficiaries from profits was slow to take off. To ensure that this happened and because C3 was not set up to support individual beneficiaries outside of some sort of community-level collective action, the LIU insisted on the formation of a Beneficiaries' Association that could fulfil a regulatory and coordinating role and take responsibility for managing the revolving fund.

During the early phases of implementation, the C3 programme in Kawempe exhibited all the classic problems of micro-finance projects and those discussed in Chapter One in relation to social funds. These included resources not reaching the poorest, elite capture of resources at the expense of more deserving residents, and support to unsuitable or unsustainable income-generating projects. Nevertheless, over time a number of positive changes took place. There were strong local-level structures in place and they were used to ensure that beneficiaries accounted for themselves and why they deserved a grant, how they would use it, and how they would ensure they contributed to a revolving fund that would benefit others, once their ventures succeeded. This was sometime a fraught process. For example, when a local politician tried to use C3 for campaign purposes by claiming to have brought C3 resources to Kawempe he was summoned by the LIU and exposed as a fraud. Even among the grantees there were tensions. For instance, the first beneficiary selected in Kawempe, who was a fishmonger, was worried that other stallholders in Kawempe Market who had not been awarded a grant would be jealous and take it out on him. In time, these problems subsided as the rate of applications and number of grantees increased. This occurred partly through word of mouth and partly because of an active LIU, which engaged in a vigorous local publicity drive. Although things got easier when more people benefited from the fund, the social mobilization aims of the fund were never very successful in Kawempe.

Kawempe Division is slowly being encouraged to shift its focus of support towards other areas. This was assisted by a visit to C3 projects in Jinja. Here, Kawempe representatives saw the possibility of doing things differently and as a result applications for projects related to social and other services started coming through. In Jinja, C3 has been implemented in Mpumudde Division, recognized as the most disadvantaged and least densely settled of Jinja's three divisions. Mpumudde is a relatively sparsely populated peri-urban area of the municipality, with a population of over 20 000 and covering an area of 1 156.5 hectares. In Mpumudde, despite having the highest level of unemployment in Jinja, the residents identified lack of shelter as a priority problem. Hence the focus of C3 in Jinja has been primarily on developing a low-cost, self-help housing programme. As in Kawempe, this was not particularly innovative – indeed, there were a number of contenders ready to present their low-cost brick-making machine for hire to the project. Hence, the ULAA and NCC also had some misgivings about C3 in Jinja but again decided to go with the community.

The C3 project in Mapumudde has the advantage of visible delivery. Houses comprise four rooms, are plastered, and have corrugated iron roofs. They were built, with a manual sand/cement block press that was the invention of a local professor, by community members taking turns on a rotation basis, with eight households building a set of eight houses. The average time to construct a house is currently 21 days. Each household is allocated a grant of £1 400, based on the cost of the materials for the house, and an additional micro-enterprise grant of £200 that householders can use to generate income to repay the costs of building. In addition, some individuals have benefited from training in block making and business skills. Grants have also been made to groups, for example, for the repair of septic tanks and for mowing machines to be used in micro-enterprise. The resources needed for housing construction, even the low-cost variety such as in Jinja, were greater than those for most micro-enterprises proposed in the Kawempe programme and it was feared that the less vocal or able might be excluded. It seems though that allocation has been fairly accountable and from the outset C3 in Jinja was more effective than in Kampala in leveraging additional resources through effective engagement with the local authority.

Unlike Kawempe, where for a long time the local council simply kept a watching brief on C3, in Mpumudde the C3 process benefited from strong commitment and personal oversight on the part of the Assistant Town Clerk. He saw in C3 an opportunity for the Jinja Municipality to be responsive to citizen priorities and to attract additional resources. The Municipality has been proactive in making links between C3 in Mpumudde and other urban and community development projects and organizations in Jinja. It has leveraged significant funds from alternative sources, while ploughing in additional resources of its own. In this way, the Council has expanded services to previously unreached urban groups in Mpumudde – co-funding an onsite primary school, inviting private companies to supply utilities, and providing social support through a clinic and a care home for street children. Kampala Municipality has been less forthcoming, which may be due to the fact that C3 got off to a rocky start in Kawempe, or that, being the capital city, Kampala's local government is much more distant than in other municipalities, or that in the capital city where donors are thicker on the ground, C3 is simply seen as too small in funding terms. Jinja is a much smaller town, and local personalities such as the Town Clerk have played an important catalytic role. Under these circumstances, C3's methodology and approach have come more swiftly to influence local authority practice although it is too early to assess with what sustainability.

Given that a decentralization process was already underway in Uganda and that the focus of activities lacked innovation, is it legitimate to ask whether C3 added any value? In both sites C3 was successful in linking local politicians to local citizens and it helped facilitate organized citizens to engage more effectively with their representative local authorities. On the C3 projects people learnt a range of things, from the best price for a bag of cement, to asking for and keeping receipts, to effective routes of access to decision-makers and how to identify and engage with the key issues on their agendas. For some officials of local councils their image improved, as they were no longer seen as being overwhelmingly preoccupied with main roads and services but also as concerned with neighbourhoods and people. One of the most positive outcomes of C3 in Uganda has been the impact of the pilot in terms of increased transparency and accountability, as people were able to hold leaders to account for C3 funds. For example, in the Kawempe Division, political capture saw some of the funds being channelled to party political supporters, many of whom failed to meet even the most lax criteria for identifying households in poverty. Nevertheless, monitoring through C3 structures, along with support from local council extension workers, served to gradually inform people of the programme and its aims, and to alert them to such examples of malfeasance. This, together with regular publicity, notably through community radio and notice boards, encouraged grantees and potential grantees to harass members of the LIU if there were problems with selection and management of the funds. Given an entrenched but imperfect decentralization process, perhaps the most important contribution of C3 was providing tangible resources, however minimal, around which people, politicians, and officials could negotiate. This proved to be an effective catalyst in a context where decentralization saw few real funds reaching the local level.

In its second phase, C3 is spreading to and being taken up by other urban centres. The focus has shifted towards using small funds as a way of strengthening institutional arrangements and enhancing local governance. There is an aim to up-scale C3 and to encourage its spread beyond an area-based approach. As the shift takes place from implementing a limited pilot project to extending C3 more widely across Uganda, the choice of the ULAA as manager of C3 becomes more strategic. The ULAA's role is changing from one of simply managing funds to one of developing and spreading the C3 approach. This is a more appropriate activity for an association of local authorities and ULAA is well placed as an organization to undertake the broad task of disseminating and rolling out the programme, given its function of representing local governments and promoting the decentralization process in Uganda. On its own, C3 is not much different from hundreds of other small grant programmes. However, as a component of a broader strategy of democratic decentralization it can provide the resources around which state society relations can begin to coalesce.

CONCLUSION

In a number of respects, NLP and the C3 in Uganda are driven by similar policy trajectories, even though in wildly different contexts that are thousands of miles apart and where the size of realistic and usable funding grants differ enormously. In the UK, the impact of a decade and a half of Conservative government was to considerably weaken traditional forms of post-War local government, and this has been firmly entrenched by two electoral terms of New Labour government. As Stoker and Wilson (2004b: 249) put it:

> The emergence of local public service agreements and local strategic partnerships confirm the drift away from the traditional form of a relatively autonomous multi-purpose system of local councils. The message to traditionalists from New Labour is: you thought it was all over; well, it is now.

According to Stoker and Wilson, this has happened amidst 'much rhetoric about the need for partnership and better community planning' with top-down tutelage and centralized policy agendas accompanied by what they call the 'new localism' whereby local councils have to share decision-making responsibility with others at the local level in a realistic response to 'the complexity of modern governance' (ibid.: 253).

In Uganda too, the challenge fund model fits in well with donor pressure on the Ugandan government towards development solutions based on multi-sector partnerships. However, despite praise by international donors for the closely connected decentralization process, this was not simply a technical exercise in Uganda and nor did it constitute a complete break with the centralizing tendencies of previous governments. President Yoweri Museveni, for more than a decade the darling of World Bank observers, has nevertheless exercised a personalized and ethnically based brand of politics that retains elements of authoritarianism. This is not to say that political spaces have not opened up following Museveni's takeover. In part this resulted from the fact that the NRM took time to consolidate its control over the country as a whole (Tripp, 2000: 55). In part, however, it resulted from ordinary people seizing the political spaces that opened up, as indeed happened in the UK. Thus one of the lessons to come out of reviewing the experiences of NLP in London and C3 in Uganda is that people respond to and make use of opportunities for cohesion and advancement where they exist. In doing so, they are not always able to respond to the challenge dimensions of small funds, particularly where exposure to different options or imaginings is limited. While even the most deprived residents of Paddington might be guided through the web sites of other regeneration areas to get ideas and draw comparisons, this was not possible in the informal settlements of Kampala and Jinja. However, in both cases exchange visits were helpful, both between the two Ugandan cities and from the other C3 pilot programme in Zambia.

Clearly some people are more adept at responding to opportunities than others and it is well known that communities can be pernicious social and political arenas that exclude as much as they generate cohesion. Important in ensuring that the most disadvantaged are not left behind in the process and that they are able to make the most of creative spaces is the role of intermediary organizations. In the absence of either the PDT in Paddington or the ULAA and its staff in Kampala and Jinja, it is doubtful whether ordinary citizens would have had the confidence or savoir-faire to effectively engage local politicians, government officials, and urban professionals and draw them into partnerships to advance their local agendas. In this context it is probably correct to say that there is no 'right' organization to play that role. The C3 pilot programme in Zambia was managed locally by a Zambian urban NGO, supported by CARE International. In Uganda, given the importance accorded to decentralization, the role of the ULAA became particularly important in terms of linking C3 into local government processes and procedures and in scaling-out the C3 approach from the pilot areas to other districts and urban centres. In London, NLP benefited from management by such an entrepreneurial and business-minded not-for-profit organization as the PDT, that was able to act as its advocate but engage on equal terms with private sector actors, Westminster Council and the LDA. The sustainability of regeneration in North Paddington will also be helped by a foresighted organization that is diversifying its funding partnerships so that it will not fall prey to the vagaries of central government policy change at any one time. Similarly, in Uganda the ULAA is not relying on continuous funding from DFID or UN-Habitat but is actively seeking support from other donors in order to consolidate its achievements in Kawempe and Mpumudde and to extend them by example to other areas of Kampala and Jinja and other parts of Uganda.

Another feature shared by NLP and C3 was the difficulty experienced in leveraging resources and support from the private sector. In Paddington, from the perspective of the PDT, it was evident that private sector involvement in local partnerships occurred only in response to carrots (such as bidding or development opportunities) or sticks (such as taxation). This is consistent with much of the thinking on CSR discussed in Chapter Three, which identifies the main business of the private sector as making profits and points out that their incentive for involvement in social development therefore remains confined to advancing if not their profits directly, then their visibility and profile. In Uganda, the ULAA was equally frustrated by efforts to leverage resources from the private sector. Apart from some interest from potential developers they have so far had to content themselves with token funds from one of the international banks operating in the country.

For all these similarities there are sufficient differences and diverging experiences to strike a note of caution when seeking to transfer lessons from one context to another. The difficulties experienced by C3 in replicating a typical urban development challenge fund model in Kampala and the hijacking of this approach by local residents towards micro-credit for income earning opportunities, speak volumes about the challenges of trying to implement projects concerned with goods of collective consumption such as infrastructure and services in contexts where people may find it difficult to feed themselves in the absence of a welfare state or even the most basic of social safety nets. There are also differences in the approaches of the two countries to community-led partnerships and their relationship with local government. In the UK there is a strong feeling that special-purpose agencies, such as the PDT, and partnership-based funding as a central policy instrument challenge local political sovereignty (Sketcher, 2004: 35). In Uganda the focus of C3 was not to undermine government at any level but to hold it to account and to ensure its lines of accountability operated both downwards towards citizens and communities as well as upwards towards central government. For local funds to animate this agenda requires that they are as autonomous as possible from government at any level, while directing their activities towards state society engagement. This in turn requires that governments and donors maintain an arm's length and hand's off approach to the management of such funds. This is not always easy to achieve. The following and last section of the book turns attention to the inside view of local funds and the challenges of management and implementation.

PART III

MANAGING LOCAL FUNDS: THE INSIDE VIEW

The delivery and management of local funds: learning by doing in Zambia and Bangladesh

INTRODUCTION

This chapter returns to some of the operational issues raised in relation to local funds in Chapter One. It traces two young local funds, the City–Community Challenge Fund (C3) for urban governance and development in Zambia and the Manusher Jonno (MJ) fund for human rights and governance in Bangladesh. Recognizing local funds both as financing instruments and as funding agencies, the focus here is on where they are best located and how they are best delivered and managed. As argued in the introductory chapter, there is little dispute that local funds are the product of external agents, whether central governments, charitable foundations, or international development agencies. However, as subsequent chapters have illustrated, there are a range of models in terms of their relationship with governments and how they should be managed. This chapter focuses on two local funds supported by DFID and managed by CARE International, a global humanitarian consortium of 12 national organizations that work with disadvantaged people in 70 of the world's poorest countries. CARE has been the implementing organization for three significant DFID-funded grant-making programmes or challenge funds, C3 in Zambia, MJ in Bangladesh, and FCS in Tanzania, profiled in Chapter Six. C3 is now funded through the Urban Management Programme (UMP) in UN-Habitat but is still managed by CARE. MJ in Bangladesh is still a DFID programme overseen by CARE but it is destined to become an independent Bangladeshi trust within a few years, along similar lines to the FCS.

Although C3 and MJ vary in their focus, structure, and size, as well as the nature of their set up, there are some interesting parallels and similar management challenges. The discussion begins with a profile of C3 in Zambia, focusing on efforts to engage local government in community led development, as well as issues of management, monitoring, and evaluation. It then turns to the experience of MJ in Bangladesh, focusing on the challenges of addressing human rights and governance with civil society organizations used to working independently of government and in a difficult external environment. Here too management issues are highlighted, alongside the demands placed on an organization preparing itself for independent trust status.

THE CITY–COMMUNITY CHALLENGE FUND IN ZAMBIA

In Zambia C3 began in October 2000 with a sum of £500 000 from DFID managed by CARE Zambia (CAREZ) and official launches in the largest city on the Copperbelt, Ndola on 31 May 2001 and in the capital city Lusaka on 1 June 2001. Unlike the area-based approach adopted in C3 in Uganda, the goal of C3 in Zambia was to ensure breadth of coverage and spread across cities. C3 Zambia was also keen for the C3 methodology to penetrate government as soon as possible. This was difficult in the case of Lusaka City Council (LCC) and like C3 in Kampala in Uganda, establishing the programme in the capital city proved to be complex. In the smaller city of Ndola, the Ndola City Council (NCC) was more receptive and from the outset it became an important partner. The other aspect of the C3 experience in Zambia that offers broader lessons is the streamlined management approach that was worked out in a sometimes difficult process of 'learning-by-doing' and the light touch management tools that were developed to ensure that red tape and bureaucracy did not exclude the busy, the illiterate, and the most needy. These are discussed in some detail below.

Zambia is the second most urbanized country in Africa and with half the country's population of over 10 million living in cities and towns characterized by sprawling informal settlements and poor infrastructure and services. Zambia's urban population is also overwhelmingly poor with about half of those of working age being unemployed. Urban poverty in Zambia is compounded by two additional contingent factors. The first is the high impact of HIV/AIDS and the second is drought, linked to weaknesses across the agricultural sector and leading to conditions that at times have bordered on famine, placing greater strain on public and private resources in the cities. Lusaka has an estimated population of 2.5 million and the poorest live in densely settled compounds or informal settlements on the outskirts of the city. Ndola was an important urban centre for the Zambian Copperbelt but its fortunes declined along with those of copper, the price of which hit rock bottom in 2001. Up to 80 per cent of the city's population is thought to be unemployed.

This scenario represents a major development challenge for cash strapped municipal governments that have found it impossible to keep up with the demand for infrastructure development and service delivery. Indeed, in Lusaka and Ndola at the time of the C3 pilot most council staff had to wait for their salaries, which were many months in arrears. As a result both the LCC and NCC were unable to deliver even the most basic services, let alone engage in developmental initiatives in poorly served areas. Strikes and go-slows were commonplace and senior management could not implement reforms or innovations in the face of crushing debts and low staff morale. These are trying conditions under which to try and initiate a challenge fund. Hence Zambia was an interesting choice of location for the piloting of an urban challenge fund.

Zambia was no stranger to social funds, notably the Zambian Social Investment Fund (ZAMSIF) funded by the World Bank to the tune of over US$64 million and focused on poverty reduction through support to District Planning. Beginning in July 2000 ZAMSIF has spent US$13 million supporting 156 community-based projects to date. Key bilateral donors are engaged in ZAMSIF, which is now providing block grants to district author-ities that can show evidence of capacity to manage local poverty reduction initiatives. An important dimension of the overall conditions in which C3 was piloted in Zambia was the desultory if not moribund decentralization process and the fact that ZAMSIF funds are being used to encourage it. This, together with its focus on the district (and city) level meant that there was a niche for C3 to work locally and at micro-level in ways that could articulate both with ZAMSIF and the city councils. Here UI and CARE Zambia were assisted by their experience and reputation in the field of urban development and the fact that both LCC and NCC had worked with them over a number of years, developing what became known as area-based organizations (ABOs) through the registration of Resident Development Committees (RDCs).

The original goal of C3 was to assist organizations of the urban poor and their representative local authorities to undertake localized poverty eradi-cation initiatives, through the provision of resources for small-scale inno-vative activities of broad community benefit. This is done through grants for small, medium, and large project funds. Small grants are for projects costing up to a maximum of the Zambian Kwacha equivalent of US$5 000. Approval for these projects is delegated the C3 management team, follow-ing criteria developed by the C3 national advisory group (NAG). They are targeted at low cost, tightly focused, and short duration projects. Simple, fast track application and approval procedures aim to encourage applica-tions from the most excluded groups. Medium cost and longer-term initia-tives are those between $5 000 and $10 000 and those over $10 000. They face tighter procedures, although delegated authority for approval still rests with C3 management. Large projects are those over $10 000 and for approval these need authorization from the NAG.

A second goal of the pilot phase was to assess the viability of challenge funds as a mechanism by which international development agencies such as DFID might reach and empower poor people, particularly within the context of direct budget support, discussed in Chapter Six. A third goal of the pilot was to develop effective and transferable mechanisms that were capable of channelling multiple small-scale funds to community-led initia-tives in the context of urban development partnerships ideally involving government agencies, CSOs, and the private sector. The general conditions that apply to all sizes of grant are as follows:

- All projects should complement City Council activities.
- All projects must have tangible (real/evident and measurable) results.
- All projects must be able to prove the need for their proposal.

- Only groups/organizations can apply and they must contribute to the project in cash or in kind from their own resources or raised from elsewhere.
- Urban INSAKA must have open access to all projects funded by C3.
- Groups/organizations must accept that their details (for example group name, address, names of leaders, size of funds received and the purpose of the funds) will be publicized (for example in the Urban INSAKA newsletter and newspapers) on receiving funds.
- There is no limit to the number of times a group can apply. Those groups that have received C3 funds before must prove that they have finalized what they applied for previously.
- All activities must be legitimate and project applicants are solely responsible for fulfilling any related statuary taxation requirements.

Projects are excluded that aim to do things that typically are within the remit of central government, i.e. government ministries, as opposed to local government.

In order to elaborate on the processes involved it is necessary to say something about the management of the C3 programme as a whole. This is illustrated schematically in Figure 9.1. Strategic management (Level 1) took place through the International Management Project Unit (IPMU), which included CARE International UK as the Fund Managers for C3 Zambia,

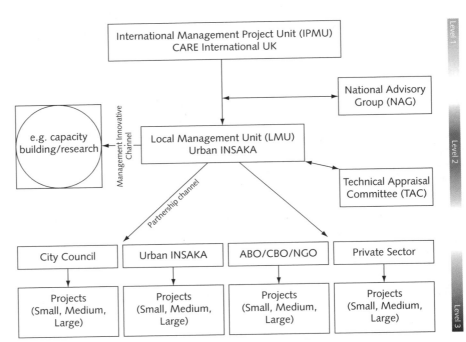

Figure 9.1   City Community Challenge Fund Management Channels
Source: CARE Zambia and Urban INSAKA (2002)

LGIB as the Fund Managers for C3 Uganda, and others. The UK external evaluator sat on the IPMU as an observer. Level 1 management subsequently fell to UN-Habitat's UMP when DFID stopped funding C3 directly. The Local Management Unit (LMU) in Zambia (Level 2) is a local NGO, Urban INSAKA (UI), supported by CARE and based in Lusaka. UI is steered by a National Advisory Group (NAG). The members were selected for their experience and expertise or organizational location, in areas that were thought would add value to the performance of C3. At present there are representatives from Barclays Bank, Canada Fund, United Nations Development Programme, University of Zambia, Zambia Chamber of Small and Medium Scale Business Associations, RDCs, the Ministry of Local Government and Housing, the LCC, and NCC and CARE (as the Secretariat). The NAG works on a voluntary basis to terms of reference they helped draw up and approved. In addition to not being paid any allowances for their services, they are not involved in the approval process of projects. UI runs a Technical Appraisal Committee (TAC) that reviews and selects proposals through two working committees, one approving grants up to US$10 000 and the other for those above US$10 000. They comprise members of the city councils, community representatives, NGOs, and CARE (as Secretariat). The process is overseen by UI, which is a Level 3 partner (see Figure 9.1). It was hoped that other Level 3 partners would emerge during the pilot phase, particularly the city councils but also some of the RDCs. However, so far only Ndola City Council has joined UI as a Level 3 partner.

C3 was designed to promote partnerships according to the challenge fund model but it was particularly concerned to engage the city councils because:

- they are permanent institutions while NGOs and CSOs tend to be time bound;
- local authorities are mandated to delivery services and should both be supported and held to account on this; and
- local authorities are meant to work with CSOs and provide support to some of these organizations.

Thus it was agreed from the outset that C3 funds in Zambia would complement or reinforce city council activities. Longer-term goals were to build the capacities of city councils to deliver services in concert with communities and of communities to confidently engage with local authorities. By narrowing the focus of projects in this way, C3 ensured that it would receive technical assistance from LCC and NCC, which had the expertise in the relevant service delivery areas. As much as possible UI tried to work through existing structures and organizations and avoid creating parallel structures. Partnership arrangements were a condition for projects above US$5 000 and applicants signed memorandums of understanding or contracts to encourage the local authority and other partners to provide support to the projects over the long run so that they could remain sustainable. Although CARE manages C3 Zambia it is implemented in partnership with the city councils for sustainability purposes and capacity building for the two city councils has been a key aspect of project implementation. One challenge has been to ensure regular funding for the C3 approach, both externally from donors but also internally from government. In Lusaka the Council has slowly increased its interest in and support for C3 whereas in Ndola the municipality was enthusiastic from the start, becoming a Level 3 partner almost immediately.

The issue of match funding is often a vexed one in low-income contexts, as pointed out in Chapter One. In Zambia, lack of resources was a problem not only for the two cash-strapped councils but also for poor urban residents, many without jobs or regular incomes. However, DFID's contract with CARE required that all applicant groups have to show a 50 per cent contribution to the projects they want implemented. The C3 management team has had to be imaginative and innovative in assessing this. Contributions are accepted in cash or kind or both. In kind contributions are calculated and recorded by C3 staff on behalf of the applicants, for example, by valuing their labour and the time they spend on C3 activities, including, for instance, preparing the proposal, community labour on projects, time spent in organizing participation and in meetings. In both cities C3 achieved buy-in from area-based organizations and community groups. As one of the aims of C3 is to leverage resources from other donors, if they support the same project as C3 is funding, this is also included as an external contribution to the 50 per cent match fund . Monitoring has shown that contributions from other donor funds have more than doubled since the start of the project (Beall, 2003).

One example of how this has worked in practice can be drawn from the informal settlement of George in Lusaka. Here community leaders engaged the LCC in assisting with a drainage project. Community members contributed labour, the council contributed expertise, and a C3 grant covered the equipment. The project was then extended through support from the Japanese who were working on another infrastructure project nearby. Another example from Ndola was the construction of an ablution block in a local market, requested by market traders and delivered through a partnership between the NCC and the NGO Habitat for Humanity. Not all projects have been as ambitious. Some groups received only a little money, for example for literacy training or to clean up a park, on the grounds that this will have a wider impact on the community and its ability to engage in governance in the longer-term. Although seeking to avoid income-generating projects and spurning any drift towards a micro-credit model, in a context of quite acute urban poverty, it was felt that some small project funds could be approved to help tie-die clothing business and tailoring groups. A list of the first round of projects funded is provided in Table 9.1.

The success of C3 in Zambia has been due in part to the determined effort to engage local government and to strengthen communities in respect of their dealings with public authorities. However, the C3 methodology itself has also contributed, along with the way it was developed and

Table 9.1   Early C3 projects approved by type and grant size

Description of project	Amount approved in Kwacha (K4 000/US$1)
Drainage clearing	13 137 800.00
Train women in Business income generating activities – poultry, tie and dye, and knitting	3 550 000.00
Feasibility study of Soweto Market	25 012 055.00
To purchase tools and equipment to help boost the work of the group in order for them to manage the solid waste in Marrapodi	7 706 700.00
To construct a public toilet at the station	3 550 000.00
To construct a cultural centre for community social activities	36 760 000.00
To co-finance national conference on Local Government for participants	20 000 000.00
To purchase a truck for communities to use to transport the garbage from their compounds to the dump site	208 000 000.00
Skills training in tie and dye	9 040 000.00
Skills training in tie and dye	3 959 500.00
Skills training in cookery	1 450 000.00
Construction of wall fence around Chawama Community Hall	28 325 500.00
Drainage digging and stone pitching	42 576 000.00
Skills training in machine knitting	2 442 000.00
To develop cultural representation and artistic skills through art work within classrooms at Chipata Open Community School	20 000 000.00
To improve existing drainage and provide culverts in the market area in Chawama	45 500 000.00
To teach 25 men, 50 women, and 70 youths how to read and write.	6 800 000.00
Institution building and local governance	9 060 815.00
For urban projects and project management in Ndola	190 250 000.00
Garbage collection in Kabanana	6 000 000.00
Rehabilitation of community hall playing field	43 576 060.00
Construction of skill training centre	2 945 000.00
Adopting a park	20 400 000.00
Provide water	36 500 000.00
Skills training in tailoring and designing	17 554 800.00
Gender training and skills centre	53 089 000.00
Maintain security and develop market	9 703 328.00
Construct VIP toilets	22 446 300.00
Market development	14 640 950.00
To purchase tools and equipment for skills training in tailoring and design	34 628 000.00
To purchase tools and equipment for skills training in tailoring and design	15 000 000.00

applied in Zambia. Avoiding prescription beyond a basic adherence to the C3 methodology, C3 facilitates local authorities and communities in jointly setting their own targets and working arrangements. The mechanisms set in place allow for upward accountability to DFID and the UK taxpayer, while emphasizing downward accountability to local governments and citizens, on the grounds that C3 funds are 'owned' by the ultimate and intended beneficiaries. With this in mind, application, approval, and monitoring procedures were kept light touch in order that grantees were spared all but the most necessary reporting requirements. The processes and procedures are described in some detail here as they constitute a useful model that cannot be exported intact as a blueprint but they can serve as a basis for learning and adaptation to other contexts.

In considering the project management tools and procedures the criteria developed for evaluating the project are a useful starting point. The external evaluation was designed in consultation with the IPMU in London, as well as the C3 team in Zambia. C3 Zambia in turn set up their monitoring system in dialogue with the external evaluators to ensure that quarterly progress reports would be directly relevant to the evaluation. The purpose of the evaluation was to:

■ assess the efficiency, cost-effectiveness, and sustainability of the C3 fund mechanisms for donor agencies;

■ evaluate how institutional arrangements between local government, civil society organizations, the private sector, and donors can be enhanced through C3;

■ provide a methodology that can track efficiency, process, and outcomes within the context of a modified Livelihoods Framework focused at the city level.

The process of the evaluation sought to strike a balance between, on the one hand, working with pre-defined indicators project results that were agreed to be significant by the evaluation team and fund managers and, on the other, being participatory and responsive to the expectations and results as defined by other groups involved in the process.

The aim was for the C3 fund to be both light in touch and fleet of foot. It was recognized that an over-prescribed evaluation would obstruct this aim, so verification of indicators was achieved through a combination of information drawn from the C3 management systems about applications and approvals, together with manageable survey work related only to those involved directly with C3 programmes, observational techniques, key informant interviews, and focus group discussions. These are discussed in more detail below.

At the time of the C3 pilot both DFID and CARE International UK used a livelihoods framework to inform their analysis of poverty reduction and pro-poor interventions. Both DFID and CARE required that a livelihoods framework, discussed in some detail in Chapter Three, informed the evaluation. Given the focus of C3 on issues of urban governance, discussed in Chapter

Two, the evaluators modified the livelihoods framework so that it focused more directly on social and political assets. This is illustrated in Figure 9.2.

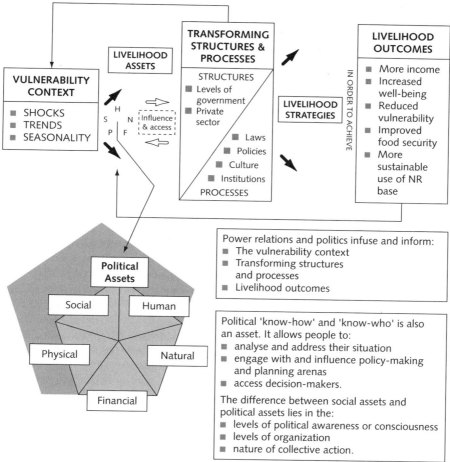

Figure 9.2   Sustainable livelihoods framework modified to incorporate politics
Source: Adapted by author

Three hypotheses were tested in the external evaluation of the C3 Fund:

- **Efficiency Hypothesis**: C3 demonstrates that there are mechanisms by which large funders can support multiple small-scale local initiatives, swiftly and cost effectively and can also leverage additional commitment and resources.
- **Process Hypothesis**: C3 demonstrates that support to community initiated interventions through local urban partnerships can enhance and support urban development and governance.
- **Outcome Hypothesis**: C3 demonstrates that support to inclusive urban development partnerships can increase the asset base of citizens in poor communities.

As illustrated in the diagram in Figure 9.3, these three hypotheses were regarded as interrelated. As can be seen, efficiency issues related to overall fund management, outcome indicators to the enhancement of social and political assets among grantees and their communities, and the process indicators to both.

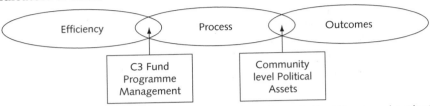

Figure 9.3   The relationship between the three hypotheses in the C3 external evaluation

Table 9.2   Selected issues, indicators, and data sources drawn from the C3 external evaluation

Hypothesis	Issue	Indicator	Data source
1. Efficiency	Ease of use of the C3F mechanism for local authorities, NGOs, and community groups	1. Length of time to establish the C3 fund to a point where grants can be distributed 2. Average application, processing, and disbursement time	■ CARE and LGIB Quarterly reports to DFID ■ C3 in-country management information system
1. Efficiency	Costs of management, e.g. time of donor staff, time for applications, disbursements, etc.	3. Ratio of overhead and administrative expenses to investments	■ DfID internal data. ■ CARE and LGIB quarterly reports ■ C3 in-country management information system
1. Efficiency	Reach and range of C3	4. Number, average size, and form of awards (e.g. grants, loans, revolving funds) 5. Percentage of C3 funds and grants awarded to groups not previously funded by international donors 6. Percentage of C3 funds and grants awarded to different **sectors** e.g. transport and sanitation or **activities**, e.g. construction and maintenance.	■ C3 in-country management information system

Hypothesis	Issue	Indicator	Data source
1. Efficiency	Local transaction cost capability (to show enhanced capacity by local fund partners, e.g. ability of local government or banks to manage multiple small funds or to identify appropriate partners to do so)	7. Number of additional bank accounts established as a result of C3 funding 8. Number and type of partners involved in handling and/or supporting C3 transactions 9. Number of people trained in small accounts management (e.g. book-keeping for beneficiaries and micro-finance management)	■ Analysis of C3 banking transactions ■ C3 in-country management information system
2. Process	Responsiveness of local authorities to citizens' priorities	10. Amount of funding provided by local government for community driven initiatives as % of total budget	■ Original research/local government accounts ■ C3 in-country management information system
2. Process	Extent to which C3F promotes buy-in from different sectors	11. Recognition of C3 brand amongst international donors, community based organizations, national government, and business 12. Match funding provided for specific C3 projects (e.g. money, venues, staff time, training, etc.) provided for C3 projects by: ■ local government; ■ business; ■ national government; ■ international donors; ■ others, e.g. academics.	■ Key informant interviews ■ C3 in-country management information system

Table 9.2 continued

Hypothesis	Issue	Indicator	Data source
		13. Other contributions (e.g. money, venues, staff time, training, etc.) by the above groups outside of match funding for specific projects (e.g. for evaluation or capacity building).	
2. Process	To assess accountability of project implementers in decision-making – both upwards and downwards	14. Mechanisms in place to make information about C3 available to potential and actual beneficiaries and partners	■ Key informant interviews
		15. Recourse available to potential and actual beneficiaries and partners if resources are not forthcoming or managed effectively (e.g. formal complaint and arbitration procedure).	
2. Process	To assess the style and inclusiveness of local C3 management and teams.	16. Number of local people community representatives attending C3 project meetings (by gender, age, and organization type)	■ Key informant interviews
2. Process	To assess the enhanced capacity of local C3 management and teams.	17. Confidence of C3 staff to run C3 type programmes effectively in the future	■ Key informant interviews
3. Outcomes	Prioritizing assets	18. Priority ranking by community members in terms of various assets (i.e. social, political, physical, human, environmental, and financial)	■ Analysis of application forms (funded or not) in terms of different sectors, (e.g. transport, sanitation) and/or activities (e.g. construction, maintenance)

Hypothesis	Issue	Indicator	Data source
3. Outcomes	Social asset base and community capacity	19. Percentage of respondents saying: I know who to contact to help me change things locally in: ■ local community groups ■ at the council ■ in other local non-governmental agencies ■ among people in the neighbourhood	■ Local community survey
3. Outcomes	Political asset base and advocacy and leadership capacity	20. Number of people who think they or their leaders could influence what happens locally	■ Local community survey ■ Key informant interviews
3. Outcomes	Gender dimensions of social and political asset base and women's empowerment	21. Number of men and women beneficiaries and rejected applicants. 22. Changes in women's confidence and participation	■ C3 in-country management information system ■ Key informant interviews

Source: Beall and Lingayah, 2001

The procedures for project proposal appraisal were set up very much with the external evaluation framework in mind. The process is represented schematically in Figure 9.4. In order to provide a flavour of how this worked in practice, the procedures for processing small grants are outlined in some detail, in order to demonstrate the lightness of touch and fleetness of foot that were applied. The procedures for medium and large funds were somewhat more onerous but not overly so. The essential conditions for a small grant are that groups are formed, that a proposal is drawn up indicating what the group is going to do and how and indicating the total budget including contributions in addition to C3 funds, whether in cash or in kind. Groups have to open a bank account before receiving funds and if necessary, information and support is given to groups in doing this. Groups have to raise their contribution in advance and proof of the bank account must be shown in order to receive the C3 funds. If the project involves the purchase of equipment, how it will be maintained or shared after the activity

Figure 9.4   City Community Challenge Fund project proposal appraisal process
Source: CARE Zambia and Urban INSAKA (2002)

should be explained. In addition to the application process being minimalist, approval for small projects is designed to be swift. Applicants are given the 'Project Outline Form and Guidelines' (Table 9.3), which they submit to UI.

Project outlines are considered weekly and groups that are eligible receive a letter or verbal confirmation alongside a full application form (Table 9.4) and they are invited for an orientation and training session on 'how to fill in the application form'. UI appraises completed application forms fortnightly. Those whose projects are not approved receive a letter explaining why they have been rejected, what could be done to improve their proposal, and details of where else they might seek assistance for their venture. Those that are approved receive letters informing them, giving details about opening a bank account and an invitation to collect the first half of the C3 grant by cheque within two weeks of submitting bank details to UI. On receipt they have to sign for the disbursement and complete the first round of monitoring forms. To receive the remaining 50 per cent of the grant from C3, applicants must produce receipts from the initial payment and an expenditure list with receipts. Further monitoring forms are also completed at this stage by UI, certifying that receipts and expenditure match monies received and to track any changes in livelihood assets, assessing whether this can be attributed directly or indirectly to the project. Final reporting involves a simple narrative report in a standard format, which is provided by the group at the end of the project. If necessary UI provides help to groups unable to complete the reporting process without assistance. A certificate of completion is given at the end of successful projects. If an approved project for some reason cannot be implemented, UI reserves the right to use the approved funds for other projects (CARE Zambia and Urban INSAKA, 2002).

Table 9.3 Checklist for Appraising Proposal for C3 Funding

Name of Group:

Name of the Proposal: Date Received:

Number of the proposal: Date Appraised:

CRITERIA	Yes	No	REMARKS
1. Are the proposed project activities complementary to City Council mandate?			Type of activities
2. Are the project outputs tangible (measurable, real/evident)?			Examples
3. Justification of project (proof of need) indicated?			How?
4. Urban INSAKA open access permitted? a) For audit of financial records by Urban INSAKA and/or other. b) For publicizing of group activities/C3 project agreed?			What has been agreed/To what?
5. Group contributions indicated (cash and/or in kind)?			% That is of total. Type of contributions.
6. Formal partnership of at least one other party indicated?			Agreement/Memorandum of Understanding attached?
7. Proof shown, of consultation and linkages with City Council, other government bodies, and/or private sector firms?			Type of proof shown? What, e.g.: letter, minutes, etc.
8. Has the group got a bank account?			Which bank?
9. Has the group received C3 funds before? And has the project being completed?			Number of previous projects and date of completion
10. Any other comments by appraiser:			
Appraised by:			

Table 9.3   continued

1: Ask for more information	☐
2: Contact to arrange meeting	☐
3: Invite for capacity building training	☐
4: Send Application Forms for: small ☐ medium ☐ large	☐
5: Send information about opening a Bank Account	☐
6. Reject and refer to another challenge fund	☐

Source: CARE Zambia and Urban INSAKA (2002)

Similarly, the monitoring tools for C3 were kept light and manageable for a busy team trying to disburse large amounts of money in small grants and multiple tranches to a large number of often novice beneficiaries. An example is provided in Figure 9.5 of the appraisal form, which was used for monitoring purposes. The existence of these simple-to-use tools and the accompanying paper trails that they generated facilitated not only the in-house monitoring process but the external evaluation as well. Furthermore, the development of these light but effective procedures has constituted an important success of C3 in Zambia, allowing control for the management of funds to be devolved to the lowest tiers of the organizational structure. Indeed, when the monitoring of multiple community level projects became too onerous for the small C3 team in UI, they put in place a procedure whereby cheques are presented at public meetings where the community at large is invited. This encourages applicants to publicly account for the money they receive and at the same time the community and C3 monitors the progress of the project as well as the use of the money (ibid.).

C3 has shown what can be achieved with small resources and minimal donor intervention. Alongside systematic and sensitive targeting and mobilization and networking on the ground, the C3 methodology is ensuring that funds reach people on the ground and that accountability mechanisms operate in their direction and not only upwards towards donors. Risk is minimized though locally developed accountability mechanisms, while stewardship is achieved through carefully constructed procedures and well maintained paper trails. None of this was achieved easily. In particular, DFID and CARE International found it difficult at first to 'let go' and to accept light touch management tools tailored to local capacities rather than international donor standards and expectations. Disbursement was also slowed down by bottlenecks higher up the chain in DFID and CARE. However, part of the innovation of C3 was that it adopted a 'learning by doing' approach and this involved the donors and international programme managers doing a lot of the learning and having to adapt their own procedures.

Disappointing has been the limited leverage of resources from the private sector and as with C3 in Uganda and New Life for Paddington in London, both discussed in Chapter Eight, public–private partnerships have

City Community Challenge Fund

Chigwirizano Partnership Ukubombela pamo

Project Outline Form

Instruction: Please answer the question in the boxes below

---

1. NAME AND DETAILS OF THE GROUP/ORGANISATION

   ■ Name of group

   ■ Number of Men [ ]   Women [ ]

   ■ Year of group formation

   ■ Is the Group registered?

   ■ Group Address: postal: Physical:

   ■ Name and Address of Contact person

   ■ Aim of Group (one sentence)

---

2. PROPOSED PROJECT TO BE FUNDED

   ■ What does the Group want to do? (Briefly describe the activity)

   ■ Why does the Group want to do this project?

---

3. WHO WILL BENEFIT

   ■ State who will benefit from the project.

---

4. WHAT IS THE TOTAL COST OF THE PROJECT

   ■ Give an estimate of the total cost of the project

Post or bring this form on any Wednesday afternoon to:
The C3 Programme Manager, Urban INSAKA, 11038 Chozi Road, Northmead, P.O. Box 36238, LUSAKA.

Figure 9.5 C3 Zambia Project Outline Form for Small Grants

City Community Challenge Fund

Chigwirizano Partnership Ukubombela pamo

Application Form for Small Projects

Instruction: Before filling in the application form, please read and follow fully the guidelines. Attach documents if necessary.

---

1. NAME OF GROUP/ORGANIZATION:

   NAME OF THE PROJECT:

---

2. CONTACT DETAILS

   ■ Physical address

   ■ Postal address

   ■ Telephone number and e-mail address (if any)

   ■ Name and address of contact person. (This should be someone we can contact about the group and the project)

---

3. BACKGROUND INFORMATION ABOUT THE GROUP/ORGANIZATION

   ■ Number of Men [   ]   Women [   ]

   ■ Year of group formation

   ■ Is the Group registered?

   ■ Aim of Group (one sentence)

   ■ Describe what the group has achieved up to now.

   ■ Has your group received C3 funds before (yes or no)? If yes, how much, from where and for what activities? Has the project been completed?

Figure 9.6   C3 Zambia Project Application Form for Small Grants

4. PROJECT DESCRIPTION

- Describe what the Group intends to do and how the activities will be done.

- Please explain who will be involved in the project and how you will organize the project.

- How long will the project take?

5. JUSTIFICATION FOR PROJECT

- Explain why the Group wants to do this project. (Attach copies of documents to support the need for this project, where necessary, for example, minutes, etc.)

- Who will benefit as a result of this project? Please try to be specific about women, children, men, disabled.

6. SUSTAINABILITY/CONTINUITY

- What will happen after the project is completed? For example, have you thought about maintenance or any follow-up activities?

7. BUDGET

No.   Item   Amount

- What is the total amount?

- How much do you want from C3?

- How much/what will you contribute?

Send your application forms to: The C3 Programme Manager, Urban INSAKA, 11038 Chozi Road, Northmead, P.O. Box 36238, LUSAKA.

been more difficult to achieve than city–community cooperation. Members of the local Rotary Club in Ndola showed some interest but so far this has been fairly desultory. Donor coordination has not been easy either, as different donors maintain their own agendas and pet programmes, despite being committed, rhetorically at least, to increased donor coordination. However, some of the smaller bilateral donors have been pleased to link up with C3 and there is some evidence that the C3 methodology has had some influence on ZAMSIF (Beall, 2003).

In terms of addressing poverty, the C3 experience in Zambia is doing this mainly indirectly through the delivery of services and projects and importantly, through advancing citizen access to decision-making and capacity to negotiate with local authorities. C3 has assisted communities in identifying needs, knowing which offices to go to in pursuit of services, engaging with their local leaders, and understanding their own roles and rights as citizens in the process. Strengthening social and political assets in this way is perhaps more sustainable in the long run. The accessible and facilitative approach of C3 has ensured the inclusion of both women and men among the beneficiaries as well as those who are not experienced or literate. One indicator of the spread of C3 and an associated growing confidence lies in the increasing uptake of C3 grants on the part of women's groups. Hence, there is little doubt that C3 has built confidence among those members of communities who have been involved in the process, not least because the C3 methodology allowed them to have free rein in managing the grants and recipients wanted to demonstrate they could be trusted. However, a challenge remains to ensure a community driven approach to urban development and governance is maintained in the longer-term (Beall, 2003).

Anxieties about misappropriation of funds have been largely misplaced, with only a few groups misusing grants. Similarly, fears that C3 funds would be siphoned off to compensate for unpaid salaries were also ungrounded. On the contrary, in Ndola the NCC used C3 as a tool to lobby the Minister of Local Government and Housing, who promised to pay salary arrears, thus allowing the local authority to get on with its tasks. Officials found themselves regaining respect from urban residents, as they were able to respond to needs that were clearly expressed in the range of their project applications, while councillors saw opportunities in the delivery of services that might help in their re-election. While there are always dangers of politicians using funds such as C3 to their own or party political advantage, this can be mitigated by the vigilance of confident citizens, as was demonstrated in the context of C3 in Uganda. Overall, the C3 experience in Zambia demonstrates that it is possible to devolve responsibility to local level partnerships in ways that are not prescriptive and without heavyweight management and conditionality. By doing just this C3 has found a niche within the wide panoply of social funds and other urban poverty reduction programmes that are targeted at the local level in Zambia. It does so by creating vehicle and a cushion for 'the missing bottom' in urban governance, without displacing existing institutional structures or substituting for government responsibilities.

MANUSHER JONNO AND HUMAN RIGHTS AND GOVERNANCE IN BANGLADESH

Manusher Jonno (MJ), meaning 'For the People', is a small funds programme established in Bangladesh in 2002 and managed by CARE International. It is currently funded by DFID to the tune of £13.5 million over five years and other donors are showing considerable interest in funding it in the future. It aims to enhance the capacity of poor women, men, and children to demand improved governance and the realization of their rights. MJ supports local and national initiatives that help build the voice of the poor and their capacity to be heard, supporting improved governance and promoting the rights of the poor and marginalized. The project does this primarily by awarding grants to NGOs who submit appropriate proposals and meet strict selection criteria. The project design envisaged that after three and a half years, MJ would become an independent national organization under Bangladeshi law. The rationale was to develop an independent, indigenous Bangladeshi institution that could address the social and political constraints that prevent disadvantaged people from achieving their social, economic, and political rights (DFID, 2004).

Projects supported by MJ include initiatives seeking to increase pressure on government, political, and other elites and to provide better access to decision-making processes, resources, and services. Sustained social mobilization efforts that make duty bearers more aware of their obligations or that raise the awareness of disadvantaged people about their civil, political, economic, and social rights are of primary concern. More difficult to get off the ground but increasingly in focus are projects aimed at building the capacity of government and other duty bearers to respond more effectively. Important in the design of MJ is that the organization be not simply a funding agency but rather a leading partner in building up organizational capacity to carry out human rights and governance programming in Bangladesh. Unlike C3, therefore, MJ was designed as an arm's length programme that would retain autonomy and distance from government institutions in order better to enhance the voice of poor and marginalized citizens. This was consistent not only with the aims of the programme but the broader context in Bangladesh where there is a long history of civil society organization and a strong local NGO sector, with some NGOs, such as the Grameen Bank and BRAC being as big in size and influence as some government departments.

When MJ was designed the political climate in Bangladesh was relatively benign and innovation and risk were stressed. However, by the time it was implemented there were serious tensions within the NGO community and between CSOs and the government. Under such circumstances the MJ

Secretariat and Steering Committee decided that initially at least, MJ would avoid funding controversial issues that might be sensitive to government and put MJ and its partners at risk, particularly as only organizations registered with the government's NGO Affairs Bureau (NGOAB) can receive MJ funds at this stage. As a result there was a bias in the first round of project appraisals towards funding known organizations with a good track record and welfare-oriented projects. This did not fit neatly with the rights-based and governance approach underpinning the rationale for MJ, although it was argued that addressing socio-economic rights was fundamental to the MJ approach to poverty reduction and livelihoods, a framework which was also applied by CARE in Bangladesh. The triangle in Figure 9.5 shows the three different entry points that MJ used for thinking about whether a proposal fitted into the MJ framework. It was recognized that most projects at the start lay along the livelihoods-rights axis and that not all the axes of the triangle would be touched by all projects. However, the challenge was to get project partners to bring the three elements together – human rights, governance, and entitlements – as well as to achieve a better balance across the MJ programme as a whole (Beall and Lewis, 2003).

In as much as the MJ team had to adapt to new ways of doing things and particularly the 'permission' to fail, so potential grant awardees and project partners were at different levels of awareness and experience in terms of human rights and governance. It became clear, therefore, that part of the assessment process in MJ required identifying the 'level of readiness' of applicant organizations to take on both their own project objectives and the more high risk rights and governance agenda being advanced by MJ in its funding priorities. It was found, for example, that at one end of the spectrum, some organizations were only just coming to terms with rights-based approaches while at the other end there were organizations that were already engaging government in policy dialogue. A four-stage typology of organizations was developed in relation to partners' readiness in undertaking human rights and governance work and is shown in Figure 9.8.

At the first step were organizations that had traditional poverty alleviation or service delivery approaches to development. They were said to have 'zero capacity' (ZC) in human rights and governance work. Second, were

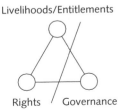

Figure 9.7   MJ approach to funding human rights and governance livelihoods/ entitlements
Source: Beall and Lewis (2003)

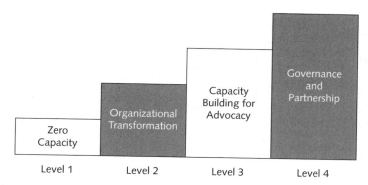

Figure 9.8 Stages of organizational competence on human rights and governance
Source: Beall and Lewis (2003)

those organizations that were increasing their capacity to engage in rights-based and advocacy work and were in a process of 'organizational transformation' (OT). Third, MJ identified organizations already engaged in a rights-based approach but still in the process of developing their capacity to engage in more advocacy-based work. These MJ referred to as 'capacity building for advocacy' (CBA) organizations. The fourth group, called 'governance and policy dialogue' (GP), comprised organizations that already had a rights-based approach and governance perspective and that were already engaged in advocacy and policy dialogue, for example with government or the private sector. This served as a way of categorizing projects and helped the MJ team identify the needs of different partners and projects in relation to capacity building on human rights and governance (ibid.).

As with C3, MJ funded projects of different sizes. However, MJ is a far bigger programme than C3 and the range of project sizes is greater as well as shown in Table 9.4. Similar to C3 as well, the MJ Secretariat went through a learning curve in terms of devising appropriate management tools and procedures. The take up of the first MJ call for projects was enormous and in order that the team could cope and not be completely swamped by an endless round of advertising, appraising, approving, and granting projects, efforts were made to streamline and speed up the mechanisms for processing applications without compromising the maintenance of a viable database for monitoring purposes. For example, by refining the project concept note, the equivalent of C3's 'project outline form' between the first and second project appraisal exercise, the processing time was reduced by half, from about 30 to 15 minutes per concept note. This was essential given that the advertisement for the second round attracted almost as many applications (see Table 9.5). Even though approximately half of the applications in the second round were rejected on the grounds that they were service delivery projects it was clear that MJ's staffing complement needed to be expanded if the team was ever to engage in the social mobilization and advocacy dimensions of MJ's mandate. This was also necessary given

Table 9.4   Range of C3 Zambia projects funded

Size of project	GBP Sterling
Micro/Small Projects	£10 000 to £55 556
Medium	£55 556 to £111 111
Large	£111 111 to £277 778
Macro	£277 778 to £555 556

Source: Beall and Lewis (2003)

their involvement in capacity building on how to develop coherent proposals among worthy but inexperienced partners and the fact that not all partners could immediately move into action and implement projects, with some requiring considerable capacity building in order to move forward, especially in relation to financial management.

Some interesting management challenges have arisen. The first related to MJ's role in counselling partner organizations. Here they have been very successful, for example by advising small and less experienced organizations to narrow their sights or to scale down their ambitions. But they stand open to accusations of favouritism by fulfilling this capacity building role. A solution being considered is contracting out this function. A second challenge relates to how MJ should respond when their partners come up against the vested interests that inevitably arise in human rights and governance work. For example, one partner organization with a project on land rights, in a well meant but perhaps over zealous initiative, encouraged a land invasion which led to a violent reaction on the part of people with counter claims, which resulted in their houses being burnt down. In this case the MJ Secretariat had to decide whether it should provide emergency relief even though this was not part of their mandate and whether MJ should express solidarity with partner organizations in situations such as this. Similar dilemmas arise when partners request MJ to intervene on controversial political issues. This goes to the heart of whether MJ is simply a funding agency or a lead organization in the field of human rights and governance. Although there is a wide consensus across the Secretariat and management team that MJ is the latter, it is recognized too that caution and prudence have to be exercised in order that the organization can continue

Table 9.5   Summary of applications submitted in first two rounds of MJ funding

	Round One	Round Two
Applications received	1 444	1 284
Requested to submit project proposal	64	51
Project proposals received	58	35
Project proposals kept aside for capacity building	34	15
Projects finally selected as MJ partners	24	20

Source: Beall and Lewis (2003)

to be a source of funding over the longer term. Given these dilemmas above all MJ needs to exercise and be seen to be exercising clear and transparent policy (ibid.).

The most pressing management issues relate to achieving readiness for the transition from a project under CARE to an independent, indigenous Bangladeshi grant-making institution. This will be done through the formation of a Trust, which is seen by DFID as integral to the achievement of the project purpose, on the grounds that 'discrete donor funded projects are no substitute for a Bangladeshi-owned and driven initiative' (DFID, 2004). In its assessment of the balance sheet to date, DFID assesses that MJ is on track and that it has:

- established bona fides, its position as lead funder in the area of civil and human rights, and ensured that the fledgling body is not aligned with any political faction;
- developed, through the first three rounds of funding, sound foundations for a project management system (appraisal, selection, and monitoring, including financial monitoring);
- developed 61 project partners, some of whom are already engaged in work capable of effecting change, and many partners with potential to develop strong programmes which advance rights with improvements in livelihoods and dignity;
- been seen by recipients primarily as a partner, not just a donor, by virtue of high levels of interaction with them; and
- been led effectively and in a manner which has generated team spirit, a sense of mission, a skilled and committed staff (ibid.).

There is nevertheless some way to go before the existing Steering Committee is transformed into a body that can direct a Trust and that provides leadership and oversight by way of a robust and independent governance system. MJ also needs to strengthen its position and impact in terms of human rights and governance, through addressing policy, networking, and advocacy issues. To do this, it is recognized that MJ needs to expand and diversify its staff in advance of becoming a fully fledged independent organization (ibid.).

It is useful to turn to the experience of the FCS in Tanzania and the way it moved to independent foundation status. There are three main tiers to the structure of the Foundation: a Council of Members, responsible for appointing the Board of Directors and giving general policy direction; a Board of Directors which has policy, advisory, and financial oversight roles and is seen as more of a management committee; and the Secretariat, made up of the day to day staff paid and employed by the Foundation, with a three person senior management team appointed by and answerable to the Board. This structure is represented schematically in Figure 9.9.

The Council is currently made up of Office Heads or Deputy Office Heads from the donor agencies supporting the FCS, as well as representatives from two potentially interested donors. The current Chair is from the Royal

Three-Tiered Organizational Structure

```
┌─────────────────────────────────┐
│      COUNCIL of MEMBERS         │
│   Appointing Board. Membership by│
│   invitation. Currently all donor│
│         funding agencies         │
└─────────────────────────────────┘
                 │
                 │                    ┌──────────────────────────┐
┌─────────────────────────────────┐  │   Executive Committee    │
│      BOARD of DIRECTORS         │  └──────────────────────────┘
│    7 to 11 Appointee Directors.  │  ┌──────────────────────────┐
│   Policy, advisory and financial │  │   Main grants committee  │
│          oversight               │  └──────────────────────────┘
└─────────────────────────────────┘  ┌──────────────────────────┐
                 │                    │  Small grants committee  │
                 │                    └──────────────────────────┘
┌─────────────────────────────────┐
│          SECRETARIAT             │
│           25 Staff               │
│  Management and Policy Services — │
│ senior members appointed by Directors│
│   Development and Capacity        │
│       Building Services           │
│        Grants Services            │
│     Administration Services       │
└─────────────────────────────────┘
```

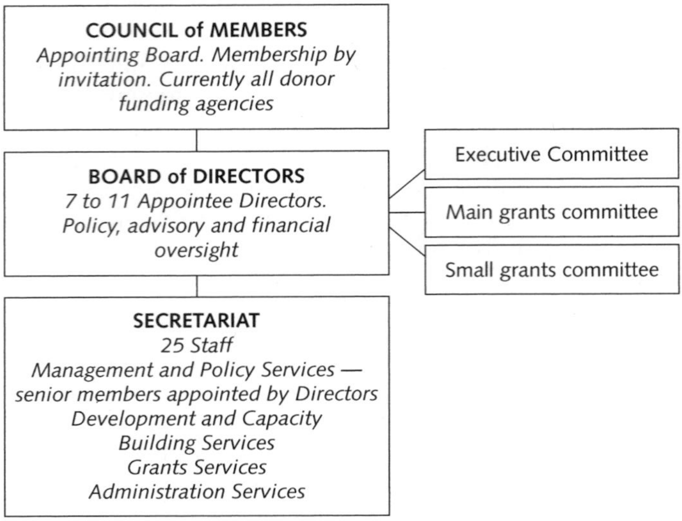

Figure 9.9   Organizational structure of the Foundation for Civil Society in Tanzania
Source: Wiseman (2004: 10)

Netherlands Embassy. Although Tanzanians are on the Council of Members and are members of the Board, both bodies are still dominated by donors. The situation is tricky. The donors have a lot at stake, not only with regard to the resources committed but also in terms of seeing through to successful hand over, an innovative project under wide and sceptical scrutiny within the development aid community. Nevertheless, a recent report includes the following quotes from Board and Foundation members (Wiseman, 2004: 11):

> *The running of the Foundation is still too donor dominated but we are slowly bringing on more Tanzanian, non-donor members . . . Last year we were so inward looking as an organisation, but now the mechanisms are in place we should be able to open up more and to connect outwards.*
>
> *(FCS Donor Board member)*

> *I understand in the future we will become independent from the donors, though we're still having teething problems at the moment. They are not quite ready to let the baby try and walk.*
>
> *(FCS staff member)*

> *The pressure from donors early on was unfair. You can't expect the baby to walk straight away.*
>
> *(Tanzanian Board member)*

The non-donor Tanzanian members of the Board certainly feel there is an imbalance in decision making. One clear example of this was a discussion that centred on taking the term 'poverty reduction' out of the vision of the Foundation. The funding agencies in this instant felt that they then would not be able to sell it to their organisations and constituents and so the decision was overturned. It was definitely felt that we used our power as funding members unfairly in this instance.

(Donor Board member)

The FCS model is by no means the only one and not necessarily the best for adaptation to Bangladesh. However, what it reveals is that the challenges for MJ are only just beginning in its incremental shift from flagship DFID project to a local social movement and foundation for civil society funding.

CONCLUSION

Common problems beset C3 and MJ and indeed FCS. These relate to the problem of having to disburse a lot of money through small grants to organizations often inexperienced in managing both projects and funds. The transaction costs are enormously high. Furthermore, it is also easy for small teams to ensure that grants reach the places where they are needed most. The organizational case studies presented here have faced little by way of poorly targeted programming or malfeasance on the part of project partners but this is precisely because of careful stewardship and sound management. Programme aims are to channel funds to small organizations at the micro-level that have not received funding in the past. This too increases the burden on staff and makes spending targets more difficult to reach than if larger grants are awarded to more experienced NGOs and CSOs. The organizations reviewed here cope by balancing their funding portfolios with small, medium, and larger projects. C3 also 'projectized' some management functions and sought to devolve these to level 3 partners. MJ sought further funding in order to contract out capacity building of partner organizations. In the face of difficult circumstances these are imaginative strategies for trying to balance stewardship with risk in ways that demonstrate trust but not naivety.

In the case of both C3 and MJ, in addition to their grant-making status they were mandated with additional normative agendas. MJ has been tasked with leading a civil society movement on human rights and governance, while C3 was designed to help transform state society relations at the local level. These are tall orders under any conditions but particularly so in the difficult social and political environments of Bangladesh and Zambia. Nevertheless, these small funds are at the cutting edge of new forms of aid delivery to the local level. They are critical in contexts where so little aid reaches the needy or where certain groups are systematically excluded. C3 and MJ are also illustrative of the changing face of special purpose agencies in the management of small funds in developing countries, demonstrating how they can be differently mandated and located in the pursuit of democracy and development. Together C3 and MJ reflect both sides of the governance coin. While from an autonomous position MJ supports CSOs in their demands and challenges to government, C3 seeks to strengthen state society relations from within by setting up level 3 partners both within and without the state. Both are radical in their own way and there are elements of risk in each.

Box 9.1   Manusher Jonno Project on Rights of Fish Processing Workers in Khulna

This project aims to improve conditions for women workers in eight export shrimp processing factories in Khulna (South West Bangladesh) in line with core ILO standards, including wage parity with men and provision of occupational reproductive health services. The goal is for the Bangladesh Department of Labour to take effective measures to implement these core labour standards. The partner is Social Activities for Environment (SAFE), a small recently formed research NGO with six or seven staff. SAFE was formed by someone who used to work for the national NGO BRAC. Most of the staff are young and local. Although they lack experience MJ has found them to be open to learning and receptive to new ideas.

This project follows on from an earlier SAFE study on the shrimp industry. They saw the MJ advertisement and attended an induction workshop in Khulna where they decided to develop a proposal, which was subsequently approved by MJ in its first round of projects in June 2003. By December 2003 SAFE had recruited project staff, completed a baseline survey, and conducted workshops with key local stakeholders such as journalists and local NGOs. They have held more than 200 preliminary one to one interviews with women workers and held a meeting with the Labour Department. As soon as they can identify suitable trainers they will begin training on labour standards issues. On request, MJ is helping them to identify these trainers.

A link has been made with an export quality control organization funded by USAID, which SAFE hopes will help them to form links with employers' organizations and 'get inside' the business. However, this is very sensitive work and the employers' association has already warned that they must be CAREful not to jeopardize this export business which is of great economic interest for the country. A key challenge for SAFE, therefore, is how to adopt a 'softly softly' approach within a polarized campaigning environment. MJ has already supported SAFE in devising a strategy which aims to have the Labour Department monitor standards with the employers' association with SAFE members present rather than CSO monitoring as originally suggested. This was judged to be both realistic in terms of meeting aims and likely to minimize confrontation. SAFE has also made a potentially useful link with another MJ partner in Khulna, which is an association of lawyers and journalists working on environmental issues.

SAFE is going for a cautious approach that pushes rights within rather than without conventional processes of governance. The prior experience of one of the MJ team in working with garments and tea garden workers under an ILO/Oxfam project helped inform MJ's advice to this partner. From MJ's perspective it is taking something of a risk by funding a small and quite inexperienced organization but it is also an organization that has clear potential to develop a well-grounded, locally informed approach to the problem of labour standards. MJ is minimizing risk by taking care to help SAFE build on local networks and contacts to give them more security and support.

Source: Beall and Lewis (2003)

CHAPTER TEN

Conclusion:
a little goes quite a long way

Local funds as a means of aid delivery have become increasingly significant in the last couple of decades. This is largely in response to the failings of earlier social funds to tackle poverty and in combination with recent drives towards decentralization and localism. Starting as Social Emergency Funds, with the aim of swiftly responding to the immediate impact of structural adjustment policies, social funds were soon turned into Social Investment Funds when it became apparent that such a short-term framework was inadequate. This change also marked a shift in policy terms from the provision of basic social protection to a concern with improving basic services. Further shifts in the nature of social funds occurred when the concept of social risk management was developed, and the idea of sustainable livelihoods and creating an enabling environment for social development became of central concern. These patterns are evident across many of the case studies profiled in this book, and in the discussion of policy trajectories in a single country, Mexico, in Chapter Four.

The challenge fund model, which gained some considerable currency over much the same period in industrialized countries, has grown to become extremely influential in the context of local funds in developing and middle income countries as well. Involving the promotion of partnerships and the involvement of the private sector and communities alongside the public sector, challenge funds allow people or groups to compete for resources by putting forward innovative project ideas. This approach now predominates in the design of local funds. Still concerned with poverty reduction and social development, making the voice of local people heard is now considered a priority among the objectives of local funds. Partnerships, where genuine and well executed, are thought to be beneficial, leading to the promotion of healthy organizations and enhanced governance, between government and citizen; between state and society. In this understanding of governance, the notion of democracy is central. This is different from the idea of 'good governance' used by organizations such as the World Bank to refer to efficiency and technical aspects of effective management. Both perspectives are controversial on a number of counts: the universal validity of democracy as a concept suitable for any society has been questioned, and critics have suggested that it is essentially predicated on market-driven principles that are at odds with the idea of development. What is useful to take from the more technicist perspective, and considered here as an outcome of voice and integral to democratic government, is transparency and accountability in service delivery.

Box 10.1   Generic features and dilemmas of local funds

a) They are a mechanism for the fast disbursement of relatively small resources towards disadvantaged or excluded groups or areas. However, disbursement can be slowed down where procedures are laborious.

b) Due to their local nature, they are better targeted. This is not uncontroversial, given that spatial communities are often heterogeneous and identities often fluid.

c) They are driven by local demand. Again this can be problematic in practice, as demand often comes from intermediary groups and the most disadvantaged groups are often ill-equipped to get their voices heard.

d) Local funds are intended to stimulate partnerships on a number of levels: between governments and donor organizations, communities and NGOs, public and private sector organizations, and state and society. Some partnerships evolve more easily than others with private sector involvement being particularly difficult.

e) Communities will provide match funding and thereby co-finance the projects assisted by local funds. However, match funding is not always easy to muster and this requirement has the potential to exclude the very poorest.

f) Local funds are intended to be delivered quickly and flexibly in response to local need. However, bureaucratic processes and the application of rigid constraints more appropriate to other forms of aid can hinder speed and efficiency.

g) Management of local funds by external agents is intended to help donors shed high transaction costs. In many ways this makes them very attractive to donors, although lack of prestige from small and localized projects can be off-putting.

In much of the literature local funds are typically considered to operate best at a distance from government. This is certainly a view advanced in many of the critiques of social funds. Whether or not such autonomy is beneficial depends on the specific situation and indeed is a source of controversy itself. In the current UK context, for example, where conventional local authorities have steadily been stripped of power and funding over several decades, local challenge funds, which are often at the initiative of central government, are viewed as a central element in the 'new localism' that threatens to undermine local representative democracy. However, as we saw in Chapter Eight with the case of New Life for Paddington, an arm's length approach on the part of the Paddington Development Trust was important for local people and organizations to remain effective, in the context of a local authority that at one time was corrupt. More generally the Trust has protected them from getting caught up more than necessary in party political rivalry and competition between different tiers of government. By contrast, the City–Community Challenge Fund in Zambia, discussed in Chapter Nine, was specifically designed to bring people closer to local government structures and to enhance local governance in a context where decentralization was being addressed only rhetorically by central government. In both Zambia and in Uganda, discussed in Chapter Eight, the C3 methodology had a noticeable impact on the transparency and accountability of local leaders. In Zambia in particular, where local government was moribund and decentralized resources negligible, challenge funds provided a valuable focus and impetus for the local state and society to re-engage.

Another source of tension raised by the examples of local funds reviewed in this book is the extent to which they are capable of and appropriate for the promotion of democracy and good governance at a local level, alongside the more traditional poverty-reduction goals of social funds. The discussion of some of the early local funds discussed in Chapter Five in relation to more conventional aid delivery mechanisms, suggests that these goals are not easy to combine. The AGETIPS in West Africa, for example, typically have a dual role of infrastructure provision and employment creation, using local labour and materials. They are criticized on the grounds that they allow governments to abdicate some areas of responsibility and can conflict with government aims. However, AGETUR in Benin, established in 1990 as an NGO with the aim of providing income to those adversely affected by Benin's first SAP, works closely with and is contracted to government to implement such projects as road and sewer construction. It also has a fairly good record of employment creation, although most jobs are temporary and low paid. They therefore serve more as a safety net than as a contribution to sustainable livelihoods. The example of AGETUR demonstrates some of the problems of combining a livelihoods approach to poverty reduction with the goals of public–private partnership and enhanced governance. A livelihoods approach, also evident in local funds managed by CARE International, is closely related to the idea of Social Risk Management as both a safety net and springboard to better opportunities. Under ideal circumstances it looks to work at longer-term asset enhancement and the causes of poverty rather than its symptoms. However, a critical issue in attaching it to local funds management is whether this is feasible in the absence of basic welfare provision. The answer is probably not if local funds are the only or principal means of poverty reduction.

A central conclusion of this book is that while local funds can help address poverty directly, this should not be their central aim. Local funds should not stand to replace social protection and welfare support. It is not fitting to expect people who are destitute or severely disadvantaged to compete for funds or to have to innovate simply in order to survive. However, for low-income communities and marginal groups that have some social resources and capabilities, local funds can work well and can address poverty indirectly. This is evident from the discussion of innovative approaches to aid delivery in Chapter Six, which shows how small funds work well when addressing issues of poverty and social exclusion indirectly, for example through policy advocacy and democracy promotion. Here the Commonwealth Education Fund and the Foundation for Civil Society in Tanzania are good illustrations, as well as Manusher Jonno in Bangladesh, discussed in Chapter Nine. Poverty reduction and social cohesion are addressed indirectly through enhanced governance and democracy promotion through participatory budgeting, discussed in Chapter Seven in relation to Brazil, Latin America and Europe. As illustrated in Figure 10.1 there are a number of variables influencing poverty and well-being. Local funds are best aimed at addressing the core development goal of democracy, and indirectly poverty reduction. Local funds undoubtedly fail when they are also expected to address social protection, sustainable livelihoods or redistribution. As small grants of finite duration they might alleviate poverty but they certainly cannot reduce inequality.

The idea that local funds improve access and distribution does not escape dispute either. There are those who are sceptical that they can really be successfully driven by demand from below and in any case, it is pointed out that local demand from below is not always compatible with broader policy goals and city-wide or district development strategies. There is also

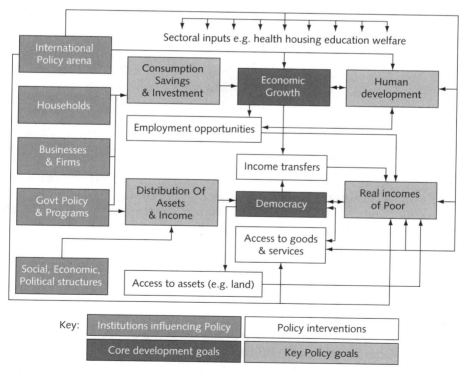

Figure 10.1   Variables influencing poverty and well-being

the critique that encouraging local participation in projects simply benefits those who already have a degree of voice. Furthermore, because of the devolutionary nature of local funds, there is considerable potential for the benefits to be absorbed by intermediary agencies rather than those at the bottom; and those local partners who do manage to engage in participatory processes may be inclined to advance their own interests over those of the community. Since the 1980s 'bottom-up' approaches have been very influential in social development and poverty reduction but there remains a tension between the democratizing goals of participation and the efficiency goals associated with the neo-liberal agenda. Whether or not participation is a good thing in the context of local funds depends very much on the presence of a democratic governance agenda.

There is little real evidence to suggest that localization necessarily leads to greater democracy. As observed in Chapter Two, decentralization is itself not uncontroversial and local fund promoters are chided for setting up parallel institutions and for creating a substitution effect, resulting in an erosion of government commitments in areas where funds are active. Decentralization has brought local governments into the frame by involving them as partners but it is nevertheless worth paying heed to argument that local funding can contribute towards a depoliticization of the local, if only to underline the importance of using local funds to help democratize decentralization. Local funds really are capable of engaging local people in decision-making processes, to foster systems of accountability, and to bring voice to marginalized communities; but in order to do so, there must be a specific emphasis on democratisation and relationships with government in their aims and design. When located at arm's length from government, this preserves autonomy and provides a safe distance for the development of voice among poor and excluded people. However, if too distant from government their voice will not be heard.

A critical question is whether donor aid should be directed at democracy promotion in the first place. Support to local governance can serve more sinister agendas such as bypassing central government or undermining state institutions more generally. One of the main criticisms of social funds was that they were often seen as pacifying civil society rather than cultivating it. While these were certainly concerns during the days of high neo-liberalism, there is now more sensitivity to domestic governance agendas and support to civil society is increasingly towards democracy promotion. Development assistance is often informed by a social exclusion perspective that appeals to a focus on the social contract, as does the growing popularity of a rights-based approach, which identifies those who have claims and those who hold duties, thus moving social development from the realm of charity to that of state society obligation.

At the present time, an increasing proportion of aid is being delivered through General (or Direct) Budget Support (GBS), generally promoted in recent years as the most suitable vehicle for the delivery of aid. The intention is that it channels assistance through the systems the recipient governments have in place, thereby empowering them and giving countries greater control over their development. This usually takes the form of General Budget Support directly to Ministries of Finance. While efficient in many ways and a less patronizing form of development cooperation than in the past, GBS is not without blemish. It is a high-risk strategy for donors as they seek to loosen their grip on recipient governments. Problems associated with GBS also include the fact that it can lead to the neglect of lower tiers of government while strengthening the hand of central government. It is important that in this context government accountability to citizens operates adequately and civil society is constantly strengthened; without proper accountability checks it is hard to monitor the effectiveness of a government's use of aid. Because it is possible that GBS can undermine local processes and institutions, it is advisable that it is combined with a range of other methods of aid delivery, such as local funds. This is beneficial for local funds because they will not be so effective without due attention to broader national poverty reduction and democratization programmes. In this way DBS and local funds can be mutually reinforcing.

Nevertheless, local funds are very diverse in form and can vary hugely in size. There are issues as to the most appropriate type of agency for the management of local funds. As was illustrated by the case of UNCDF in Mozambique and UNDP LIFE in Asia, discussed in Chapter Five, UN agencies are often too bureaucratically bulky and lack the necessary flexibility and agility to implement small-scale and responsive funding programmes, unless they transfer responsibility to intermediary organizations. With the AGETUR in Benin responsibility was devolved by the World Bank and ILO to a newly created special purpose agency with NGO status. The model adopted by DFID with the Commonwealth Education Fund, profiled in Chapter Six, was to rely on existing international NGOs and their local partners and networks. In Tanzania and Bangladesh DFID has opted for the creation of special purpose organizations that are incrementally supported towards the development of independent foundation status, under the interim management and tutelage of an international NGO. In Uganda and Tanzania efforts were made to locate the C3 local fund within or closely alongside local government. Here the nature of government, as well as the strength and ingenuity of organized civil society are important factors in deciding how and through which institutional mechanisms local funds are best delivered.

In recognizing the variety of local funds, it is clear that some are more strictly controlled from above than others. As demonstrated in Chapter Six with the FCS in Tanzania, there is an inherent difficulty in reconciling the power and inclination of the donors to control the process with an increasingly prevalent impetus towards demand-led and locally coordinated projects. The same tensions are evident in those organizations managing local funds. For example, in Chapter Nine it was shown that it was at first very hard for DFID and CARE to take a step back and accept light touch and locally determined management in the context of the local funds in Zambia and Bangladesh. For CARE, it faced a learning curve in achieving a balance between stewardship and risk. Within the local fund management teams as well, it has involved a long and sometimes painful learning process to realize that paring down the bureaucracy, simplifying the procedures, and speeding up delivery does not mean abdicating management responsibility.

Nowhere is a blueprint or 'one-size-fits-all' approach less appropriate than in relation to local funds and governance. If nothing else the examples profiled in this book demonstrate that the political, policy, and institutional context differs dramatically from one place to another. This is perhaps best illustrated through the discussion of participatory budgeting in Chapter Seven. Unlike many other ways of funding local governance, PB is a model which explicitly brings local citizens and government together through the process of allocating funds. First developed in Brazil, PB can be seen both as a means of improving efficiency in the management of local resources and as a way of empowering local people and fostering democracy and wealth redistribution. It is hard to evaluate the overall achievements of PB in Brazil, but clearly there have been some impressive advances and indicators point to positive side-effects such as a reduction in local tax evasion. Problems and criticisms of PB centre on its potential to exclude women and minorities and the fact that it often only deals with small proportions of the budget and is generally short-termist. There is also little to suggest that it really addresses chronic poverty. Overall, however, it seems fair to say that in parts of Brazil it has allowed citizens to genuinely participate rather than just passively be consulted and thus has helped to set progressive agendas.

Some would argue that PB is the child of Porto Alegre and does not transplant well, that it is only successful when adopted by leftist parties and is likely to be compromised by party political changes in government. Its association with the left would seem to be confirmed by the alacrity of its take up by socialist mayors in Southern Europe. However, in Brazil the experience of Belo Horizonte serves to contradict this and PB has equally been taken up outside of a strongly leftist political context in Salford in the UK. What is clear is that for PB to be successful its supporters must be to willing embrace conflict, it must be carefully situated within broader planning processes, and it must allow citizens to participate in actually shaping the agenda.

The PB experience also indicates that local funds can work well in close proximity to government. In the case of PB as in so many aspects of local fund design and delivery, the implication to be drawn is that while lessons can usefully be learned across different initiatives, this must be with adaptability rather than replicability in mind. Moreover, local funds, whether in the form of PB or otherwise, are no panacea. They cannot in themselves solve the problems of poverty and bad governance and should not be expected to do so. They have to be part of broader social and economic policy repertoires and can only marginally contribute towards the advancement of democracy. Nevertheless, they can do very valuable work towards these ends when well-executed. Under such circumstances local funds can provide an important supplementary strategy and go a considerable way towards compensating for the shortcomings of other forms of development aid.

References

Abers, R. (1998a) Learning Democratic Practice: Distributing Government Resources through Popular Participation in Porto Alegre, Brazil, in: Douglass, M. and Friedmann J. (eds), *Cities for Citizens*, John Wiley and Sons, Chichester and New York, pp. 39–65.

Abers, R. (1998b) From Clientelism to Cooperation: Local Government, Participatory Policy, and Civic Organizing in Porto Alegre, Brazil, *Politics & Society*, 26(4): 511–37.

Abers, R. (2000) Overcoming the Dilemmas of Participatory Democracy: The Participatory Budget Policy in Porto Alegre, Brazil, paper presented at Latin American Studies Association 2000, Miami, 16–18 March.

Abrahamsen, R. (2000) *Disciplining Democracy, Development Discourse and Good Governance in Africa*, Zed Books, London.

ActionAid-Nigeria (2002) Strategic Programme of Work and Budget for Funding Under the Commonwealth Education Fund, ActionAid, London.

Ahikire, J. (2003) Gender Equity and Local Democracy in Contemporary Uganda: Addressing the Challenge of Women's Political Effectiveness in Local Government, in: Goetz, A.M. and Hassim, S. (eds), *No Shortcuts to Power, African Women in Politics and Policy Making*, Zed Books, London, pp. 213–39.

Alcock, P., Erskine, A. and May, M. (eds) (1998) *The Student's Companion to Social Policy*, Blackwells, Oxford.

Allegretti, G. (2002) An Overview of On-going Changes in Participatory Budgeting Practices, presentation, University of Florence, Italy, March.

Alsop, R., Clisby, S. and Craig, G. (2001) *Young, Urban and Female*, Young Women's Christian Association (YWCA), Oxford.

Alvarez, S., Dagnino, E. and Escobar, A. (1998) Introduction: The Cultural and the Political in Latin American Social Movements in Alvarez, S., Dagnino, E. and Escobar, A. (eds), *Cultures of Politics/Politics of Cultures: Revisioning Latin American Social Movements*, Westview Press, Boulder, Colorado, pp. 118–37.

Amis, P. (1995) Making Sense of Urban Poverty, *Environment and Urbanization*, 7(1): 145–57.

Archer, R. (1994) Markets and Good Government: The Way Forward for Economic and Social Development, UN Non-Governmental Liaison Service (NGLS), Geneva.

Arizpe, L. (1982) *Etnicismo, Migracion y Cambio Economico*, El Colegio de Mexico, Mexico City.

Arrossi, S., Bombarolo, F., Hardoy, J., Mitlin, D., Coscio, L.P. and Satterthwaite, D. (1994) *Funding Community Initiatives*, Earthscan, London.

Avritzer, L. (1999) Corruption and political reform in Brazil: the impact of Collor's impeachment, in Rosenn, K.S. and Downs, R. (eds), *Corruption and Political Reform in Brazil*, North–South Center Press, Coral Gables, Florida.

Avritzer, L. (2000a) Civil Society, Public Space and Local Power: A Study of the Participatory Budget in Belo Horizonte and Porto Alegre, report for the IDS/Ford

Foundation Project: Civil Society and Democratic Governance, unpublished mimeo, Institute of Development Studies, Sussex.

Avritzer, L. (2000b) Democratisation and Changes in the Pattern of Association in Brazil, *Journal of Inter-American Studies and World Affairs*, 42: 59–76.

Avritzer, L. (2002) *Democracy and the public space in Latin America*, Princeton University Press, Princeton.

Baierle, S.G. (1998) The Explosion of Experience: The Emergence of a New Ethical–Political Principle in Popular Movements in Porto Alegre, Brazil, in: Alvarez, S., Dagnino, E. and Escobar, A. (eds), *Cultures of Politics/Politics of Cultures: Revisioning Latin American Social Movements*, Westview Press, Boulder, Colorado, pp. 118–37.

Bailey, N. with Barker, A. and MacDonald, K. (1995) *Partnership Agencies in British Urban Policy*, University College London (UCL) Press, London.

Baiocchi, G. (2001) Participation, Activism, and Politics: The Porto Alegre Experiment and Deliberative Democratic Theory, *Politics and Society*, 29(1): 43–72.

Balabanis, G., Phillips, H. and Lyall, J. (1998) Corporate Social Responsibility and Economic Performance in the top British Companies: are they Linked? *European Business* Review, 98(1): 25–44.

Baldock, J., Manning, N., Miller, S. and Vickerstaff, S. (eds) (1999) *Social Policy*, Oxford University Press, Oxford.

Bartlett, W., Roberts, J. and Le Grand, J. (eds) (1998) *A Revolution in Social Policy, Quasi-market Reforms in the 1990s*, Policy Press, Bristol.

Batkin, A. (2001) Social Funds: Project and Program Issues, in: Ortiz, I. (ed.) *Social Protection in Asia and the Pacific*, Asian Development Bank: Manila, Philippines, pp. 461–80.

Baum, W.C. (1982) *The Project Cycle*, World Bank, Washington D.C.

Beall, J. (ed.) (1997a) *A City for All, Valuing Difference and Working with Diversity*, Zed Books, London.

Beall, J. (1997b) Social Capital in Waste – A Solid Investment?, *Journal of International Development*, 9(7): 951–61.

Beall, J. (1998) Trickle Down or Rising Tide? Lessons on Mainstreaming Gender Policy from Columbia and South Africa, *Social Policy and Administration*, 32(5): 513–35.

Beall, J. (2002a) The DFID Supported City–Community Challenge Fund (C3F) Pilot Programme: Lessons from the Interim External Evaluation Report. Presentation to the International Workshop on Reducing Urban Poverty Through Innovative Local Funds: Sharing Donor Experiences, held at the London School of Economics, 28 February–1 March.

Beall, J. (2002b) Globalization and Social Exclusion in Cities: Framing the Debate with Lessons from Africa and Asia, *Environment and Urbanization*, 14(1), April: 41–52.

Beall, J. (2002c) Living in the Present, Investing in the Future: Household Security Among the Urban Poor, in: Rakodi, C. with Lloyd-Jones, T. (eds), *Urban Livelihoods, A People-Centred Approach to Reducing Poverty*, Earthscan, London, pp. 71–87.

Beall, J. (2002d) 'A New Branch can be Strengthened by an Old Branch': Livelihoods and Challenges to Inter-generational Solidarity in South Africa, in Townsend, P. and Gordon, D. (eds), *World Poverty, New Policies to Defeat an Old Enemy*, The Policy Press, Bristol, pp. 325–48.

Beall, J. (2003) 'City-Community Challenge Fund External Evaluation Report', Department for International Development, London.

Beall, J. (2004) Decentralisation and Engendering Democracy: Lessons from Local Government Reform in South Africa, *Crisis States Research Centre Working Paper No. 54*, Development Studies Institute, London School of Economics, London.

Beall, J., Crankshaw, O. and Parnell, S. (2000) Victims, Villains and Fixers: The Urban Environment and Johannesburg's Poor, *Journal of Southern African Studies*, 26(4): 803–55.

Beall, J. and Lewis, D. (2003a) 'Report on LSE Advisory Team to Manusher Jonno, Bangladesh 14th–21st June 2003', London School of Economics, London, June.

Beall, J. and Lewis, D. (2003b) 'Third Visit Report of LSE Advisory Team to Manusher Jonno, Bangladesh 8th–15th December 2003', London School of Economics, London, December.

Beall, J., D. Lewis and C. Sutherland (2003) 'Supporting Human Rights and Governance: A Background Paper on Conceptual and Operational Approaches for Manusher Jonno', unpublished mimeo.

Beall, J. and Lingayah, S. (2001) 'C3F External Evaluation Framework', unpublished mimeo, Department for International Development, London.

Beall, J. and Todes, A. (2004) Gender and Integrated Area Development Projects: Lessons from Cato Manor, Durban, *Cities* 21(4): 301–10.

Bebbington, A. (1999) Capitals and capabilities: A framework for analyzing Peasant viability, rural livelihoods and poverty, *World Development*, 27(12): 2021–44.

Beneria, L. (1991) Structural Adjustment, the Labour Market and the Household: The case of Mexico, in: Standing, G. and Tokman, V. (eds), *Towards Social Adjustment, Labour Market Issues in Structural Adjustment*, International Labour Organisation, Geneva.

Beneria, L. and Roldan, M. (1987) *The Crossroads of Class and Gender: Industrial Homework, Subcontracting and Household Dynamics in Mexico City*, University of Chicago Press, Chicago.

Bigio, A.G. (ed.) (1998) *Social Funds and Reaching the Poor, Experiences and Future Directions*, International Bank of Reconstruction and Development (IBRD) 906, World Bank, Washington D.C.

Blair, T. (1998) *Leading the Way: A New Vision for Local Government*, Institute for Public Policy Research, London.

Booth, D., Holland, J., Hentschel, J., Lanjouw, P. and Herbert, A. (1998) *Participation and Combined Methods in African Poverty Assessment: Renewing the Agenda*, Social Development Division, Department for International Development, London, February.

Boyle, R. and Eisenger, P. (2001) The US empowerment zone program. The evolution of a national urban program and the failure of local implementation in Detroit, Michigan, Paper presented to the European Urban Research Association Conference on Integrated Based Initiatives in Contemporary Urban Policy, Copenhagen.

Brennan, A., Rhodes, J. and Tyler, P. (1998) Evaluation of the Single Regeneration Challenge Fund Budget: A Partnership for Regeneration – An Interim Evaluation, Department of Land Economy, University of Cambridge, Cambridge.

Brett, E.A. (1996) The Participatory Principle in Development Projects: The Costs and Benefits of Co-operation, *Public Administration and Development*, 16(1): 5–19.

Brock, K. and McGee, R. (eds) (2002) Knowing Poverty, Critical Reflections on Participatory Research and Policy, Earthscan, London.

Brown, A., Foster, M. and Naschold, F. (2000) The Status of Sector-Wide Approaches, ODI Working Paper No. 142, Centre for Aid and Public Expenditure, Overseas Development Institute, London, October.

Brownill, S. (2000) Regen(d)eration: Women and Urban Policy in Britain, in: Dark, J., Ledwith, S. and Woods, R. (eds), *Women and the City. Visibility and Voice in Urban Space*, Palgrave, Basingstoke.

Brownill, S. and J. Darke (1998) *Rich Mix: Strategies for Inclusive Regeneration*, Policy Press, Bristol.

Burnell, P. (1997) *Foreign Aid in a Changing World*, Open University Press, Milton Keynes.

Burnell, P. (2000) Democracy Assistance: The State of the Discourse, in: Burnell, P. (ed.), *Democracy Assistance, International Cooperation for Democratization*, Frank Cass, London, pp. 3–33.

Cabannes, Y. (2003) Participatory Budgeting and Municipal Finance: Participatory Perspectives in Cities of Europe and Latin America, Urban Network Seminar No. 9, UN-Habitat, Porto Alegre.

Cabral, J.T. and Moura, A.S.d. (1996) City Management, Local Power, and Social Practice: An Analysis of the 1991 Master Plan Process in Recife, *Latin American Perspectives*, 23(4): 54–70.

Care Zambia and Urban INSAKA (2002) 'C3 Funding and Disbursal Procedures', unpublished mimeo.

Carney, D. with Drinkwater, M., Rusinow, T., Neefjes, K., Wanmali, S. and Singh, N. (1999) Livelihoods Approaches Compared, DFID, London, November.

Carothers, T. and Ottaway, M. (2000) The Burgeoning World of Civil Society Aid, in: Ottaway, M. and Carothers, T. (eds), *Funding Virtue, Civil Society Aid and Democracy Promotion*, Carnegie Endowment for International Peace, Washington D.C., pp. 3–20.

Castells, M. (1998) *The End of the Millenium*, Blackwells, Oxford.

Chambers, R. (1983) *Rural Development, Putting the Last First*, Longman Group, UK Harlow.

Chambers, R. (1993) *Challenging the Professions: Frontiers for Rural Development*, Intermediate Technology Publications London.

Chambers, R. (1995) 'Poverty and Livelihoods: Whose Reality Counts?' *Environment and Urbanization*, Vol. 7, No. 1, pp. 173–204.

Chambers, R. (1996) 'Participatory Rural Appraisal and the Reversal of Power', *Cambridge Anthropology*, Vol. 19, No. 1, pp. 5–23.

Chambers, R. (1997) *Whose Reality Counts? Putting the First Last*, IT Publications, London.

Chambers, R. and Conway, G. (1992) Sustainable Rural Livelihoods: Practical Concepts for the 21st Century, *IDS Discussion Paper 296*, Institute of Development Studies, Brighton.

Chant, S. (1991) *Women and Survival in Mexican Cities: Perspectives on Gender, Labour and Low-income Households*, Manchester University Press, Manchester.

Chant, S. (1992) *Gender and Migration in Developing Countries*, Belhaven Press, London.

Chant, S. (1994) Women's Work and Household Survival Strategies in Mexico 1982–1992: past Trends, Current Tendencies and Future Research, *Bulletin of Latin American Research*, 13(2): 203–33.

Chant, S. (1996) Recession and Adjustment: gendered outcomes and implications in Mexico and the Phillipines, *Research Papers in Environmental and Spatial Analysis*, Department of Geography, London School of Economics, London.

Chant, S. (1997) *Women-headed Households: Diversity and Dynamics in the Developing World*, Macmillan, Basingstoke.

Chronic Poverty Research Centre (2004) *The Chronic Poverty Report 2004–2005*, The Chronic Poverty Research Centre, Institute for Development Policy and Management, University of Manchester, Manchester.

Cleaver, F. (2001) Institutions, Agency and the Limitations of Participatory Approaches to Development in Cooke, B. and Kothari, U. (eds), *Participation, The New Tyranny?*, Zed Books, London, pp. 36–55.

Clert, C. (1999) Evaluating the Concept of Social Exclusion in Development Discourse, *European Journal of Development Research*, 11(2), December: 176–99.

Clert, C. (2000) Policy Implications of a Social Exclusion Perspective In Chile: Priorities, Discourse And Methods In Question. PhD Thesis. Social Policy Department, London School of Economics and Political Science, London.

Commonwealth Education Fund (2002) The Commonwealth Education Fund (CEF), A Brief Overview, http://www.commonwealtheducationfund.org.

Commonwealth Education Fund (2004a) Global Summary to Date: CEF Narrative Report to the Department for International Development, London: CEF UK Management Committee, March.

Commonwealth Education Fund (2004b) Sustainability: Agreements and Options, London: CEF UK Management Committee, April.

Conmujer (1999) *Informe de Avances de Ejecucion: 8 de Marzo*, Comision Nacional de la Mujer, Mexico.

Conmujer (2000) *Informe Nacional sobre el Grado de Avance de la Plataforma de Acion: Pekin + 5*, Comision Nacional de la Mujer, Mexico.

Consejo Consultivo del Programa Nacional de Solidaridad (1994) *El Programa Nacional de Solidaridad: Una Vision de la Modernizacion de Mexico*, Fondo de Cultura Economica, Mexico City.

Conyers, D. (1983) Decentralization: The Latest Fashion in Development Administration?, *Public Administration and Development*, 3: 97–109.

Cooke, B. and Kothari, U. (eds) (2001) *Participation, The New Tyranny?*, Zed Books, London.

Cornia, G.A. (1999) Social Funds in Stabilization and Adjustment Programmes, WIDER Research for Action Paper No. 48, World Institute for Development Economics Research, United Nations University, Helsinki.

Cornia, G.A. (2001) Social Funds in Stabilization and Adjustment Programmes: A Critique, *Development and Change*, 32: 1–32.

Cornia, G.A., Jolly, R. and Stewart, F. (eds) (1987) *Adjustment with a Human Face*, Vol. 1, Oxford University Press, Oxford.

Correia, M. and Katz, E. (eds) (2001) *The Economics of Gender in Mexico: Work, Family, State and Market*, The World Bank, Washington, D.C.

Cos-Montiel, F. (2003) The Empress' New Clothes: Lessons from Gender Mainstreaming in Mexico, *Debate Feminista*, Mexico.

Cos-Montiel, F. (2001) The effects of globalisation on child farm workers in Mexico, in: del Rio, N. (ed.), *Children in a Globalising World*, UNICEF-UAM, Mexico.

Crook, R. and Manor, J. (2000) Democratic Decentralization, *Operations Evaluation Department Working Paper*, Washington D.C.: World Bank, June.

Cunningham, W. and Cos-Montiel, F. (2003) Crossroads of Gender and Culture: Impediments to Economic Development in Oaxaca, Chiapas, and Guerrero, in: Giugale, M. (ed.), *A Development Agenda for the South of Mexico*, The World Bank, Washington D.C.

Davey, K., Batley, R., Devas, N., Norris, M. and Pasteur, D. (1996) *Urban Management, The Challenge of Growth*, Avebury, Aldershot.

Deacon, B. (2000) Globalisation: A Threat to Equitable Social Provision? *IDS Bulletin*, 31(4), October: 32–41.

Deacon, B., with Hulse, M. and Stubbs, P. (1997) *Global Social Policy: International Organizations and the Future of Welfare*, Sage, London.

De Haan, A. (1998) Social Exclusion: an Alternative Concept for the Study of Deprivation? *IDS Bulletin*, 29(1): 10–21.

De Haan, A. and Maxwell, S. (1998) Poverty and Social Exclusion in North and South, *IDS Bulletin*, 29(1): 1–9.

Department for International Development (n.d.) Sustainable Livelihoods Guidance Sheets, Section One, available from: http://www.livelihoods.org/info/guidance_sheets_pdfs/section1.pdf.

Department for International Development (1997) *Eliminating World Poverty: A Challenge for the 21st Century*, Department for International Development White

Paper on International Development, Her Majesty's Stationery Office, London and http://www.dfid.gov.uk/policieandpriorities/files/whitepapers_main.htm.

Department for International Development (2000) *Eliminating World Poverty: Making Globalisation Work for the Poor*, Department for International Development White Paper on International Development, Her Majesty's Stationery Office, London and http://www.dfid.gov.uk/policieandpriorities/files/whitepapers_main.htm.

Department for International Development (2003) DFID Country Assistance Plan for Tanzania, June 2003–December 2004, London: Department for International Development.

Department for International Development (2004) 'Output to Purpose Review Manusher Jonno, Bangladesh', Department for International Development, Dhaka, December.

Devas, N. (1993) Evolving Approaches, in: Devas, N. and Rakodi, C. (eds), *Managing Fast Growing Cities, New Approaches to Urban Planning and Management in the Developing World*, Longman, Harlow, Essex.

Devas, N., Amis, P., Beall, J., Grant, U., Mitlin, D., Rakodi, C. and Satterthwaite, D. (2001) *Urban Governance and Poverty – Lessons from a Study of Ten Cities in the South*, University of Birmingham and Department for International Development, Birmingham and London.

Diaz-Cayeros, A. and Magaloni, B. (2003) The politics of public spending – Part II, *Programmea Nacional de Solidaridad* (Pronasol), Mexico. Prepared as a Background Paper for the World Bank *World Development Report 2004*, World Bank, Washington D.C.

Doornbos, M. (2003) Good Governance: The Metamorphosis of a Policy Metaphor, *Journal of International Affairs*, 57(1), Fall: 3–17.

Dresser, D. (1991) Neopopulist Solutions to Neoliberal Problems: Mexico's National Solidarity Program, *Current Issues Brief Series, No. 3*, Center for U.S.-Mexican Studies, La Jolla and University of California, San Diego.

Dresser, D. (1994a) Pronasol y política: combate a la pobreza como fórmula de gobernabilidad, in: Vélez, F. (ed.) *La Pobreza en México: Causas y Políticas para Combatirla*, Fondo de Cultura Económica, México, pp. 262–99.

Dresser, D. (1994b) Bringing the Poor Back In: National Solidarity as a Strategy of Regime Legitimation, in: Cornelius, W., Craig, A. and Fox, J. (eds), *Transforming State–Society Relations in Mexico: The National Solidarity Strategy* Center for U.S.–Mexican Studies, UCSD, La Jolla.

Ellis, F. (2000) *Rural Livelihoods and Diversity in Developing Countries*, Oxford University Press, Oxford.

Elson, D. (1989) The Impact of Structural Adjustment on Women: Concepts and Issues, in: Onimode, B. (ed.), *The IMF, the World Bank and the African Debt Vol. 2: The Social and Political Impact*, Zed Books, London.

Elson, D. (ed.) (1991) *Male Bias in the Development Process*, Manchester University Press, Manchester.

Elson, D. and A. Norton (2002) What's behind the Budget? Politics, Rights and Accountability in the Budget Process, paper commissioned by the Department for International Development, Overseas Development Institute, London.

Esping-Andersen, G. (1990) *Three Worlds of Welfare Capitalism*, Polity Press, Cambridge.

Etzioni, A. (1993) *The Spirit of Community: Rights, Responsibilities and the Communitarian Agenda*, Crown Publishers, New York.

Evans, P. (1996a) Introduction: Development Strategies across the Public–Private Divide, *World Development*, 24(6): 1033–37.

Evans, P. (1996b) Government Action, Social Capital and Development: Reviewing the Evidence on Synergy, *World Development*, 26(6): 1119–32.

Evans, P. (2002) Political Strategies for More Livable Cities, in: Evans, P. (ed.), *Livable Cities? Urban Struggles for Livelihood and Sustainability*, University of California Press, Berkeley, Los Angeles and London, pp. 222–46.

Faguet, J.P. (2004) Does Decentralisation Increase Government Responsiveness to Local Needs? Evidence from Bolivia, *Journal of Public Economics*, 88: 867–93.

Fanou, B. with Grant, U. (2000) Poverty Reduction and Employment Generation, The Case of Agetur, Benin, *Urban Governance, Partnership and Poverty Working Paper No. 29*, International Development Department, School of Public Policy, University of Birmingham, Birmingham.

Feldstein, M. (1987) El curso probable de la economia en los proximos años, in M. de la Madrid, *Cambio Estructural en Mexico y el Mundo*, Fondo de Cultura Economica/Secretaría de Programación y Presupuesto, Mexico City.

Ferguson, J. (1990) *The Anti-politics Machine, 'Development', Depoliticization and Bureaucratic Power in Lesotho*, Cambridge University Press, Cambridge.

Fine, B. (2001) *Social Capital versus Social Theory: Political Economy and Social Science at the Turn of the Millennium*, Routledge, New York.

Foster, M. (2000) New Approaches to Development Co-operation: What can we learn from experience with implementing Sector Wide Approaches?, Centre for Aid and Public Expenditure, Overseas Development Institute (ODI), London, October.

Foster, M. and Fozzard, A. (2000) Aid and Public Expenditure: A Guide, ODI Working Paper No. 141, Centre for Aid and Public Expenditure, Overseas Development Institute, London, October.

Foweraker, J. and Craig, A. (1990) *Popular Movements and Political Change in Mexico*, Westview Press, Boulder, Colorado.

Fox, J. (1994) The Difficult Transition from Clientalism to Citizenship: Lessons from Mexico, *World Politics*, 46(2), January: 151–84.

Friedman, M. (1988) The Social Responsibility of Business is to Increase its Profits, in: Donaldson, T. and Werhane, P.H. (eds), *Ethical Issues in Business: A Philosophical Approach*, Prentice-Hall Inc., New Jersey, pp. 217–28.

Fumo, C., de Haan, A., Holland, J. and Kanji, N. (2000) Social Fund: An Effective Instrument to Support Local Action for Poverty Reduction?, *Social Development Working Paper No. 5*, Department for International Development, London.

Galbraith, K. (1998) *The Socially Concerned Today*, University of Toronto Press, Toronto, Buffalo and London.

Ghai, D. (ed.) (1991) *The IMF and the South: the Social Impact of Crisis and Adjustment*, Zed Books, London.

Glennester, H., Lupton, R., Noden, P. and Power, A. (1999) *Poverty, Social Exclusion and Neighbourhood: Studying the Area Bases of Social Exclusion*, CASEpaper 22, Centre for Analysis of Social Exclusion, London School of Economics and Political Science, London.

Goetz, A.M. and Gaventa, J. (2001) Bringing Citizen Voice and Client Focus into Service Delivery, *IDS Working Paper No. 138*, Institute of Development Studies, Brighton, UK.

Goetz, A.M. and O'Brien, D. (1995) Governing for the Common Wealth? The World Bank's Approach to Poverty and Governance, *IDS Bulletin*, 26(2), April: 17–26.

Goldfrank, B. and Schneider, A. (2002) Budgets and Ballots in Brazil: Participatory budgeting from the City to the State, *IDS Working Paper No. 149*, Institute of Development Studies, Sussex.

Golub, S.J. (2000) Democracy as Development: A Case for Civil Society Assistance in Asia, in Ottaway, M. and Carothers, T. (eds), *Funding Virtue, Civil Society Aid and Democracy Promotion*, Carnegie Endowment for International Peace, Washington D.C., pp. 135–58.

Gore, C. and Figueiredo, J. (eds) (1997) *Social Exclusion and Anti-Poverty Policy: A Debate*, IILS Research Series 110, International Labour Organisation, Geneva.

Gray, J. (1996) *After Social Democracy*, Demos, London.

Gray, R., Owen, D. and Maunders, K. (1987) *Corporate Social Reporting: Accounting and Accountability*, Prentice-Hall, Engelwood Cliffs, New Jersey.

Hall, N. and Dirie, I. (2002) Local Funds as an Aid Instrument, unpublished mimeo.

Hall, A. and Midgeley, J. (2004) *Social Policy for Development*, Sage, London.

Hardiman, M. and Midgley, J. (1982) *The Social Dimensions of Development*, Wiley, Chichester.

Harriss, J. (2002) *Depoliticizing Development: The World Bank and Social Capital*, Anthem Press, London.

Heller, P. (2001) Moving the State: The Politics of Democratic Decentralization in Kerala, South Africa and Porto Alegre, *Politics and Society*, 29(1): 131–63.

Hewitt, M. (1992) *Welfare Ideology and Need: Developing Perspectives on the Welfare State*, Harvester Wheatsheaf, Hemel Hempstead.

Holzmann, R. and S. Jørgenson (2000) *Social Risk Management: A New Conceptual Framework for Social Protection and Beyond*, Social Protection Discussion Paper No. 0006, The World Bank, Washington, D.C.

Hutton, W. (ed.) (1997) *Stakeholding and its Critics*, Vol. 36, *Choice in Welfare*, IEA Health and Welfare Unit. London.

IILS/UNDP (1996) *Social Exclusion and Anti-Poverty Strategies*, International Labour Organisation, Geneva.

Jack, W. (2001) Social Investment Funds: An Organizational Approach to Improved Development Assistance, *World Bank Research Observer*, No. 16, pp. 109–24.

Jackson, C. (1996) Rescuing Gender from the Poverty Trap, *World Development*, 24(3): 489–504.

Jørgensen, S.L. and Van Domelen, J. (2001) Helping the Poor Manage Risk Better: The Role of Social Funds, in: Lustig, N. (ed.), *Shielding the Poor, Social Protection in the Developing World*, Brookings Institution Press and Inter-American Development Bank, Washington D.C., pp. 91–107.

Kabeer, N. (2000) Social Exclusion, Poverty and Discrimination, Towards an Analytical Framework, *IDS Bulletin*, 31(4), October: 83–97.

Kabeer, N. (1998) 'Money Can't Buy Me Love'? Re-evaluating Gender, Credit and Empowerment in Rural Bangladesh, *IDS Discussion Paper No. 363*, University of Sussex, Institute of Development Studies, Brighton.

Kabeer, N. (1997) Editorial: Tactics and Trade-offs: Revisiting the Links between Gender and Poverty, *IDS Bulletin*, 28(3), July: 1–13.

Kabeer, N. (1994) *Reversed Realities: Gender Hierarchies in Development Thought*, Verso Press, London.

Kanji, N. (1995) Gender, Poverty and Economic Adjustment in Harare, Zimbabwe, *Environment and Urbanization*, 7(1), April: 37–56.

Kanji, N. (2002) Social Funds in sub-Saharan Africa: How Effective for Poverty Reduction?, in: Townsend, P. and Gordon, D. (eds), *World Poverty, New Policies to Defeat an Old Enemy*, The Policy Press, Bristol, pp. 233–50.

Kanji, N. and Manji, F. (1991) From Development to Sustained Crisis: Structural Adjustment, Equity and Health, *Social Science and Medicine*, 33(9): 985–93.

Kaufman, R. and Trejo, G. (1996) Regionalismo, Transformación del Régimen y Pronasol: la Política del Programmea Nacional de Solidaridad en Cuatro Estados Mexicanos, *Política y Gobierno*, 3(2): 245–80.

Kitching, G. (1982) *Development and Underdevelopment in Historical Perspective*, Methuen, London.

Kiyaga, J. (2002) Local Governance for Poverty Reduction: Uganda's Experience, 1993–2002, Country paper for the Fifth African Governance Forum, Maputo, Mozambique, 22–25 May.

Korten, D. (1995) *When Corporations Rule the World*, Kumarian Press and Berrett-Koehler Publishers, Connecticut and California.

Le Grand, J. and Bartlett, W. (eds) (1993) *Quasi-markets and Social Policy,* Macmillan, Basingstoke and London.

Lenoir, R. (1974) *Les Exclus. Un Francais Sur Dix,* Le Seuil, Paris.

Levine, A. (ed.) (2000) Social Funds: Accomplishments and Aspirations, *Proceedings from the Second International Conference on Social Funds, June 5–7,* World Bank, Washington D.C.

Lewis, D. (2002) On the Difficulty of Studying 'Civil Society': Reflections on NGOs, State and Democracy in Bangladesh, paper presented at South Asian Anthropologists Group Annual Meeting, University College, London, 13–14 September.

Leys, C. (2001) *Market-Driven Politics, Neoliberal Democracy and the Public Interest,* Verso, London.

LIFE (1999) Global Evaluation Results and Recommendations of Locality Initiative Facility for Urban Environment (LIFE), United Nations Development Programme and LIFE, New York.

Lipton, M. and Maxwell, S. (1992) *The New Poverty Agenda: An Overview,* Institute of Development Studies, Sussex University, Brighton.

MacPherson, S. and Midgley, J. (1987) *Comparative Social Policy in the Third World,* Wheatsheaf, London.

Mainwaring, S. (1999) *Rethinking the Party System in the Third Wave of Democratization: the Case of Brazil,* Stanford University Press, Stanford, California.

Manor, J. (1999) *The Political Economy of Democratic Decentralization,* The World Bank, Washington D.C.

Marc, A., Graham, C., Schacter, M. and Schmidt, M. (1995) Social Action Programs and Social Funds, A Review of Design and Implementation in sub-Saharan Africa, *World Bank Discussion Paper No. 274,* World Bank, Washington D.C.

Massolo, A. (1992) Por Amor y por Coraje, Mujeres en movimientos urbanos de la Ciudad de Mexico, Programa Interdisciplinario de Estudios de la Mujer, El Colegio de Mexico, Mexico City.

Mayoux, L. (1995) *From Vicious to Virtuous Circles?: Gender and Micro-enterprise Development,* United Nations Research Institute for Social Development (UNRISD), Geneva.

Melo, M., Rezende, F. and Lubambo, C. (2000) Urban Governance, Accountability and Poverty: The Politics of Participatory Budgeting in Recife, Brazil, *Urban Governance, Partnership and Poverty Working Paper No. 27,* International Development Department, School of Public Policy, University of Birmingham, Birmingham.

Midgley, J. (1993) Ideological Roots of Social Development Strategies, *Social Development Issues,* 15(1): 1–13.

Midgley, J. (1995) *Social Development: The Developmental Perspective in Social Welfare,* Sage, London.

Mishra, R. (1998) Beyond the Nation State: Social Policy in an Age of Globalization, *Social Policy and Administration,* 32(5): 481–500.

Mitlin, D. and Satterthwaite, D. (2004) *Squatter Citizen, Local Government, Civil Society and Urban Poverty Reduction,* Earthscan, London.

Mohan, G. and Stokke, K. (2000) Participatory Development and Empowerment: The Dangers of Localism, *Third World Quarterly,* 21(2): 247–68.

Moser, C. (1989) The Impact of Structural Adjustment at the Micro-level: Low-income Women and their Households in Guayaquil, Ecuador, in: UNICEF (ed.), *Invisible Adjustment Vol 2,* UNICEF Americas and Caribbean Regional Office: New York.

Moser, C. (1992) Adjustment from Below: Low Income Women, Time and the Triple Role in Guayaquil, Ecuador in Ashfar, H. and Dennis, C. (eds), *Women and Adjustment Policies in the Third World,* Macmillan, Basingstoke.

Moser, C. (1993) *Gender Planning and Development: Theory, Practice and Training*, Routledge, London.

Moser, C. (1996) *Confronting Crisis: A Comparative Study of Household Responses in Four Poor Urban Communities*, Environmentally Sustainable Development Studies and Monograph Series No. 8, The World Bank, Washington D.C.

Moser, C. (1998) The Asset Vulnerability Framework: Reassessing Urban Poverty Reduction Strategies, *World Development*, 26(1): 1–19.

Moser, C. and Norton, A. (2001) To Claim our Rights: Livelihood Security, Human Rights, and Sustainable Development, Overseas Development Institute, London.

Mosley, P., Harrigan, J. and Toye, J. (1991) *Aid and Power, The World Bank and Policy-based Lending, Volume One*, Routledge, London.

Mosse, D. (2001) People's Knowledge, Participation and Patronage: Operations and Representations in Rural Development, in: Cooke, B. and Kothari, U. (eds), *Participation, The New Tyranny?*, Zed Books, London, pp. 16–35.

Mullard, M. and Spicker, P. (1998) *Social Policy in a Changing Society*, Routledge, London.

Mutizwa-Mangiza, N.D. and Conyers, D. (1996) Decentralisation in Practice, with Special Reference to Tanzania, Zimbabwe and Nigeria, *Regional Development Dialogue*, 17(2): 77–93.

Narayan, D. with Patel, R., Schafft, K., Rademacher, A. and Koch-Schulte, S. (2000a) *Voices of the Poor, Can Anyone Hear Us?*, The World Bank and Oxford University Press, Oxford.

Narayan, D., Chambers, R., Shah, M.K. and Petesch, P. (2000b) *Voices of the Poor, Crying out for Change*, The World Bank and Oxford University Press, Oxford.

Narayan, D. and Ebbe, K. (1997) Design of Social Funds Participation, Demand Orientation and Local Organizational Capacity, *World Bank Discussion Paper No. 375*, World Bank, Washington D.C.

Ndegwa, S.N. (2002) *Decentralization in Africa: A Stocktaking Survey*, World Bank Africa Working Paper Series No. 40, The World Bank, Washington D.C.

Norton, A. with Bird, B., Brock, K., Kakane, M. and Turk, C. (2001) *A Rough Guide to PPAs: Participatory Poverty Assessments – An Introduction to Theory and Practice*, Department of International Development, London.

Norton, A. and Stephens, T. (1995) *Participation in Poverty Assessments*, Social Policy and Resettlement Division, World Bank, Washington D.C.

Nunnenkamp, P. (1995) What Donors Mean by Good Governance: Heroic Ends, Limited Means, and Traditional Dilemmas of Development Cooperation, *IDS Bulletin*, 26(2), April: 9–16.

Nylen, W.R. (2001) Testing the empowerment thesis: The Participatory Budget in Belo Horizonte and Betim, Brazil, *Comparative Politics*, 34(2): 127–45.

OECD (1985) *Twenty-five Years of Development Cooperation: A Review*, Development Assistance Committee, Organisation for Economic Cooperation and Development, Paris.

OECD (1996) *Shaping the 21st Century: the Role of Development Cooperation*, The Development Assistance Committee, Organisation for Economic Cooperation and Development, Paris, May download from http://www.oecd.org/dac/htm/stc.htm.

O'Neill, W. (2003) An Introduction to the Concept of Rights-based Approach to Development: A Paper for Interaction, available on http://www.interaction.org/files.cgi/2495_RBA_1.5.04.pdf.

Osborne, S. (ed.) (2000) *Public–Private Partnerships Theory and Practice in International Perspective*, Routledge, London and New York.

Ostrom, E. (1996) Crossing the Great Divide: Coproduction, Synergy and Development, *World Development*, 24(6): 1073–87.

Painter, J. (2000) State and governance, in: Sheppard, E. and Barnes, T. (eds), *A Companion to Economic Geography*, Blackwell, Oxford, pp. 359–76.

Parker, A. and Serrano, R. (2000) Promoting Good Local Governance through Social Funds and Decentralization, paper presented at the second World Bank Conference on Social Funds, World Bank, Washington D.C. Document can be accessed through http://www.worldbank.org.

Parrra, L.P. (2004) *Personal Communication with Francisco Cos-Montiel.*

PDT (2002) New Life for Paddington Mid Programme Review October 1999–March 2002, Executive Management Team, Paddington Development Trust, London.

PDT (2004) Enabling Social and Economic Independence in Paddington, Paddington Development Trust Business Plan Review 2003–2009, Paddington Development Trust, London.

Penrose, A. (2000) Partnership, in: Robinson, D., Hewitt, T. and Harriss, J. (eds), *Managing Development, Understanding Inter-organizational Relationships,* Sage Publications in Association with the Open University, London and Milton Keynes, pp. 243–60.

Pereira, M. (1996) Experiências de Orçamento Participativo na Democratização de Gastão Urbana' A Dimensão Politico-Eleitoral, paper presented at the ANPOCS 1996, Caxambu, 20–22 October.

Peters, B. (1998) 'With a Little Help from our Friends': Public–private Partnerships as Institutions and Instruments, in: Pierre, J. (ed.), *Partnerships in Urban Governance: European and American Experience,* Macmillan, Basingstoke, pp. 11–33.

Pinker, R. (1973) *Social Theory and Social Policy,* Heinemann Educational Books, London.

PPRU (2001) New Life for Paddington Evaluation, Public Policy Research Unit, Queen Mary and Centre for Urban and Community Research, Goldsmiths, University of London, London.

Presidencia de la República (1993) *Cuarto Informe de Gobierno, Discurso del Presidente Constitucional de los Estados Unidos Mexicanos,* Presidencia de la República, Mexico.

Presidencia de la República, (2001) *Plan Nacional de Desarrollo 2001–2006,* Presidencia de la República, Mexico.

Putnam, R. (1993) *Making Democracy Work, Civic Traditions in Modern Italy,* Princeton University Press, Princeton, New Jersey.

Putzel, J. (1998) The Business of Aid: Transparency and Accountability in European Union Development Assistance, *Journal of Development Studies,* 34(3), February: 71–96.

Rakodi, C. (2002) A Livelihoods Approach – Conceptual Issues and Definitions, in: Rakodi, C. with Lloyd-Jones, T. (eds), *Urban Livelihoods, A People-Centred Approach to Reducing Poverty,* Earthscan, London.

Robinson, M. (1995) Introduction, *IDS Bulletin,* 26(2), April: 1–8.

Rodgers, G., Gore, C. and Figueiredo, J.B. (eds) (1995) *Social Exclusion: Rhetoric, Reality, Responses,* International Institute of Labour Studies, Geneva.

Rondinelli, D. (1992) *Development Projects as Policy Experiments,* Routledge, London.

Rondinelli, D., McCullough, J. and Johnson, R.W. (1989) Analysing Decentralization Policies in Developing Countries: A Political-Economy Framework, *Development and Change,* 20: 57–87.

Samoff, J. (1990) Decentralization: The Politics of Interventionism, *Development and Change,* 21: 513–30.

Santos, B. (1998) Participatory Budgeting in Porto Alegre: Toward a Redistributive Democracy, *Politics and Society,* 26(4): 461–510.

Satterthwaite, D. (2002) Local funds, and their potential to allow donor agencies to support community development and poverty reduction in urban areas: Workshop Report, in *Environment and Urbanization,* 14(1), April: 179–88.

Schumaker, E.F. *Small is Beautiful*, Harper and Row, New York, 1974.

Schuurman, F.J. (1997) The Decentralisation Discourse: Post-Fordist Paradigm or Neo-liberal Cul-de-Sac?, *European Journal of Development Research*, 9(1): 150–66.

Scoones, I. (1998) Sustainable Rural Livelihoods: A Framework for Analysis, *Working Paper 72*, Institute of Development Studies, Brighton.

Sedesol (1994) *Solidaridad: Seis Anos de Trabajo*, Secretaría de Desarrollo Social, Mexico, Mexico City.

Sedesol (2004) Principales Logros de los Programas Sociales de la Sedesol Primer Semestre de 2004, Secretaría de Desarrollo Social, Mexico City. Document can be found at http://www.sedesol.gob.mx/acciones/logros2004.htm.

Segel, K. (2004) State–Corporate Social Development in South Africa: The Role of the State in Advancing Corporate Social Engagement. PhD thesis submitted to the London School of Economics.

Seltzer, M. (2000) Democratizing Urban Brazil: Institutional Legacies and Determinants of Accountability in Local Elections and Legislatures, paper presented at Latin American Studies Association 2000, Miami, 16–18 March.

Sen, A. (2001) *Development as Freedom*, Oxford University Press, Oxford.

Sen, A. and Drèze, J. (1999) *The Amartya Sen and Jean Drèze Omnibus*, Oxford University Press, Oxford.

Sharma, K. (2000) *Governing our cities – Will people power work?*, The Panos Institute, London.

SHCP (1991) *Informe de Gobierno*, Secretaría de Hacienda y Crédito Público, Mexico.

SHCP (1998) *Informe de Gobierno*, Secretaría de Hacienda y Crédito Público, Mexico.

SHCP (2000) *Informe de Gobierno*, Secretaría de Hacienda y Crédito Público, Mexico.

SHCP (2003) *Informe de Gobierno*, Secretaría de Hacienda y Crédito Público, Mexico.

Siegel, P. and Alwang, J. (1999) *An Asset-Based Approach to Social Risk Management: A Conceptual Framework*, Social Protection Discussion Paper No. 9926, The World Bank, Washington, D.C.

Skelcher, C. (2004) The New Governance of Communities, in: Stoker, G. and Wilson, D. (eds), *British Local Government into the 21st Century*, Palgrave Macmillan, Basingstoke: pp. 25–42.

Slater, D. (1989) Territorial Power and the Peripheral State: The Issue of Decentralization, *Development and Change*, 20: 501–31.

Somarriba, M. and Dulci, O. (1997) A Democratização do Poder Local e seus Dilemas: A Dinâmica Actual da Participação Popular em Belo Horizonte, in: Diniz, E. and Azevedo, S. (eds), *Reforma do Estado e Democracia no Brasil*, Editora UnB, Brasilia.

Sousa Santos, B.d. (1998) Participatory Budgeting in Porto Alegre: Toward a Redistributive Democracy, *Politics & Society*, 26(4): 461–510.

Souza, C. (1996) Redemocratisation and Decentralisation in Brazil: The Strength of the Member States, *Development and Change* 27: 529–55.

Souza, C. (2000) Participatory Budgeting in Brazilian Cities: Limits and Possibilities in Building Democratic Institutions, *Urban Governance, Partnership and Poverty Working Paper No. 28*, International Development Department, School of Public Policy, University of Birmingham, Birmingham.

Souza, C. (2001) Participatory Budgeting in Brazilian cities: Limits and Possibilities in Building Democratic Institutions, *Environment & Urbanization*, 13(1): 159–84.

Stewart, F. (1985) *Planning to Meet Basic Needs*, MacMillan, London and Basingstoke.

Stewart, F. (1995) *Adjustment and Poverty: Options and Choices*, Routledge, London.

Stoker, G. (1998) Public–private Partnerships and Urban Governance, in: Pierre, J. (ed.), *Partnerships in Urban Governance: European and American Experience*, Macmillan, Basingstoke, pp. 34–51.

Stoker, G. and Wilson, D. (2004a) Introduction, in: Stoker, G. and Wilson, D. (eds), *British Local Government into the 21st Century*, Palgrave Macmillan, Basingstoke, pp. 1–8.

Stoker, G. and Wilson, D. (2004b) Conclusions: New Ways of Being Local Government, in: Stoker, G. and Wilson, D. (eds), *British Local Government into the 21st Century*, Palgrave Macmillan, Basingstoke pp. 247–62.

Stoesz, S. (2000) *Poverty of Imagination: Bootstrap Capitalism, Sequel to Welfare Reform*, University of Wisconsin Press, Madison, Wisconsin.

Streeten, P., Burki, J., ul Haq, M., Hicks, N. and Stewart, F. (1981) *First Things First: Meeting Basic Human Needs in Developing Countries*, Oxford University Press, Oxford.

Sullivan, H. (2004) Community Governance and Local Government: A Shoe that Fits or the Emperor's New Clothes?, in: Stoker, G. and Wilson, D. (eds), *British Local Government into the 21st Century*, Palgrave Macmillan, Basingstoke, pp. 182–98.

Tacher, L. and Mondragon Padilla, L. (1997) Women in Solidarity in Mexico, in: Beall, J. (ed.), *A City for All*, Zed Books, London, pp. 268–75.

Taylor-Gooby, P. and Dale, J. (1981) *Social Theory and Social Welfare*, Edward Arnold, London.

Tendler, J. (1997) *Good Government in the Tropics*, The Johns Hopkins University Press, Baltimore and London.

Tendler, J. (2000) Why are Social Funds so Popular?, in: Yusuf, S., Evenett, J. and Wu, W. (eds), *Local Dynamics in the Era of Globalization*, The World Bank and Oxford University Press, New York, pp. 114–29.

Tendler, J. and Serrano, R. (1999) The Rise of Social Funds: What are they a Model of?, Mimeo for the United Nations Development Programme (UNDP) Department of Urban Studies and Planning, Massachusetts Institute of Technology, Boston.

Thomas, A. and Allen, T. (2000) Agencies of development, in: Allen, T. and Thomas, A. (eds), *Poverty And Development Into the 21st Century*. Oxford University Press, Oxford, pp. 189–216.

Titmuss, R.M. (1974) *Social Policy: An Introduction*, Allen and Unwin, London.

Tjonneland, E.N., Harboe, H., Jerve, A.M. and Kanji, N. (1998) *The World Bank and Poverty in Africa: A Critical Assessment of the Bank's Operational Strategies for Poverty Reduction*, Evaluation Report 7.98 undertaken by Christian Michelsen Institute Norway and the Comparative Research Programme on Poverty (CROP), Royal Ministry of Foreign Affairs, Oslo.

Townsend, P. and Gordon, D. (eds) (2002) *World Poverty, New Policies to Defeat an Old Enemy*, Policy Press, Bristol.

Toye, J. (1987) *Dilemmas of Development*, Blackwells, Oxford.

Tripp, A.M. (2000) *Women and Politics in Uganda*, James Currey, Oxford.

Turok, I. (1999) Localisation or mainstream bending in urban regeneration?, *Local Economy*, May: 72–86.

UNCDF (2003) *Independent Programme Impact Assessment (PIA) of the UNCDF Local Development Programme, Companion Report: Mozambique*, United Nations Capital Development Fund, UNDP, New York.

UNDP (1997) *Manual for the Analysis of Poverty in Benin*, United Nations Development Programme, New York.

UNDP (1998) *Human Development Report for Benin*, United Nations Development Programme, New York.

UNDP (2003) *Human Development Report 2003: Millennium Development Goals: A Compact Among Nations to End Human Poverty,* United Nations Development Programme, New York.

United Nations (2003) The Human *Rights Based* Approach to *Development:* Towards a Common Understanding Among the UN Agencies, United Nations, New York.

United Nations World Summit for Social Development (1995) *The Copenhagen Declaration and Programme of Action,* United Nations Department of Public Information, New York.

UNRISD (1994) *World Summit for Social Development: Social Integration: Approaches and Issues,* UNRISD Briefing Paper Series 1, Geneva: United Nations Research Institute on Social Development.

Uphoff, N. (1992) *Local Institutions and Participation for Sustainable Development,* Gatekeeper Series No. 3, International Institute for Environment and Development, London.

Van der Hoff, R. and F. Steinberg (1993) The Integrated Urban Infrastructure Development Programme and Urban Management Innovations in Indonesia, *Institut* for Housing and Urban Development Studies Working Paper 7, IHUDS, Rotterdam.

Vibe, M. (2002) From Bird Watching to Budget Negotiations: Participatory Budgeting, Social capital, and the Question of Causality, dissertation presented in partial fulfilment of the MSc in Development Management, London School of Economics and Political Science.

Wampler, B. (2000) A guide to Participatory Budgeting, http://www.international budget.org.

Wempe, J. (1998) *Market and Morality: Business Ethics and the Dirty and Many Hands Dilemma,* Eburon, Amsterdam.

Wilson, F., Kanji, N. and Braathen, E. (eds) (2001) *Poverty Reduction, What Role for the State in Today's Globalized Economy?* Zed Books, London.

Wiseman, K. (2004) *Letting the Baby Grow: Lessons in Establishing a National Local Fund for Civil Society: The Foundation for Civil Society, Tanzania,* Care International UK and Foundation for Civil Society, London.

Wodon, Q. (1999) Government Programs and Poverty in Mexico, *Report No. 19214–ME,* World Bank, Washington D.C.

Wolfensohn, J.D. (1997) The Challenge of Inclusion, President's Address to the World Bank-International Monetary Fund Annual Meeting in Hong Kong, China, 23 September, http://www.worldbank.org/html/extdr/am97/jdw-sp/jwsp97e.htm.

World Bank (1990) World Development Report 1990: Poverty: World Development Indicators, Oxford University Press, Oxford and New York.

World Bank (1992) *Governance and Development Report,* World Bank, Washington D.C.

World Bank (1993) *The World Bank Annual Report,* World Bank, Washington D.C.

World Bank (1994) *World Development Report 1994: Infrastructure for Development,* Oxford University Press, Oxford and New York.

World Bank (1997) *World Development Report 1997: The State in a Changing World,* Oxford University Press, Oxford and New York.

World Bank (1998) Making Development more Inclusive and Effective, 28 May, Washington D.C.: World Bank, www.worldbank.org Social Development Topic.

World Bank (2000) Gender Equity Project, Project Appraisal Document, World Bank, Washington, D.C. Document can be found at http://www.worldbank.org/ servlet/WDSContentServer/WDSP/IB/2000/06/27/000094946_00061005312682 /Rendered/PDF/multi_page.pdf.

World Bank (2000) *World Development Report 2000/2001: Attacking Poverty,* Oxford University Press, Oxford and New York.

World Bank (2001) *Social Protection Sector Strategy: From Safety Net to Springboard,* The World Bank, Washington D.C.

World Bank (2002) *Social Funds: Assessing Effectiveness,* World Bank Operation Evaluation Department, World Bank, Washington D.C.

World Bank, (2004a) World Bank Recognizes Mexican Government Efforts To Combat Poverty, World Bank, Washington, D.C. Document can be found at http://web.worldbank.org/WBSITE/EXTERNAL/COUNTRIES/LACEXT/ MEXICOEXTN/0,,contentMDK:20206798~menuPK:338403~pagePK: 141137~piPK:141127~theSitePK:338397,00.html.

World Bank, (2004b) Gender Equity Project, Midterm Evaluation, World Bank, Washington, D.C. Document can be found at http://lnweb18.worldbank.org/ LAC/LAC.nsf/ECADocByUnid/5564900AD558C0D485256E68005ED58D? Opendocument.

Yeates, N. (2001) *Globalization and Social Policy,* Sage, London.

Index